Hockey Hall of Fame
TRUE
STORIES

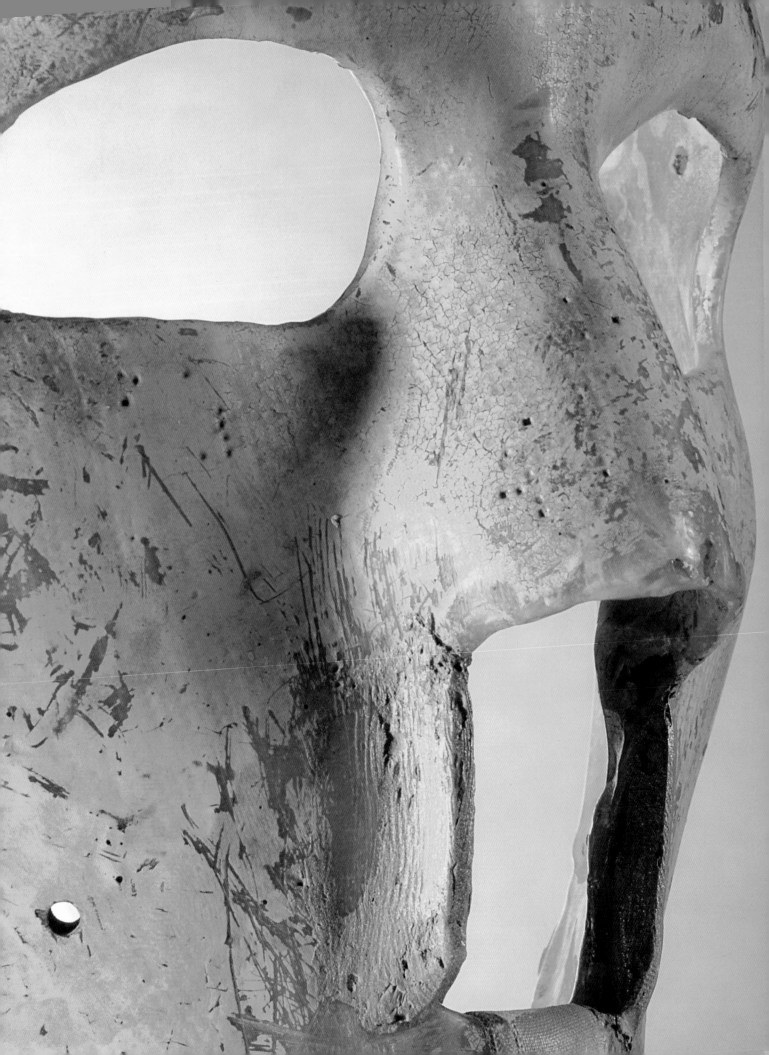

Hockey Hall of Fame
TRUE STORIES

Eric Zweig

FIREFLY BOOKS

Dedication

In memory of Bill Fitsell (1923–2020), founding president of the Society for International Hockey Research. A friend and a mentor to many.

A Firefly Book

Published by Firefly Books Ltd. 2022
Copyright © 2022 Firefly Books Ltd.
Text copyright © 2022 Hockey Hall of Fame and Eric Zweig
Images copyright as listed in the photo credits

First printing

Library of Congress Control Number: 2021944666

Library and Archives Canada Cataloguing in Publication
Title: True stories / Eric Zweig.
Other titles: Hockey Hall of Fame.
Names: Zweig, Eric, 1963- author. | Hockey Hall of Fame.
Description: Includes index.
Identifiers: Canadiana 20210289961 | ISBN 9780228103554 (softcover)
Subjects: LCSH: National Hockey League—Anecdotes. | LCSH: Hockey—Anecdotes. | LCSH: Hockey players—Anecdotes.
Classification: LCC GV847.8.N3 .Z84 2021 | DDC 796.962/64—dc23

Published in the United States by
Firefly Books (U.S.) Inc.
P.O. Box 1338, Ellicott Station
Buffalo, New York 14205

Published in Canada by
Firefly Books Ltd.
50 Staples Avenue, Unit 1
Richmond Hill, Ontario L4B 0A7

Cover and interior design: Hartley Millson

Printed in China

Canada ■♦■ *We acknowledge the financial support of the Government of Canada.*

Contents

Introduction and Acknowledgements

▼

There's a line from the days of classic Hollywood that I think of a lot when I'm working:

"When the legend becomes fact, print the legend."

The line is usually attributed to director John Ford and his 1962 film *The Man Who Shot Liberty Valance.* In truth — since it doesn't appear in the original 1953 short story by Dorothy M. Johnson — the line should probably be credited to screenwriters James Warner Bellah and Willis Goldbeck. Then again, the attitude expressed is so similar to the sentiments at the end of Ford's 1948 film *Fort Apache* (screenplay by Frank S. Nugent) that perhaps the director deserves the credit.

But whoever is responsible for the line, it has certainly stood the test of time.

I've written about this before, but for years "print the legend" was all that most writers of hockey history could do. There was, of course, no television in the early days of hockey, and even after some games started to be filmed in the 1920s and '30s, it wasn't easy to access the footage. So, there were only newspaper reporters writing about what they'd seen.

As the years went by, it wasn't even all that easy to check on the old written copy. It meant either a trip to the "morgues" to find saved clippings in newspaper offices or to the library to pore over microfilm. So, most writers simply relied on their own memories or the stories they'd heard from older reporters. Or from the players themselves. It often made for entertaining reading, but it wasn't always accurate. And so, the legends became the facts.

These days so many old newspapers have been digitized, and feature such effective search engines, that it's simple to read them without leaving one's desk. The vast number of sources available makes it so much easier to differentiate fact from fiction. Hence the *True Stories* title of this book. It's not so much about proving the old legends wrong as it is about trying to get the facts right. Or at least more right than they've usually been.

Two of the best tellers of old hockey tales in my lifetime have been Stan Fischler and Brian McFarlane, whose books I began reading as a boy. I have met a few famous people over more than 30 years of writing about hockey (although not as many as some may think), and I consider it quite a privilege that Stan and Brian have become my friends.

Bill Fitsell was a friend too.

He's not as well known as Stan and Brian, but Bill spent more than 40 years as a journalist after serving in the Royal Canadian Navy in World War II. Bill loved hockey in general, and hockey history in particular. He famously took a photograph back in 1961 of a just-turned-13-year-old Bobby Orr when he was still a mostly unknown prodigy and his Parry Sound bantam team played a provincial semifinal playoff game in Gananoque, Ontario, where Bill was a reporter.

In March 1977 Bill began floating the idea of an association of hockey historians and researchers to Lefty Reid, then the curator of the Hockey Hall of Fame in Toronto. The Society for International Hockey Research (SIHR) finally took shape in Kingston in 1991, with Bill as its founding president and 16 other founding members. Among them was James Duplacey, whom I would later work with at Dan Diamond & Associates, creator of the modern *NHL Official Guide & Record Book* and publisher of *Total Hockey* among many titles.

Two other founding SIHR members — Ernie Fitzsimmons and Glen Goodhand — have also become my friends. Glen collects stories from the early days of the game, and Ernie's work accumulating statistics from all manner of amateur and professional hockey leagues was pioneering. Both have always been quick to help when I have called on them over the years, and I have always appreciated that. Both have helped make this book — and so much of what I do — possible.

I try to answer any professional queries people send me as quickly as I can. (Mainly because when I ask questions for my work, I'm hoping the answers come just as fast.) Many fellow authors and journalists were quick to respond when I contacted them with questions for this book. So, thank you to Paul Patskou, the foremost expert on archival hockey footage and a well-respected researcher; Stephen Smith (*Puckstruck:*

Distracted, Delighted and Distressed by Canada's Hockey Obsession); Todd Denault (*Jacques Plante: The Man Who Changed the Face of Hockey* and others); Marc Durand (*La Coupe à Québec : les Bulldogs et la naissance du hockey* and others); Mikael Lalancette (*Georges Vezina: L'habitant silencieux*); Richard J. Bendell (*1972 The Summit Series: Canada vs. USSR, Stats, Lies and Videotape, The UNTOLD Story of Hockey's Series of the Century*); Craig Bowlsby (*Empire of Ice. The Rise and Fall of the Pacific Coast Hockey Association, 1911–1926*), Stephen J. Harper (*A Great Game: The Forgotten Leafs & the Rise of Professional Hockey*) and Kevin Shea, who is the author of numerous hockey books and has been the editorial and education facilitator for the Hockey Hall of Fame since 2001. Also Robert Lefebvre, who is working on a biography of Newsy Lalonde.

Finally, thank you to Darcy Shea and Lionel Koffler of Firefly.

And thank you to you for reading this book. I hope you enjoy it.

Chapter 1

Scoring Sprees

Setting Off a Time Bomb

The Maple Leafs were slumping in early February 1976. Since recording back-to-back wins on January 14 and 15, Toronto had just one win, with four losses and three ties, in eight games. The Leafs' overall record was still a winning one, at 21-20-11, and since the California Golden Seals played with them in the Adams Division, the chances of falling out of the playoffs were low. Still, Toronto was 13 points behind second-place Buffalo, so catching the Sabres was also unlikely. The Bruins were in first place, with a record of 32-10-9, and Boston was on a seven-game winning streak heading to Toronto to take on the Leafs on a Saturday night in early February.

Like his team, the new Leafs captain that season was slumping too. Darryl Sittler still led Toronto in scoring, but since missing a game after bruising his shoulder in a two-goal effort against the Kansas City Scouts on January 15, Sittler had gone six games without a goal, and managed just one assist in that time. He finally looked better in the game on February 4, with a goal and an assist in a 4–4 tie with the Washington Capitals.

Leafs owner Harold Ballard was unhappy with his team's recent failures. Coach Red Kelly had his system, but Ballard complained that it was nothing like the one Fred Shero had with the Philadelphia Flyers. "Obviously, there's no comparison," griped Ballard. "How many Stanley Cups have we won in the last two years?"

Ballard was also unhappy with goalie Doug Favell, who was barely playing anymore behind Wayne Thomas and Gord McRae despite earning $150,000 for the season. "What can you do with a guy making that kind of money?" asked Ballard. "Some teams have shown interest in Dougie, but when they hear what he's making they turn and run. There's no use giving him away."

Ballard wasn't happy with the play of the Leafs' top line, either. "I'd been in a little slump," admitted Sittler, "not producing the way I want, and working with different wingers all the time hadn't helped."

The top line was supposed to be Sittler playing with Lanny McDonald and Errol Thompson, but

10, Top 10, and 100

Darryl Sittler's 10-point night gave him 63 points on the season with 27 goals and 36 assists in the 52 of 53 Leafs games he'd played. The performance vaulted him into the top 10 in scoring in the NHL. Sittler finished the season ninth in scoring and became the first Leafs player ever to reach 100 points, with 41 goals and 59 assists in 79 games.

Darryl Sittler celebrates after his 10-point night in 1976.

Spirit of '76

Darryl Sittler had two more big nights during the calendar year of 1976. On April 22 he scored five goals against Bernie Parent and the Philadelphia Flyers to tie an NHL playoff record in an 8–5 Maple Leafs victory. Then on September 15, 1976, he scored the winning goal in overtime to give Canada a 5–4 victory over Czechoslovakia in the championship game of the first Canada Cup hockey tournament.

Darryl Sittler scores as a member of Team Canada in 1976.

Ballard claimed that he was determined to find "a sensational center" to put between the two high-flying wingers.

"Can you imagine the time bomb we'd set off if we had a hell of a center in there? Sure, they're hard to find but it would be like another Kid Line," said Ballard, referencing the Leafs trio of Joe Primeau, Charlie Conacher and Busher Jackson from the 1930s.

But on the night of February 7, 1976, Sittler wouldn't just beat one of the oldest Leafs scoring records set by Jackson back in 1934 (most points in one period), he would rewrite the NHL record book entirely with a 10-point game in Toronto's 11–4 win over Boston.

Sittler got started fast and early that night, with a long pass that set up McDonald at 6:19 of the first period, followed by a quick move to get the puck to Thompson, who passed to Ian Turnbull for a goal at 7:01. The first 20 minutes ended with Toronto ahead 2–1, but things would really get interesting in the second period for the customary capacity crowd of 16,485 at Maple Leaf Gardens. Borje Salming set up Sittler for a goal at 2:56, and then Sittler set up Salming four seconds into a Leafs power play at 3:33. Sittler scored twice more and helped set up Salming again for a team-record five-point period, which gave him three goals and four assists on the night and the Leafs an 8–4 lead.

"I remember from the game," Salming would say in a tribute film when the Leafs honored the 40th

Most Points, One NHL Game

Points	Player	Team	Date	G	A	Score
10	Darryl Sittler*	Toronto Maple Leafs	Feb. 7, 1976	6	4	TOR 11 BOS 4
8	Maurice Richard*	Montreal Canadiens	Dec. 28, 1944	5	3	MTL 9 DET 1
8	Bert Olmstead*	Montreal Canadiens	Jan. 9, 1954	4	4	MTL 12 CHI 1
8	Tom Bladon	Philadelphia Flyers	Dec. 11, 1977	4	4	PHI 11 CLE 1
8	Bryan Trottier*	New York Islanders	Dec. 23, 1978	5	3	NYI 9 NYR 4
8	Peter Stastny*	Quebec Nordiques	Feb. 22, 1981	4	4	QUE 11 WSH 7
8	Anton Stastny	Quebec Nordiques	Feb. 22, 1981	3	5	QUE 11 WSH 7
8	Wayne Gretzky*	Edmonton Oilers	Nov. 9, 1983	3	5	EDM 13 NJD 4
8	Wayne Gretzky*	Edmonton Oilers	Jan. 4, 1984	4	4	EDM 12 MIN 8
8	Paul Coffey*	Edmonton Oilers	Mar. 14, 1986	2	6	EDM 12 DET 3
8	Mario Lemieux*	Pittsburgh Penguins	Oct. 15, 1988	2	6	PIT 9 STL 2
8	Patrik Sundstrom°	New Jersey Devils	Apr. 22, 1988	3	5	NJD 10 WSH 4
8	Bernie Nicholls	Los Angeles Kings	Dec. 1, 1988	2	6	LAK 9 TOR 3
8	Mario Lemieux*	Pittsburgh Penguins	Dec. 31, 1988	5	3	PIT 8 NJD 6
8	Mario Lemieux*°	Pittsburgh Penguins	Apr. 25, 1989	5	3	PIT 10 PHI 7
8	Sam Gagner	Edmonton Oilers	Feb. 2, 2012	4	4	EDM 8 CHI 4

* Member of the Hockey Hall of Fame   ° Playoffs

anniversary of that night in 2016, "we knew after the second period that he had seven points and he could tie the record with Maurice Richard."

"We were aware after he got six points," remembered McDonald, "let alone seven ending the second period, and we're in the dressing room thinking, 'Oh my gosh, come on, Darryl. You've got 20 minutes left.'"

Sittler wasted no time in tying the record.

Standing on the edge of the Boston crease, the Leafs captain stuffed in a pass from Salming just 44 seconds into the third to give him eight points. He broke the record at 9:27 with a soft 40-foot wrist shot that caught Bruins goalie Dave Reece off-balance. He then capped his 10-point night with his sixth goal of

Gerry Cheevers makes a save.

the game when an attempted pass from behind the net bounced off the skate of Boston defenseman Brad Park and past Reece.

Sittler was modest about his accomplishment afterward, saying that getting 10 points in one game was really a team achievement. "I had plenty of help," he said. And, yes, he got some lucky bounces. "It was a night when every time I had the puck, something seemed to happen. In other games, you can work as hard and come up empty. That's why hockey is frustrating. Some games the puck goes in the net for you; the next game it won't do anything you want no matter how hard you try."

As for Ballard, Sittler said, "Maybe now he won't have to hunt quite so hard for that center he wants."

For his part, the Leafs owner was gracious. "Mr. Ballard congratulated me very warmly," Sittler told reporters. "He gave my wife a big kiss and seemed really happy I'd done it."

Ballard called Sittler's feat "a greater thing than what Paul Henderson did in Moscow" scoring the winning goals in the last three games of the 1972 Canada–USSR series. "We'll certainly be rewarding him for it. We'll give him a gift [a silver tea service, it turned out], which can be an heirloom in his family."

Back-to-Back ... the Long Way!

A night after the Leafs crushed the Bruins 11–4 in Darryl Sittler's 10-point game, Gerry Cheevers made 22 saves for Boston in a 7–0 shutout of the Detroit Red Wings on February 8, 1976. It was his second straight shutout for the Bruins ... although the last one had come nearly four years earlier.

Cheevers' previous Boston shutout was on May 11, 1972, when the Bruins blanked the New York Rangers for a 3–0 victory to claim the Stanley Cup in Game 6 of that year's final. During the time since then, Cheevers

Five Different Ways

During his eight-point game against New Jersey on New Year's Eve 1988, Mario Lemieux scored five goals in five different ways: one at even strength, one short-handed, one on a power play, one on a penalty shot and the last into an open net.

had played with the Cleveland Crusaders of the World Hockey Association. But he quit the Crusaders on January 25, 1976, after reportedly being fined $1,000 and suspended indefinitely by the team because of his poor play. Though he would later deny the story, Cleveland general manager Jack Vivian had been quoted as saying the reason for the fine and suspension was that "we haven't been getting $200,000 goalkeeping from him," in reference to what was then considered Cheevers' huge $1.4 million, seven-year contract with the Crusaders.

Two days later Cheevers secured his release from Cleveland. He signed with Boston on February 3 and was at practice with the Bruins the next day. It was thought that Cheevers might take a week to 10 days to get back into game shape, but with Bruins starter Gilles Gilbert injured, and Dave Reece getting bombed in Toronto, Cheevers was rushed back into action. Reece would never play in the NHL again and ended his career after playing in the minors in 1976–77. Cheevers would star in Boston through the 1979–80 season and then coach the Bruins from 1980–81 until midway through the 1984–85 season.

Moving Day?

When Maurice Richard first set the NHL record of eight points in one game on December 28, 1944, it was said at the time that he'd spent the entire day lugging furniture while his family moved. As the story was always told, Richard arrived at the Montreal Forum that night telling coach Dick Irvin that he was exhausted and not to expect too much from him. But in truth, the story was a little different.

Richard had actually cleared it up himself years ago. In Montreal's *La Presse* newspaper on October 16, 1959, Richard explained that while he was helping to set up his new place on Papineau Avenue the day of the game and was tired that night, he'd actually moved the day before. Richard also told the story to Peter Gzowski on *90 Minutes Live* on CBC television in 1977, saying that he had gotten only about two or three hours' sleep the previous night but that he'd moved the day before the game, not the day of it.

Dave Stubbs helped set the record straight with a story on NHL.com in 2020. Even then, some members of Richard's family still believed that he'd had his eight-point night after having moved all that day.

Seven Goals and ... Silence?

It's the oldest major NHL record still on the books. Having lasted now for more than 100 years, it may never be broken. Then again, it seems to be just achievable enough to hold out the possibility at least of tying it. Imagine what would happen if someone ever does?

On January 31, 1920, Joe Malone scored seven goals to lead the Quebec Bulldogs past the Toronto St. Pats 10–6. What kind of attention would it generate today if Alex Ovechkin, Auston Matthews or any of the NHL's other top snipers were to score seven goals in one game? Or break the record with eight!

Given that one of the greatest players of his day set a record that has stood for over 100 years, you'd think it was probably a pretty big deal in his time too. But it wasn't. Malone's seven-goal game got little coverage in the newspapers. There are several reasons why.

First of all, Malone set his record in a meaningless midseason game. More meaningless than most midseason games at any time since 1922. That's because from 1917–18 through 1920–21, the NHL used a split-season format to determine playoff teams. Schedules were split in two, with the first-place team from the first half of the season playing the team that finished first in the second half. (If one team won both halves, as the Ottawa Senators would do in 1919–20, there were no playoffs.)

So on the night of January 31, 1920, a playoff spot was on the line when the 8-and-3 Ottawa Senators hosted the 8-and-3 Montreal Canadiens. Meanwhile, the 5-and-6 Toronto St. Pats were out of contention when they traveled to Quebec City to face Malone's woeful 1-and-10 Bulldogs. The results of Ottawa's 11–3 win over Montreal attracted much more press coverage the following day than did Malone's seven-goal game.

Attendance at the game in Quebec would likely have been sparse anyway, but the coldest night of the winter attracted the smallest crowd of the year. Only about 1,200 fans witnessed Malone's scoring spree. The game report in the *Toronto Star* stated that it was -29°F (-34°C). "So cold that the goalkeepers froze their hands, and Corbett Denneny [of the St. Pats] had two fingers and three toes on the same list."

At least there was plenty of action to keep things warm.

Malone tested Toronto's Ivan "Mike" Mitchell early, but the netminder kept him off the score sheet until 6:50 of the first period. It was 3–2 Quebec when the first 20 minutes ended, though Malone had nearly scored a second goal late in the frame. (If it hadn't been called back — for reasons that are unclear — the NHL's single-game record would be eight goals, not seven.)

Malone officially got goal number two 55 seconds into the second period, with three and four coming later as Quebec's lead grew to 6–4 after 40 minutes. Toronto replaced Mitchell in net with Howard Lockhart for the third period, and the St. Pats pulled to within 7–6 before Cully Wilson took a major penalty. Malone scored goals five and six while the St. Pats were shorthanded. Goal number seven came late in the game and closed out the 10–6 Bulldogs victory.

"For the locals," stated reports of the game in most Canadian newspapers, "Joe Malone was the bright star. The lanky forward had his biggest night of the year, setting up an individual performance that has not yet been equaled this year. He scored seven tallies, and played a great game."

That's it.

McGee's Magic

When Joe Malone was starring in the NHL, goalies didn't have much in the way of equipment by modern standards. Of course, the sticks and skates he used

Phantom Joe

A sportsmanlike player in the rough early days of the game, Joe Malone was known as "Phantom," or "Phantom Joe," because of his uncanny ability to slip past opposing players. It's said that he skated with a unique upright style, but Malone was deceptively quick and a prolific scorer.

According to Marc Durand, a Quebec journalist and sports reporter who has written a book and maintains a website about the Bulldogs, the earliest reference to Malone as Phantom comes when his Quebec team was in New York for a postseason tournament with the Montreal Wanderers and Ottawa Senators in 1913. In the final game, on March 15, the Bulldogs beat the Wanderers 5–3 in a rough contest. Malone scored all five goals.

The *New York Times* of March 16, 1913, describes much of the game as being played in a heavy fog that "hung like a blanket over the ice." The players "were invisible to the spectators" who packed the St. Nicholas Rink.

Joe Malone was lightning fast. He glided over the ice phantomlike in the heavy mist. His ghost-like figure seemed to be in front of every Wanderer skater and never did he fail to steal the rubber from an opponent. His hockey stick was like a thing alive, for it poked its way between skates and under falling players in a way which brought Malone the puck every time. He wiggled through the roughest scrimmages and always brought [the puck] in front of the Wanderers' net.

Most Goals, One Game: NHL

Goals	Player	Team	Date	Score
7	Joe Malone*	Quebec Bulldogs	Jan. 31, 1920	QUE 10 TOR 6
6	Newsy Lalonde*	Montreal Canadiens	Jan. 10, 1920	MTL 14 TOR 7
6	Joe Malone*	Quebec Bulldogs	Mar. 10, 1920	QUE 10 OTT 4
6	Corb Denneny	Toronto St. Pats	Jan. 26, 1921	TOR 10 HAM 3
6	Cy Denneny*	Ottawa Senators	Mar. 7, 1921	OTT 12 HAM 5
6	Syd Howe*	Detroit Red Wings	Feb. 3, 1944	DET 12 NYR 2
6	Red Berenson	St. Louis Blues	Nov. 7, 1968	STL 8 PHI 0
6	Darryl Sittler*	Toronto Maple Leafs	Feb. 7, 1976	TOR 11 BOS 4

* Member of the Hockey Hall of Fame

would seem primitive too. Forward passing was only allowed in the neutral zone, between the two blue lines, during the 1919–20 season and wouldn't be allowed everywhere on the ice until 1929–30. Still, high-scoring performances were far from rare in hockey's early days. Stars often played the full 60 minutes, or close to it, so scoring opportunities were plentiful. Newsy Lalonde had scored six goals in a game for the Canadiens just three weeks before Malone scored seven. Malone scored six himself only six weeks later.

So there was little reason to expect Malone's record would last more than 100 years. Even less so because it would have been impossible for anyone to believe that the NHL itself would last for 100 years. Leagues had come and gone fairly regularly in hockey's early days, and the NHL was only in its third season. Fans would barely have differentiated it from its forerunner, the National Hockey Association, or any of the other top leagues that had come before.

And Malone himself had already scored seven goals in an NHA game back in 1913. He'd topped that with eight in one game during that league's final season of 1916–17. But even that wasn't Malone's best effort. On March 8, 1913, he scored nine goals to lead the Quebec Bulldogs to a lopsided 14–3 win over the Sydney Millionaires in a Stanley Cup game. Yet even nine goals in a Stanley Cup game wasn't unprecedented. Many fans in 1913 and in 1920 would still have recalled that Frank McGee scored 14 goals for Ottawa in a 23–2 win over Dawson City in a Stanley Cup game on January 16, 1905.

So what was the big deal about scoring seven?

McGee had a brief career at hockey's highest level, playing only a handful of games over four short seasons from 1902–03 to 1905–06. But his Ottawa team — remembered today as "the Silver Seven" — won the Stanley Cup in each of those years (although they lost it before the 1905–06 season ended). McGee averaged nearly three goals per game during his career, and his name has lived on forever because of his Dawson City scoring spree.

The Dawson City team traveled some 4,400 miles

Frank McGee as a member of the 1905 Ottawa Hockey Club, nicknamed the "Silver Seven."

(7,200 km) on foot, by bicycle, by boat and by train for the strangest series in Stanley Cup history. In the first game of the best-of-three set, the Silver Seven won 9–2. By most accounts, the game was closer than the score indicates. "McGee did not exert himself," noted the *Ottawa Journal*. He only scored once.

According to legend, the Klondike team was unimpressed by McGee, even though he was widely recognized as the greatest player in hockey. Before the second game, on January 16, "Word was whispered around that McGee was 'not so hot,' and that all those stories of the country's greatest center were a lot of rubbish," said sportswriter Gordon Headley in a retrospective for the *Journal* on December 12, 1936.

"Incensed over these remarks, McGee put on a one-man show ... that was brilliant in the extreme."

There are also stories that McGee had a personal dislike for Joe Boyle, the Klondike businessman who had organized the Dawson City adventure. Whatever it was that inspired him, McGee was brilliant that night.

The score was already 4–0 Ottawa when McGee got his first of the game about 19 minutes into the 30-minute first half. (Games would not have three 20-minute periods until the 1910–11 season.) Before the half ended, McGee scored three more times and Ottawa had a 10–1 lead.

McGee scored his fifth goal just 30 seconds into the second half and scored again about 10 minutes later. Then things got crazy. According to summaries in the newspaper the next day, McGee scored his seventh goal just 30 seconds after his sixth. One minute later he scored again, followed by another goal 10 seconds after that. Over a span of about 8:30 of playing time, McGee scored eight straight goals, giving him 13 on the night and putting Ottawa ahead 20–1. His 14th and final goal upped the lead to 22–1, with both teams scoring once more before the game ended a few minutes later.

"Those Yukon boys were nice fellows," said a story in the *Ottawa Citizen* a few days later on January 19, 1905. "Too bad they can't play hockey."

One-Eyed Wonder

What makes Frank McGee's scoring feats throughout his career even more remarkable is the fact that he accomplished all that he did despite being blind in one eye. Still, references to him as "One-Eyed Frank McGee" exaggerate the facts a little bit.

McGee had been cut badly in a game in 1899 while playing for the Aberdeens in Ottawa when he took a puck over the eye. He was hurt worse a year later during an exhibition game in Hawkesbury, Ontario, to raise funds for families of soldiers serving in the Boer War. On that night, March 21, 1900, McGee was struck in the face by a stick or maybe a puck. According to

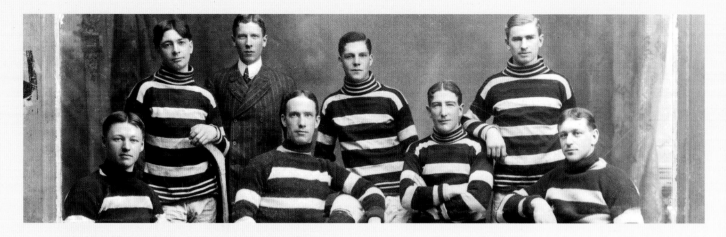

Most Goals, One Game: Other Leagues

These are the highest-scoring single-game performances by players in leagues that once competed for the Stanley Cup. All are in the Hockey Hall of Fame except for Herb Jordan, Harry Smith and Skene Ronan:

Frank McGee, 14 goals — January 16, 1905
Ottawa Silver Seven 23 vs. Dawson City Nuggets 2
(Stanley Cup game)

"Dawson Hockey Team Gets the Big Wallop at Ottawa Last Night"
> — *Whitehorse Daily Star*; Whitehorse, Yukon. January 17, 1905

Harry Trihey, 10 goals — February 4, 1899
Montreal Shamrocks 13 vs. Quebec Bulldogs 4
(Canadian Amateur Hockey League)

"One of the features of the game was the ease with which Trihey scored."
> — *The Gazette*; Montreal, Quebec. February 6, 1899

Marty Walsh, 10 goals — March 16, 1911
Ottawa Senators 13 vs. Port Arthur HC 4
(Stanley Cup game)

"Stanley Cup Remains in Ottawa ... Marty Walsh Distinguished Himself by Scoring Ten Goals"
> — Ottawa Citizen; Ottawa, Ontario. March 17, 1911

Tommy Smith, 9 goals — January 28, 1909
Brantford Indians 14 vs. Galt Professionals 8
(Ontario Professional Hockey League)

"The feature of the game was the wonderful work of Tommy Smith ..."
> — *The Globe*; Toronto, Ontario. January 29, 1909

Newsy Lalonde, 9 goals — March 11, 1910
Renfrew Millionaires 15 vs. Cobalt Silver Kings 4
(National Hockey Association)

"Newsy Lalonde, the Renfrew center, jumped into first place in the National League scoring list last night when he notched nine goals ..."
> — *Ottawa Evening Journal*; Ottawa, Ontario. March 12, 1910

Joe Malone, 9 goals — March 8, 1913
Quebec Bulldogs 14 vs. Sydney Millionaires 3
(Stanley Cup game)

"Joe Malone Scored Nine Goals Against Maritime Champions"
> — *Ottawa Citizen*; Ottawa, Ontario. March 10, 1913

Tommy Smith, 9 goals — January 21, 1914
Quebec Bulldogs 12 vs. Montreal Wanderers 6
(National Hockey Association)

"A new goal scoring record was created for this season in the NHA ..."
> — *The Gazette*; Montreal, Quebec. January 22, 1914

Herb Jordan, 8 goals — January 9, 1904
Quebec Bulldogs 13 vs. Montreal Shamrocks 5
(Canadian Amateur Hockey League)

"The Quebec team was a vast improvement over any septette which has represented the Rock City during past seasons."
> — *The Gazette*; Montreal, Quebec. January 11, 1904

Harry Smith, 8 goals — February 17, 1906
Ottawa Silver Seven 13 vs. Montreal Shamrocks 2
(Eastern Canada Amateur Hockey Association)

"The Ottawas simply practiced and now and then
... Harry Smith, Ebbs or McGee would slam the
puck into the net."
    – *Ottawa Citizen*; Ottawa, Ontario. February 19, 1906.

Tommy Smith, 8 goals — February 23, 1906
Ottawa Victorias 14 vs. Brockville HC 8
(Federal Amateur Hockey League)

"Smith showed up in good style ..."
    – *Ottawa Citizen*; Ottawa, Ontario. February 24, 1906

Frank McGee, 8 goals — March 3, 1906
Ottawa Silver Seven 14 vs. Montreal AAA 9
(Eastern Canada Amateur Hockey Association)

"McGee, Alf Smith and Westwick put up splendid
games ..."
    – *Ottawa Citizen*; Ottawa, Ontario. March 5, 1906

Russell Bowie, 8 goals — January 16, 1907
Montreal Victorias 16 vs. Montreal Shamrocks 3
(Eastern Canada Amateur Hockey Association)

"Bowie was in his best scoring form and landed
eight of the sixteen goals."
    – *The Gazette*; Montreal, Quebec. January 17, 1907

Ernie Russell, 8 goals — February 20, 1907
Montreal Wanderers 18 vs. Montreal Shamrocks 5
(Eastern Canada Amateur Hockey Association)

"Russell, with 8 goals out of Wanderers' total 18,
did the feature work in the scoring line."
    – *The Gazette*; Montreal, Quebec. February 21, 1907

Ernie Russell, 8 goals — March 6, 1907
Montreal Wanderers 16 vs. Montreal Shamrocks 5
(Eastern Canada Amateur Hockey Association)

"Russell, who scored eight goals during the match,
was the only man in the Wanderer lineup who
worked at all in [the second] half."
    – *The Gazette*; Montreal, Quebec. March 7, 1907

Newsy Lalonde, 8 goals — February 29, 1908
Toronto Professionals 12 vs. Brantford Indians 3
(Ontario Professional Hockey League)

"When Lalonde came back to the ice he proceeded
to carve holes through the Brantford aggregation."
    – *Toronto Daily Star*; Toronto, Ontario. March 2, 1908

Skene Ronan, 8 goals — February 14, 1912
Ottawa Senators 17 vs. Montreal Wanderers 5
(National Hockey Association)

"Ottawas Played Brilliant Hockey – Ronan Gets
Eight Goals"
    – *Ottawa Evening Journal*; Ottawa Ontario.
      February 15, 1912

Harry Hyland, 8 goals — January 25, 1913
Montreal Wanderers 10 vs. Quebec Bulldogs 6
(National Hockey Association)

"Wanderers Back to Old Time Form ... Harry
Hyland Scored Eight Goals"
    – *The Gazette*; Montreal, Quebec. January 26, 1913

Joe Malone, 8 goals — February 28, 1917
Quebec Bulldogs 17 vs. Montreal Wanderers 6
(National Hockey Association)

"Joe Malone beat Hague eight times and with the
rest of the Bulldogs played in such an irresistible
manner that no team could have held them."
    – *Quebec Telegraph*; Quebec City, Quebec.
      March 1, 1917

Duke Keats, 8 goals — January 23, 1922
Edmonton Eskimos 15 vs. Saskatoon Sheiks 3
(Western Canada Hockey League)

"The Duke had a perfectly rotten night, thank you,
with only eight goals and one assist to his credit."
    – *Edmonton Journal*; Edmonton Alberta.
      January 24, 1922

a story in the *Ottawa Journal* on September 17, 1936, commemorating the 20th anniversary of McGee's death during World War I, McGee's injuries had not caused the removal of his eye, but his vision was impaired to the extent that he could only distinguish between light and darkness with it.

"For hockey purposes," says the story, "the eye was useless."

McGee took much of the season off from hockey in 1900–01, but he returned to play at the intermediate level the following year and would soon launch his brief but brilliant career with the Silver Seven.

First to 50

During the hockey season of 1940–41, Maurice Richard had begun playing with the Montreal Canadiens... of the Quebec Senior Hockey League, not the NHL team. It was there that Richard began to earn a reputation for being injury prone.

Richard missed practically the full season with a broken left ankle and then most of 1941–42 with a broken wrist. Even so, the NHL Canadiens invited him to training camp in 1942, and he was the only rookie to make the team.

"I still can't figure what the Canadiens saw in me," admitted Richard years later. "I was hopelessly awkward and fragile."

But he could put the puck in the net.

Dink Carroll's column in the *Gazette* on November 14, 1942, quoted Newsy Lalonde — the Canadiens' first scoring star in the earliest days of franchise history — as saying Richard was "the best looking rookie to show in a long time." Lalonde added that the youngster "had hockey instinct and does everything right. Even when he falls down, he looks good."

In 1942–43 Richard had five goals and six assists in 16 games through late December, but he did not look good when he fell down after Boston's Johnny Crawford elbowed him into the boards in the third period of a 4–2 win over the Bruins on December 27. He was carried off the ice and taken to hospital, where x-rays revealed a fracture in his right ankle. The rookie had already missed five games, and the injury would keep him out for the rest of the season.

Canadiens general manager Tommy Gorman worried that Richard was too fragile, but coach Dick Irvin argued to keep him around. When a healthy Richard turned up at training camp for the 1943–44 season, Irvin began to play him with center Elmer Lach and left winger Toe Blake. The trio of Lach, Blake and right winger Joe Benoit had already been dubbed "the Punch Line" by Montreal writers in 1942–43. With Benoit now in the Canadian military for World War II, the addition of Richard gave the line even more punch.

Richard played 46 of 50 games for the Canadiens in 1943–44 and led the team with 32 goals. Blake was next with 26. Lach was second in the NHL with 48 assists and fifth in scoring with 72 points. As a team, the Canadiens were 38-5-7, and their 83 points were 25 more than second-place Detroit. In the playoffs Richard scored 12 goals in nine games as the Canadiens romped to the Stanley Cup. The highlight came on March 23, 1951, when he tied Lalonde's postseason record with five goals in a single game. Richard led the Canadiens to a 5–1 win over the Maple Leafs and was rewarded by being named all three stars.

"The Rocket" entered the 1944–45 season with a contract that called for a bonus if he could score 30 goals again. Richard would earn an enormous $500 if he scored 50 during the 50-game schedule. According to author D'Arcy Jenish in his book *The Montreal Canadiens: 100 Years of Glory*, the 50-goal clause was added "almost in jest because few thought such a thing was possible."

The NHL record for goals in a season was 44, set

The Rocket

Who was it who dubbed Maurice Richard "the Rocket?" Credit is often given to Baz O'Meara of the *Montreal Star*. Also to Harold Atkins of the same paper. Still, the first person to use the word *Rocket* in connection with Richard may have been his teammate Ray Getliffe.

Getliffe was the oldest living former Montreal Canadiens player before passing away at age 94 in 2008. He recalled the Rocket story shortly after Richard's death on May 27, 2000. Getliffe remembered it as occurring during Richard's second season of 1943–44: "I was on the bench when he got the puck at the blue line, deked two guys and streaked in with that fire in his eyes to score. I said, 'Jeez, he went in like a rocket.' Dink Carroll [sportswriter for the *Montreal Gazette*] was standing behind the bench and that's when he publicly became Rocket Richard."

Accurate or not, Carroll was certainly using the nickname *Rocket* in his columns by December 1944, and he wrote that Richard's teammates knew it as early as that spring. An earlier attempt by French-speaking reporters to dub Richard "le Comet" hadn't caught on, but "Rocket" certainly did.

Maurice Richard in the dressing room in 1945.

by Joe Malone of the Canadiens during the league's first winter of 1917–18. Malone scored those goals in just 20 games. In 1929–30 Boston's Cooney Weiland scored 43 goals in a 44-game season, and that was considered the NHL's modern record. Richard left both marks behind with his 45th goal in his 42nd game of the 1944–45 season. Still, many people considered Richard to be a wartime wonder, putting up such big numbers while many of the league's stars were away. Others scoffed because Richard had played so many more games than Malone. Malone wasn't among them. He was there at the Montreal Forum that night when the Canadiens beat the Maple Leafs 5–2. He presented Richard with the record-breaking puck and was generous with his praise to the press afterward: "This Richard is a great hockey player. He's fast, game, and powerful. Really strong. Look at the way he fights off checks, tears loose from them, fights for the puck.

Richard, I tell you, would be a great hockey player in any day, age or league."

With 49 goals heading into his 49th game of the season on March 17, Canadiens fans hoped to see Richard hit 50 at home, but he was kept off the score sheet in a 4–3 win over Chicago. The milestone came on the road at Boston in the season finale the next night. Richard scored his 50th with just 2:15 remaining in the third period, beating Boston's Harvey Bennett and sparking a quick three-goal rally that saw the Canadiens win 4–2.

First to 500

Maurice Richard scored his first NHL goal on November 8, 1942, in a 10–4 win at home over the New York Rangers. Ten years to the day later, on November 8, 1952, Richard scored goal number 325 in a 6–4 win

Mike Bossy poses in the dressing room with his 50th goal puck.

over Chicago at the Forum. That tally moved him past Nels Stewart as the leading goal-scorer in NHL history.

From then on, every goal Richard scored set a new record. And he kept scoring plenty. Entering the 1957–58 season Richard had 493 goals. By then Gordie Howe had also passed Stewart and was a distant second to the Rocket with 353.

At 36, Richard was now the oldest player in the NHL, but he came out flying when play began. Richard scored six goals in the Canadiens' first five games and had 499 heading into a game at the Forum against Chicago on October 19, 1957. He was determined to reach 500 at home that night, and did so when he put the puck past Glenn Hall at 15:52 of the first period. The home crowd burst into cheers while the organist played "Il a gagné ses épaulettes" (He's Earned His Stripes).

50 in 50

After Maurice Richard scored 50 goals in 1944–45, it would take a while for anyone to match his feat. A few came close. Richard himself scored 45 in a 60-game season in 1946–47. Gordie Howe scored 47 in 70 games in 1951–52 and 49 the next year. It wasn't until 1960–61 that the NHL got its second 50-goal-scorer, when Bernie Geoffrion accomplished the feat in 64 games. A year later, Bobby Hull did it in 70 games to become the third.

Through 1979–80 there were 24 players who had scored 50 goals in a season — several more than once. Mike Bossy of the New York Islanders had become the first rookie to score 50 goals when he notched 53 in 1977–78. Bossy led the NHL with 69 goals the next year, but "slumped" to 51 in 1979–80. He was looking for something new to motivate him entering the 1980–81 season. No NHL player since Richard had managed to

Highest Goals-Per-Game, Career (minimum 200 goals)

Player	GP	G	G/GP
Mike Bossy*	752	573	.762
Mario Lemieux*	915	690	.754
Cy Denneny*	329	247	.751
Babe Dye*	272	203	.746
Pavel Bure*	702	437	.623
Auston Matthews†	379	232	.612
Alex Ovechkin†	1,247	761	.610
Wayne Gretzky*	1,487	894	.601
Brett Hull*	1,269	741	.584
Bobby Hull*	1,063	610	.574

* Member of the Hockey Hall of Fame
† Through February 20, 2022

score 50 goals in just 50 games, and that was the target Bossy set for himself. He didn't go public with it at first, but did confide in a few friends and teammates.

After scoring three goals in a 9–0 win over Chicago on December 21, 1980, Bossy had 37 goals in 36 games. It was around then, when a journalist asked him if he was shooting for Phil Esposito's single-season scoring record of 76 goals, set 10 years earlier in 1970–71, that Bossy went public with what had been driving him. "Rocket's record is what I'm aiming for," he said.

With the spotlight now on him, Bossy soon hit a slump. Through 45 games, he had scored 41 goals and the chance at 50 in 50 seemed to be slipping away. Then a four-goal night in a 6–3 win over Pittsburgh on January 13 put him at 45 in 46, and three goals in his next game in a 6–4 win against Washington gave him 48 in 47. Scoreless nights in his next two games left Bossy at 48 heading into the Islanders' 50th game of the season, at home against the Quebec Nordiques on January 24, 1981.

Remarkably, Bossy was not the only player in the NHL with a chance to reach 50 goals in 50 games that day. Playing in Los Angeles with Dave Taylor and future Hall of Famer Marcel Dionne on the Kings' "Triple Crown Line," Charlie Simmer had scored 46 goals through 49 games. Simmer had scored 56 the year before but had not spoken much about the 50-in-50 milestone. He was "amazed" that Bossy had put so much pressure on himself. "I'd love to do it," admitted Simmer, "but I'm not obsessed by it."

Simmer had the first chance, with the Kings playing an afternoon game in Boston that day. Four goals was a big ask, but Simmer had already done it once that season — in a 7–4 win over Bossy's Islanders back on November 1. He would score three against the Bruins that afternoon, although the third came into an empty net with just one second remaining so there was no real chance of getting another.

Bossy now had the stage to himself, in front of a capacity crowd of 15,008 at the Nassau County Coliseum. But through two periods against the Nordiques that night, he was all but invisible. Coach Al Arbour was sending him out on extra shifts, and his teammates kept looking to set him up, but Bossy didn't even manage a shot on goal during the first 40 minutes.

"It felt like my hands were taped together," he told reporters. "I wondered if I'd ever score a goal again."

How the NHL Sees It

The NHL doesn't keep a record for the fewest games to score 50 goals. Instead, it notes a record for the most goals scored in 50 games played from the start of a season:

Goals	Player	Team	Season	(Reached 50 in)
61	Wayne Gretzky	Edmonton	1981–82	(39 games)
61	Wayne Gretzky	Edmonton	1983–84	(42 games)
54	Mario Lemieux	Pittsburgh	1988–89	(46 games)
53	Wayne Gretzky	Edmonton	1984–85	(49 games)
52	Brett Hull	St. Louis	1990–91	(49 games)
50	Maurice Richard	Montreal	1944–45	(50 games)
50	Mike Bossy	NY Islanders	1980–81	(50 games)
50	Brett Hull	St. Louis	1991–92	(50 games)

(All are members of the Hockey Hall of Fame)

Bossy began to look more like his usual self in the third period, but he still couldn't get a shot past goalie Ron Grahame. Finally, on a setup from his future Hall of Fame center Bryan Trottier and defenseman Stefan Persson with just 4:10 to play, Bossy put in a backhander for number 49. Then with just 1:29 remaining, Bossy took a long cross-ice pass from Trottier, paused for just an instant and fired a wrist shot through the goalie's legs. Bossy jumped and the crowd went into a frenzy as the scoreboard flashed "50 50 Bossy 50 Fifty" over and over.

It was a remarkable moment ... even if, just one year later, Wayne Gretzky would obliterate both Bossy's accomplishment and Esposito's single-season record when he scored 50 goals in 39 games en route to 92 goals and 212 points in 1981–82.

Unofficial 50 in 50

It's team games that matter for the 50-in-50 scoring feat, not player games. So although these players reached the milestone too, they don't actually count:

▶ Jari Kurri of the Oilers scored his 50th goal in his 50th game in 1984–85, but it was Edmonton's 53rd game of the season. Kurri finished with 71 goals in 73 games during an 80-game season.

Alexander Mogilny gets tripped up by Ken Daneyko.

► Alexander Mogilny of the Sabres scored his 50th goal in his 46th game in 1992–93, but it was Buffalo's 53rd game. Mogilny scored 76 goals in 77 games during an 84-game season.

► Mario Lemieux of the Penguins scored his 50th goal in his 48th game in 1992–93, which was Pittsburgh's 72nd game. Lemieux had 69 goals in 60 games that season.

► Cam Neely of the Bruins scored his 50th goal in his 44th game in 1993–94, which was Boston's 66th game. Neely finished with 50 goals in 49 games during an 84-game schedule.

► Lemieux scored his 50th goal in his 50th game in 1995–96, but it was the Penguins' 59th game. Lemieux had 69 goals in 70 games that year during an 82-game schedule.

Near Misses

► Bobby Hull of the Chicago Black Hawks scored his 50th goal in his 52nd game in 1965–66. He finished with 54 goals, a new single-season record at the time, in 65 games played during the 70-game season.

► Charlie Simmer scored 49 goals in 50 games for Los Angeles in 1980–81 and got his 50th in his 51st

WHA 50 in 50

Playing for the Winnipeg Jets of the World Hockey Association in 1974–75, Bobby Hull became the first major pro hockey player since Maurice Richard to score 50 in 50. Hull had 47 goals entering his 50th game and scored three goals to hit the milestone. Hull finished with 77 goals in 78 games, surpassing what was then the single-season NHL record of 76 goals scored by Phil Esposito in 1970–71.

Also playing for the Winnipeg Jets, Anders Hedberg scored 51 goals in 49 games in 1976–77, becoming the first player in either the WHA or the NHL to score 50 goals in fewer than 50 games. Hedberg finished that season with 70 goals in 68 games.

game. Simmer finished with 56 goals in 65 games after a season-ending injury.

- ▶ Mario Lemieux scored his 50th goal in his 51st game in 1987–88 and finished the season with 70 goals in 77 games played.
- ▶ Bernie Nicholls of the Los Angeles Kings scored his 50th goal in his 51st game in 1988–89 and finished with 70 goals in 79 games played.

Scoring Streaks

During the 1921–22 NHL season, Punch Broadbent of the Ottawa Senators scored in 16 straight games during the 24-game schedule. After notching his first of the season with the game-winning goal in overtime when Ottawa beat the Hamilton Tigers 3–2 on opening night on December 17, 1921, Broadbent was shut out in the second game when the Senators lost 5–4 to the Toronto St. Pats. After that, he scored in every game played from December 24 through February 15, 1922. Broadbent never scored more than three in a game, which he did with back-to-back hat tricks against the Canadiens and Hamilton on January 18 and 21, but during his streak he scored 26 times in 16 games.

NHL records used to show Broadbent as the league leader in 1921–22 with 32 goals and 46 points. But when the league revealed its revamped statistical records in 2017, it knocked one off Broadbent's goal-scoring total, meaning he tied Babe Dye for the lead that season with 31 goals, although his 45 points still tops that list.

As to Broadbent's scoring streak, newspapers didn't appear to give it much play at the time. In fact, there seems to be almost no mention of it at all until 1963.

From December 15, 1962, through January 5, 1963, future Hall of Famer Andy Bathgate of the New York Rangers scored goals in 10 straight games. When Bathgate scored in his ninth straight game, it was

Andy Bathgate poses for a portrait as a member of the New York Rangers.

announced that he had tied an NHL record shared by Maurice Richard, Bernie Geoffrion and Bobby Hull, who had each done it during the three 50-goal seasons

Old Elbows

Born in Ottawa with the given names Harold Lawton Broadbent, he usually went by Harry. Broadbent was being referred to as "Punch" in local newspapers as early as 1910 when he was just a 17-year-old kid playing with a couple of different Ottawa amateur clubs. No reason seems to be given, but Broadbent was tough as well as talented. During his NHL heyday he was sometimes known as "Old Elbows" too. At a Lions Club sports dinner in Ottawa in 1965, Broadbent admitted that nickname was no accident, but he wasn't taking all the blame either. "I was merely protecting myself at all times," he said, "but somehow other fellows kept running into them with their faces. People could never understand."

Quote ... Unquote

"I'm glad it's over. Now I can just start a new one. There's a little disappointment in not scoring. I was tight. They checked us pretty good. I can forget about Punch Broadbent now. Maybe I can get back down to playing a normal game."

— **Charlie Simmer**, after being held scoreless for the first time in 14 games in the Kings' 4–3 win over the Minnesota North Stars on December 29, 1979

Longest Goal Streaks, One Season

Games	Player	Team	Season	Dates	Goals
16	Punch Broadbent*	Ottawa Senators	1921–22	Dec. 24/1921 to Feb. 15/1922	26
14	Joe Malone*	Montreal Canadiens	1917–18	Dec. 19/1917 to Feb. 6/1922	35
13	Newsy Lalonde*	Montreal Canadiens	1920–21	Jan. 22/1921 to Mar. 2/1921	25
13	Charlie Simmer	Los Angeles Kings	1979–80	Nov. 24/1979 to Dec. 27/1979	17
12	Cy Denneny*	Ottawa Senators	1917–18	Dec. 19/1917 to Jan. 26/1918	23
12	Dave Lumley	Edmonton Oilers	1981–82	Nov. 21/1981 to Dec. 16/1981	15
12	Mario Lemieux*	Pittsburgh Penguins	1992–93	Oct. 16/1992 to Nov. 1/1992	18
11	Babe Dye*	Toronto St. Pats	1920–21	Jan. 17/1921 to Mar. 19/1921	22
11	Babe Dye*	Toronto St. Pats	1921–22	Jan. 14/1922 to Feb. 18/1922	15
11	Marcel Dionne*	Los Angeles Kings	1982–83	Feb. 26/1983 to Mar. 22/1983	14
11	Pat LaFontaine*	New York Islanders	1989–90	Dec. 15/1989 to Jan. 11/1990	18
11	Mario Lemieux*	Pittsburgh Penguins	1992–93	Mar. 18/1993 to Apr. 4/1993	21
11	Teemu Selanne*	Anaheim Ducks	1997–98	Oct. 21/1997 to Nov. 10/1997	17

* Member of the Hockey Hall of Fame

to that point in NHL history. But on the day Bathgate would score in his 10th straight game came news that the NHL had recently been apprised of the true record.

Fans of hockey history may recognize the name Charles Coleman. Coleman spent years compiling the statistics of early era hockey players and would publish them during the mid-1960s in a three volume set called *The Trail of the Stanley Cup*. Coleman provided the NHL with the numbers from Broadbent's streak, as well as those from Joe Malone, Newsy Lalonde, Cy Denneny and Dye, who'd all had scoring streaks of more than 10 games between 1917 and 1922.

Gretzky's Streaks

Wayne Gretzky's longest goal-scoring streak ran nine games, from December 9 through December 30, 1981. He scored 19 goals during his streak, including five on the final night in a 7–5 win over Philadelphia in which he scored his 50th goal of the season in his 39th game. Gretzky scored points in a record 51 straight games during the 1983–84 season from the first night of play on October 5, 1983, through to January 27, 1984. He also holds the record for the longest assist streak, setting up goals in 23 consecutive games from February 8 through March 24, 1991.

Boom Boom

Bernie Geoffrion, the NHL's second 50-goal-scorer, was known as "Boom Boom." While it's often said that he invented the slap shot, there were others who had used it before him … although never with such impressive results. Still, the stories of how Geoffrion got his nickname reveal something about the disdain coaches and fans had for the slap shot in his time. It was said that "Boom Boom" came from the booming sound that was made when Geoffrion's stick hit the puck … and then by the second boom when the puck hit the boards behind the net.

Geoffrion tells the story of his nickname in a Legends Spotlight by Kevin Shea on the Hockey Hall of Fame website: "There was a sportswriter named Charlie Boire who used to work for the *Montreal Star*. I was always practicing my slap shot. I was at the Forum after a practice and Charlie came up to me and said, 'Do you mind if I call you Boom Boom?' I said, 'I don't care' … I realized that nicknames are always recognized if you produce, but if you don't produce, no one cares about a nickname."

Malcolm Moran, writing in the *New York Times* on December 3, 1979, reveals more of the sarcasm behind the nickname:

He was 16 when he became Boom Boom, in his first season with the Palestre Nationales, a junior team owned by the Canadiens. Already

he was using an unconventional method to shoot the puck. Instead of flicking it with his forearms and wrists, he brought his stick back farther, leaned his upper body, hips and legs into the shot, and slapped at the puck. One day the slap shot would change the game.

Back then, all it did was discourage people from sitting behind the net. He was a third-string forward, and his shot needed lots of work. Which is what he did. He would stay after practice, a half hour and more, trying to put his shot on net and not succeeding very often.

Charlie Boire, a writer for The Montreal Star, was watching all this from the catwalk at the top of the Forum one day as he sat with Russ Taylor, the public-address announcer.

A shot missed, and crashed against the boards. 'Boom,' Boire said.

Another miss, another crash. 'Boom,' Taylor said.

A shot missed again, and again. 'Boom, boom,' Boire said. He thought it sounded catchy so he used it in his next story.

An article in the *Ottawa Citizen*, from March 29, 1948, tells a slightly different story, crediting the nickname to Geoffrion's teammates. Geoffrion had recently turned 17 and was playing with the Montreal Nationales, who had crushed the Quebec Red Wings 11–0 the night before to advance to the Eastern Canada junior semifinals: "Best scoring effort of the day was provided by Geoffrion. Nicknamed 'Boom-Boom' by his teammates, the speedy wingman lived up to the name on Nationales' sixth goal. He picked up a loose puck at center ice, skirted the Quebec defense and blasted a high hard one behind a surprised Lucien Gauthier in the Red Wings' cage."

Assistance, Please

The Pacific Coast Hockey Association became the first league to tabulate assists as an official statistic during its second season of 1912–13. The National Hockey Association began tracking assists in 1913–14, but the NHL did not continue it as an official statistic during the league's first season, and only began doing so in its second season of 1918–19. Counting up to two assists for each goal would soon become the standard, but from 1930–31 through 1935–36 the NHL allowed three assists per goal. In one instance, in a game on January 10, 1935, four assists were counted on a single goal.

The game was a 5–5 tie between the Toronto Maple Leafs and the New York Americans at Madison Square Garden. At 13:52 of the second period, with Red Dutton in the penalty box for the Americans, Joe Primeau scored for the Leafs, with assists given to his "Kid Line" mates Busher Jackson and Charlie Conacher, as well as Harold "Baldy" Cotton and Andy Blair. *The New York Daily News* on January 11, 1935, described the situation: "The official scorer doled out assists to Conacher, Blair, Cotton, and Jackson on the Primeau goal, and then apparently ran out of names. It was a crazy scramble and no one could have told accurately how many men had a hand in it."

Three Goals in 21 Seconds

Bill Mosienko played 12 full seasons in the NHL and parts of two others between 1941 and 1955. In an era when 20 goals was still considered a major achievement, Mosienko topped that plateau five times, including two seasons with more than 30. Playing right wing during the heyday of Maurice Richard and Gordie Howe, he earned only two selections as a Second-Team All-Star, yet when he left the league in 1955 only six men in NHL history — Richard (422), Nels Stewart (324), Howe (271), Howie Morenz (271), Aurele Joliat

Bill Mosienko set an NHL record by scoring 3 goals in 21 seconds.

(269) and Ted Lindsay (264) — had scored more goals than his 258. He was elected to the Hockey Hall of Fame in 1965.

No less an authority than Doug Harvey, a six-time Stanley Cup champion and seven-time winner of the Norris Trophy as the league's best defenseman, told Marv Moss of the *Montreal Gazette* in 1970 that Mosienko gave him more difficulty than any other player he faced. "He liked to wind up behind his own net and come down my side," explained Harvey. "He would let go of the puck, jump around you on either side, and beat you to it."

Yet if Mosienko is remembered at all by hockey fans today, it is for scoring the fastest hat trick in NHL

The Pony Line

At just 5-foot-8 and 160 pounds, Bill Mosienko was sometimes known as "Wee Willie," but fans and teammates mostly called him "Mosie." In 1945–46 and 1946–47, Mosienko played with brothers Max and Doug Bentley. The high-flying trio was dubbed "the Pony Line" because of their small size and great speed. Max Bentley won the NHL scoring title both seasons the line played together.

history: 21 seconds. He did it on the last day of the 1951–52 season — March 23, 1952.

Mosienko scored his three goals at 6:09, 6:20 and 6:30 of the third period, sparking his Chicago Black Hawks to a 7–6 comeback win over the New York Rangers. The goals were all set up by center Gus Bodnar. On each one, Mosienko sped around Rangers defenseman Hy Buller and beat goalie Lorne Anderson, first with two shots low to the left side and then one high to the right.

By strange coincidence, Mosienko told *Hockey Digest* in 1974 that just three days before the game, he'd been looking through the NHL record book with a friend, "and I remarked how nice it would be to have my name in there with some of the hockey greats."

"Funny thing is," he said in the *Hockey Digest* story, "that 45 seconds later, I could have had a fourth goal. I was alone again, I faked Anderson out of position and had an open net to hit, but I missed the far post by a matter of inches. When I went back to the bench after missing that one, [coach Ebbie] Goodfellow yelled at me. 'Hey, what's the matter, Mosie? Are you slowing down?'"

Jean Beliveau and the Canadiens Rule

Jean Beliveau was in just his second full season with the Montreal Canadiens in 1955–56, but most fans and writers thought he was already the best player in the NHL. A First-Team All-Star at center in 1954–55, Beliveau would earn that honor again in 1955–56, adding the Hart Trophy as NHL MVP, leading the league with a career-high 47 goals, and winning the Art Ross Trophy as the scoring champion with 88 points.

Heading into a game with the Boston Bruins a month into the season on November 5, 1955, Beliveau had scored just three goals in 12 games but had collected 11 assists. That night, he scored all four goals as the Canadiens rallied from a 2–0 deficit after the first period to beat the Bruins 4–2. Three of Beliveau's goals came during a stretch of just 44 seconds between 0:42 and 1:26 of the second period. At the time the Bruins were two men short, with Cal Gardner off for charging at 19:50 of the first period and Hal Laycoe for hooking just 17 seconds into the second. (Newspaper accounts show Laycoe's penalty at 16 seconds, but NHL records show 17.)

Both charging and hooking are minor penalties, calling for two minutes in the box — but in those days players serving a two-minute sentence were not allowed to return to the ice if the team with a power play scored a goal. As such, the Bruins were two men short the entire time Beliveau scored his three quick goals.

After the season, in a meeting of the NHL rules committee on June 4, 1956 (which kicked off two days of NHL meetings, followed by a governors' meeting on June 6), the rules regarding minor penalties were changed to allow a player to return to the ice if the other team scored. The rule has often been referred to as the Montreal Canadiens rule because of how efficient the combination of Beliveau centering Maurice Richard and Bert Olmstead with Doug Harvey and Tom

Le Gros Bill

Writing a feature about Jean Beliveau that appeared in *Maclean's* magazine on March 3, 1956, Trent Frayne noted that "for years he has been called Jean Marc Beliveau in the newspapers, but he has in fact no middle name and has no idea where the Marc originated." However, according to his baptismal record, Beliveau's name was actually Joseph Arthur Jean Beliveau. As to his nickname, Frayne wrote that Beliveau was first called "le Gros Bill" around 1950 by Quebec City newspaperman Roland Sabourin. The name came from the title of an old French-Canadian folk song, "Voila le Gros Bill," which translates as Here Comes Big Bill.

Johnson on defense was on the power play. (The NHL has only tracked teams' power-play percentages since 1977–78, so it's difficult to get an official read on this.)

The fact that the six NHL teams voted 5–1 in favor of the rule change, with Canadiens assistant general manager Ken Reardon the only one to vote against it, helped enforce the idea — at the time, and ever since — that this rule was passed to hamper the Canadiens. Dink Carroll of the *Montreal Gazette* quoted Bruins general manager Lynn Patrick addressing the issue just three days after the rule had been passed: "That's a lot of nonsense. I'll tell you the reasoning behind the rule. If a player draws a minor penalty for doing something illegal which may have saved a goal — like tripping or holding or hooking — and while he is off the opposing team scores, there is no reason why he shouldn't be allowed to return to action immediately. The opposing team got the goal he may have saved by doing the thing he did which led to the penalty."

Frank Boucher was a longtime member of the New York Rangers who had starred with the team from 1926 until 1938, and later served as the team's coach and general manager until 1955. "The new rule makes sense," he said. "We tried it out in the Western Hockey League last winter and everybody liked it." Boucher also pointed out that the Canadiens weren't just outvoted 5–1 but actually 19–1. "The [American Hockey League], the WHL, and the other five NHL clubs voted for it."

Patrick also added that Jack Adams of the Red Wings had advocated for the rule change three years before, "when Detroit had the best power-play in hockey." He did it, said Patrick, "because he thought it would improve the game."

"There's always resistance to suggested rule changes," said Patrick, "but once they're adopted the criticism stops because it becomes obvious that they did work an improvement."

Still, in an era as low-scoring as the mid-1950s actually were, critics of the rule change wondered if it would take some of the excitement out of the game. Patrick referenced Beliveau's hat trick in his response: "It depends on which rink you're in. I can remember a night in the Forum last season when we had a 2–0 lead over Canadiens. Then we got a penalty and while we were short-handed Jean Beliveau scored three goals. Sure, the crowd liked it, but suppose the Canadiens had been leading and it was the Bruins who scored three goals because of a penalty. How do you think the crowd would have felt?"

Carroll also reported that Richard had no problem with the rule change. "I think it's all right," said the Rocket. "How many times do you think we scored more than one goal while the other team was a man short?" When someone replied that he remembered quite a few times, Richard laughed and said: "It may seem like that to you, but I think if you checked back you'd find it didn't happen very often. Think of all the times we didn't score when we had a man advantage."

Chapter 2
Multisport Hockey Stars

Bo Didn't Know

Remember that first "Bo Knows" commercial for Nike? It originally aired during the Major League Baseball All-Star Game on July 11, 1989. Bo Jackson played in the game that year. In 1990 the two-sport star would play in the NFL Pro Bowl.

The ad begins with Jackson taking swings in his Kansas City Royals uniform. It then cuts to Kirk Gibson, reigning National League MVP and 1988 World Series hero for the Los Angeles Dodgers.

"Bo knows baseball," says Gibson confidently.

After some guitar licks by blues legend Bo Diddley (who provides the soundtrack throughout the ad), the scene shifts to Jackson running upfield in his L.A. Raiders gear.

"Bo knows football," says Los Angeles Rams quarterback Jim Everett.

Next up, Jackson stuffs a slam dunk. Michael Jordan says, "Bo knows basketball too."

Then a few shots of Jackson in his whites playing on a different court.

John McEnroe seems confused.

"Bo knows tennis?" he asks.

Next, American Olympic marathon champion Joan Benoit confirms that Bo knows running. Later, a professional women's cycling team, followed by a group of bodybuilders — over more clips of Jackson in action — maintain that Bo knows their sports too.

After the running segment, Jackson is seen in the uniform of the Los Angeles Kings, helmet-less, but crunching an opponent heavily into the boards. Wayne Gretzky, similarly attired after his first season in L.A. (and also without a helmet), skates into the scene. Gretzky stops and shakes his head. With a sly grin, he says:

"No."

Diddley chuckles.

Bo Jackson knew a lot of things, but he didn't know hockey. He filmed those scenes wearing socks on his feet in a rink with no ice.

After all, skating is hard.

"Have you ever considered that the game of hockey is unique?" asked future NHL executive Wren Blair in a 1965 article by Trent Frayne for *Maclean's* about Bobby Orr when he was with the Oshawa Generals.

"A good hockey player can play all games well," continued Blair, then known as the man who'd signed Orr for the Boston Bruins organization, "but few stars of another sport can play hockey at all. Can you imagine Mickey Mantle or Cassius Clay or Arnold Palmer or Johnny Unitas able to make even a high school hockey team?

"The point is," said Blair, "every hockey player must have the attributes of the top athletes in any game, except he must then add the encumbrance of skates. We grow up taking these things for granted in Canada, but the truth is that hockey is the most difficult of all games to master."

Wayne Gretzky as a member of the Los Angeles Kings.

Lionel Conacher debuted as a professional wrestler in May 1932 at the Arena Gardens in Toronto, Ontario.

Lionel Conacher's Sporting Life

With all the money available to athletes in recent years, it's not surprising that most now specialize in one sport. Even young kids can play hockey nearly 12 months a year. In the old days multisport athletes used to be the rule, rather than the exception. Generally speaking, sports seasons were much shorter, and games were played according to the seasons in nature: hockey in the winter, baseball and lacrosse in the spring and summer, football in the fall. Other sports were on the calendar when appropriate, and a good athlete stayed in shape year-round by playing many of them. Still, there were some who took this to the extreme. None more so than Lionel Conacher.

Born on May 24, 1900, Lionel Conacher was the second child, and oldest boy, in a family of 10 who grew up poor in a working-class Toronto neighborhood. Canadians and citizens all across the British Empire were marking the last birthday that Queen Victoria would celebrate in her lifetime, and troops fighting the Boer War were marching on Pretoria in South Africa. The Boer capital would soon be captured and would provide Conacher with an unusual middle name. He was, according to Ontario birth records registered on June 30, 1900, Lionel Joseph Pretoria Conacher.

Conacher attended Jesse Ketchum school in Toronto, where the principal believed that playing organized sports helped keep children out of trouble. Conacher had to quit school after grade 8 to go to work with his father, but he never stopped playing sports, and he was a champion at almost everything he tried, be it football, baseball, boxing, lacrosse, wrestling and others. He was, however, a latecomer to hockey.

It's usually said that Conacher didn't start skating until he was 16. But in a story in the Brooklyn *Daily Eagle* on January 26, 1929 (when he was in the NHL with the New York Americans), Conacher told writer Harold C. Burr, "I didn't have hockey skates on my feet until I was 15."

"I couldn't think much about hockey," added Conacher. "I had to go to work for a living. But it's a night game, and by and by the bug bit me. I had the kid's regulation dream of making one of the [Ontario Hockey Association junior] teams in my home town of Toronto. I and hundreds of other kids went to the arena for the tryouts. I went home with 'em too — and wasn't asked to come back. But I kept coming back."

Stamp of Approval

Canada issued its first hockey-themed stamp on January 23, 1956. The 5 cent stamp is blue and white and depicts a goalie and two players heading up the ice. They are wearing jerseys that say CANADA across the chest. A Canadian Press story on December 9, 1955, announcing the upcoming release said that former Liberal Member of Parliament for Toronto Trinity Lionel Conacher had given "strong sponsorship" to the hockey stamp.

The Big Train

Considered the fastest pitcher anyone had ever seen, Walter Johnson was known as "the Big Train" for his power and speed in the age of the locomotive as a future Baseball Hall of Fame star with the Washington Senators from 1907 to 1927. Lionel Conacher was known as "Big Train" as early as 1921 because of his combination of power and speed as a ball carrier when he was starring in football with the Toronto Argonauts. In Conacher's case, the nickname might also have been a bit of wordplay involving his first name and the Lionel Train company that made toy train sets.

Interestingly, on the same day Conacher was leading the Toronto Argos to the 1921 Grey Cup championship, future Hockey Hall of Famer Sprague Cleghorn signed with the Montreal Canadiens after spending the previous three seasons with the Ottawa Senators. In reporting on the deal on December 5, 1921, the *Ottawa Citizen* referred to Cleghorn as "the Big Train."

At the age of 16, Conacher played juvenile hockey with the Century Rovers, who won the championship of the Beaches Hockey League (forerunner of today's Greater Toronto Hockey League). By 17 Conacher was playing OHA junior hockey with Toronto's Aura Lee team. When he was 19 he joined the hockey team from the Toronto Canoe Club along with several other future NHLers, including future Hall of Fame goalie Roy Worters, and led them to the second ever Memorial Cup championship in 1920.

But football and lacrosse were Conacher's favorite games. In 1920 he joined the Toronto Argonauts of the Ontario Rugby Football Union. In 1921 he joined the senior Argonauts in the Interprovincial Rugby Football Union with the Hamilton Tigers, Ottawa Rough Riders and Montreal Football Club. The IRFU was known as the "Big Four" and was the forerunner of the East Division of the Canadian Football League. Conacher was a star, and he led the Argos to the Grey Cup that season with a 23–0 win over the Edmonton Eskimos (now the Edmonton Elks) in the first East–West Canadian football championship. He accounted for 15 of Toronto's 23 points with two touchdowns (worth five points at the time), a field goal and a pair of singles on long punts.

During 1921 and 1922 Conacher was offered professional contracts to play hockey in the NHL. But since most of the sports he competed in required him to be an amateur, he turned them down. In 1923 Conacher played intermediate hockey for the North Toronto Athletic Association. He scored six goals in a 16–4 win over Midland in a playoff game on February 8, 1923, which happened to be the first hockey game ever broadcast on the radio.

With his amateur status still intact, Conacher went to Pittsburgh in the fall of 1923, hoping to play football at Pittsburgh University. His academic status wasn't up to it, however, so he attended the Bellefonte Academy prep school instead. Conacher got to play football against American colleges while at Bellefonte and enjoyed the American-style game. He also played hockey in Pittsburgh, joining several Torontonians and Canadians (including Worters, as well as Baldy Cotton, who was also attending Bellefonte) on the Pittsburgh Yellowjackets. The team won the U.S. Amateur championships in 1924 and 1925.

Before the 1925–26 season Pittsburgh was admitted to the NHL. Conacher finally decided to go pro, and he and several of his Yellowjacket teammates (including Cotton and Worters) were included on the Pittsburgh Pirates roster. He would play in the NHL with the Pirates, the New York Americans, the Montreal Maroons and the Chicago Black Hawks for 12 seasons through 1936–37.

As a hockey player, Conacher was never a great skater, but he had a hard shot, was a tough checker and could block shots too. Through determined effort, he made himself into an All-Star defenseman, earning Second-Team selections in 1933 and 1937, and a First-Team nod in 1934. He also played with other NHL stars in the Ace Bailey Benefit Game in 1934 and was second in Hart Trophy voting for NHL MVP in 1934 and 1937. He won the Stanley Cup with Chicago in 1934 and with the Maroons the following year.

During most of his time in the NHL, Conacher still played other sports too. He was with the Toronto Maple Leafs baseball team during the 1926 season and played pro football against American teams with Toronto-based clubs in 1933 and 1934. (His 1934 team also featured his brother Charlie). In the summer of 1931 he was the star player when the Montreal Canadiens, Montreal Maroons, Toronto Maple Leafs and a team from Cornwall, Ontario, created box lacrosse by moving the game indoors from fields to hockey arenas. In 1932 he wrestled professionally during the NHL off-season.

In 1936 Conacher wrote an article for *Maclean's* titled "You've Got to Be Tough." In it he spoke of his many injuries: nose broken eight times, leg and arm broken, several broken bones in his hands, 10 cracked ribs, a skate gash near his jugular, two smashed knee cartilages resulting in operations, and more than 500 stitches in his face and head to go with another 150 or so across the rest of his body.

"Has it been worthwhile?" asked Conacher. "I answer that question simply by stating that if I had it to do all over again, there would be no alteration to the course I've set. It cost me plenty to become a tough athlete, but I've reaped plenty of dividends in thrills, happiness, and financial security. A career in the Big Time is worthwhile because, to make a success of it, you must build your body, think clearly, and lead a regular life."

Out of sports by 1937 Conacher won election as a Member of Provincial Parliament from Toronto that October and served until 1943. He ran for the Federal Liberal Party in 1945 and was defeated, but he later won election in 1949 and 1953.

On May 26, 1954, two days after his 54th birthday (although many newspapers reported he was only 52), Conacher was playing in the annual softball game between Members of Parliament and the press corps. Bucko McDonald, another former NHL player turned politician, was also playing. In the second inning Conacher hit a single and stretched it into a triple when a reporter bobbled the ball. In the fourth he made a nice running catch in left field from his position at second base.

Just before he came to bat in the sixth inning, Conacher complained of a slight pain in his chest. He thought it was probably indigestion.

"C'mon, Lionel, we're not getting as many homers as we used to," called out teammate George Hees, a Progressive Conservative MP from Toronto, as Conacher stepped to the plate.

"I guess we're getting older," replied Conacher.

It was the last thing he ever said.

After swinging hard and missing at two pitches, Conacher hit a drive over the infield and down the right field line. McDonald had been on base, and as he came around to score, Conacher raced into third with an RBI triple.

Maurice Jefferies of the *Windsor Star* was playing third base for the press gallery team. "Quite a clout," said Jefferies.

Charlie Conacher (9), Bert Conacher (3) and Lionel Conacher (12) pose in 1952.

Conacher only mumbled a reply. Jefferies thought he looked gray.

A moment later Conacher eased himself to his knees and then fell forward.

Jefferies and future prime minister Lester B. Pearson, who was coaching at third base, tore off calling for a doctor. The first one on the scene diagnosed coronary thrombosis: a heart attack.

"It was apparent to all he was dying," said Jefferies.

Within 10 minutes Conacher was given oxygen from the crew of an Ottawa Fire Department emergency truck. Less than 10 minutes after that, he was pronounced dead on the way to Ottawa General Hospital.

After a funeral on May 29, 1954, Lionel Conacher was laid to rest at St. John's York Mills Anglican Church Cemetery in the Toronto suburb of North York.

Family Affair

Lionel Conacher is a member of the Hockey Hall of Fame, Canada's Sports Hall of Fame, the Canadian Football Hall of Fame and the Lacrosse Hall of Fame. Brother Charlie, a scoring star and Stanley Cup champion with the Toronto Maple Leafs in the 1930s, is a member of the Hockey Hall of Fame and Canada's Sports Hall of Fame. Youngest brother Roy, who played with Boston, Detroit and Chicago in the NHL from 1938 until 1952 (and served in the Royal Canadian Air Force during World War II as well), is also a member of the Hockey Hall of Fame.

Another brother, Bert, was a twin of Roy. Bert played hockey in Toronto in the 1930s and '40s and won the Memorial Cup playing with Roy on the West Toronto Nationals — under coach Hap Day, a teammate of Charlie's — in 1936. Bert may well have followed his brothers into the NHL, and perhaps into the Hall of Fame too, but he had lost the sight in his left eye as a 16-year-old when he was clipped by the blade of Charlie's stick playing road hockey.

Lionel's son Lionel Conacher Jr. played a year of football with the Montreal Alouettes of the CFL in 1960. Son Brian played hockey for Canada at the 1964 Winter Olympics and won the Stanley Cup with the Maple Leafs in 1967. Charlie's son Pete played in the NHL with Chicago, Toronto and the New York Rangers between 1951 and 1957. Murray Henderson, the son of sister Catherine Conacher, played with the Bruins from 1945 through 1952 and was a teammate of his uncle Roy during the final four games of the 1945–46 season.

Iron Man: Part 1

In the January 26, 1929, story about him in the *Brooklyn Daily Eagle*, Lionel Conacher spoke about his biggest day in sports. Hockey played no part in it. It had happened in the summer.

"I was doubling at baseball and lacrosse," explained Conacher. "Hillcrest started their baseball games at 2 o'clock to give me a chance to do some lacrosse playing for the Maitland Club before dark. It so happened that both teams played for the championship on the same afternoon.

"The baseball team had already won the city title and was playing the Monarchs for the championship of Ontario. The game was shortened to seven innings by agreement. In the last half of the seventh we were two runs behind. I came up with the bases filled, hit a triple and touched third, ending the game.

"My next stop was a taxi. I jumped out of my baseball uniform and into my lacrosse suit. Maitland was trailing, 3–0, when I got into the game. I shot four goals, which left the score 5–3, beating Brampton for the [Ontario] championship."

Unless it happened more than once (which it might have), Conacher seems to have gotten some of the details wrong. Though both the Hillcrests and the Maitlands did win championships later that season, Conacher's "Iron Man Stunt" (as a headline in Toronto's *Globe* newspaper called it) occurred earlier in the season.

On Saturday, June 4, 1921, Conacher did help his Hillcrest team win a game to reclaim first place in the league. When he arrived at the Maitlands game afterward, his team was trailing Brampton 2–1 at half-time. "Conacher began the second half on the home field, and from then till full-time Brampton were able to score only once, while the local team added [four] to their total. Conacher displayed stick handling ability as well as speed and used his superior weight to advantage on numerous occasions."

Conacher scored twice in a three-minute stretch during the final period "and was an essential factor in the play that accounted for a third" as the Maitlands rallied for a 5–3 victory.

Iron Man: Part 2

Though he didn't mention it at all in his *Brooklyn Eagle* interview, Lionel Conacher pulled off another impressive double on December 3, 1921, which the *Toronto Daily Star* this time referred to as "Conny's Iron Man Stunt." This one did involve hockey... although perhaps the fact that his hockey team lost its game made the moment less memorable for him.

On the same day that Conacher led the Argonauts to the Grey Cup, he left the season's final football game at Varsity Stadium on Bloor Street near St. George in downtown Toronto (leaving, perhaps, a little bit early, as the game was well in hand) to prepare for the first senior hockey game of the season that evening a short distance away at the Arena Gardens on Mutual Street, just south of Dundas near Jarvis.

Lionel Conacher waits for the ball with Crosse and Blackwell Chefs in 1934.

Conacher's Aura Lee team featured another future Hockey Hall of Famer, with Billy Burch also in the lineup, but it was in tough that night against the future 1924 Olympic gold medalists from the Toronto Granite Club. Led by amateur scoring sensation — and another future Hall of Famer — Harry Watson (although without another Hall of Famer due to the absence of Hooley Smith that night), plus future

NHLers Dunc Munro, Bert McCaffrey and goalie John Ross Roach, the Granites came away with a 4–2 victory.

Despite having played in the Grey Cup game that afternoon, Conacher played all 60 minutes on defense for Aura Lee and scored one of the team's goals. And, remarkably, he wasn't the only football champion on the ice that night. Alex Romeril of the Argonauts played for the Granites. Romeril would miss the 1924 Winter Games because of work commitments, but he would make his mark in the NHL as a referee and, briefly, in 1926–27 as a coach for part of the season in Toronto during the time when the St. Pats were bought by Conn Smythe and renamed the Maple Leafs.

Conacher in the Ring

One of the more remarkable stories from the extraordinary career of Lionel Conacher is his boxing exhibition with Jack Dempsey, the heavyweight champion of the world. Dempsey was 27 years old when the two met in Toronto on October 10, 1922. He had become the champ in 1919 and would hold the belt until 1926. Conacher was 22 years old and hadn't done a lot of boxing.

Conacher had won the welterweight wrestling championship of Ontario when he was only 16 years old but had trained in boxing for only a short time when he stepped into the ring for his first career fight at the Canadian amateur boxing championships, which were held in Ottawa on April 23–24, 1920. He won the light heavyweight title by defeating Harry Lomas of Montreal. "It was a splendid bout," said the *Montreal Gazette*, "with both boys landing some tremendous punches." Lou Marsh, writing in the *Toronto Star*, said Conacher, "forced Lomas to the ropes on different occasions, landing hard rights and lefts to the face."

While noting that Conacher was "green" as a fighter, Marsh said that he "had the punch and the fighting spirit and he hammered out a brilliant

Lionel Conacher and Jack Dempsey in the late-1930s.

victory." Conacher also fought for the heavyweight title against fellow Torontonian Charlie McDoulton that same day. The *Gazette* referred to this as an "iron-man stunt," but just 49 seconds into the bout, "during which he had rocked McDoulton with a wicked swing to the face," Conacher tore the ligaments in one of his wrists and was unable to continue.

Conacher fought at least once more as a heavy-weight in 1921 but hadn't spent much time in the ring when Jack Dempsey arrived in Toronto for a week of work at a local vaudeville theater. Conacher was there at a luncheon for Dempsey at the King Edward Hotel on October 9, 1922, and the two met in a four-round exhibition bout the next day at the Christie Street

Military Hospital before a crowd of disabled veterans of World War I.

The two were a good match physically, with the *Toronto Star* story on October 11 reporting that they weighed within two pounds of one another. "Dempsey is more slender below the waist but his arms were larger and chest deeper than that of the rugby star, but Conacher lost nothing by the physical compari-son." Still, the fight wasn't much to begin with.

"Conacher," said the *Star*, "started off like he thought Dempsey was a cream puff. Everybody thought it was going to be a petting party or a kissing bee. Dempsey wasn't for mussing up the village hero and getting himself in dutch so they slapped and

Wrestling Against the Great Depression

Just a couple of weeks after helping the Toronto Maple Leafs win their first Stanley Cup on April 9, 1932, future Hall of Famers Hap Day, the team captain, and fellow defenseman Red Horner were back at Maple Leaf Gardens on the evening of April 25. They weren't playing hockey this time. Day and Horner faced each other in front of 4,500 fans "in a wild exhibition of wrestling" as part of an Unemployment Benefit Show. Their bout ended in a draw.

hugged and waltzed and the boys were getting the yawns when the first bell rang."

"Dempsey was just wonderful," said Conacher, telling the story in the *Brooklyn Daily Eagle* on January 26, 1929. "Wonderful fighter and a wonderful fellow. I thought I wasn't scared after I got in the ring, but the referee thought I was after the first round. He came over to me on my stool. 'Are you afraid of him?' he snarled. Then I began to realize I was afraid—just a little."

In the *Star* story, it was said that a friend encouraged Conacher to take a shot at Dempsey in the second round. In the *Brooklyn* story, he said he was there with Billy Burch, so it might have been him. Whoever it was, when the second round started, "Jack came in, bobbing around the way he does, and I managed to cut his lip."

The *Star* story says Conacher punched Dempsey on the chin, which rocked him onto his heels and "jarred his brain pan." Then, "Dempsey sent one back that made Conacher think the hospital was a midway

merry-go-round ... Of course Dempsey did not try to hurt Conacher, but he hit him hard enough to teach him not to get fresh with a champeen."

"I wobbled about, I guess," recalled Conacher in the *Brooklyn* newspaper. "Dazed, I felt his arms close about me. I heard his voice whisper in my ear, 'Are you all right, kid?' Now that was a mighty fine thing. I hadn't any business hitting him like that. Another fellow would have sent me to the refrigerator."

"The third round was lively," said the *Star*, "and both left the ring blowing and sweating." There is no recap of the fourth, but "Conacher lost several square inches of skin from his face and ribs and he has a lump on his chin he wouldn't trade for a new Ford."

Dempsey, who also went two rounds that day with University of Toronto middleweight champion Les Black, came away impressed with Conacher. "[He's] a good one," said the champ. "If he would get into the [fight] game I'm sure he would make good. They tell me he has all sorts of courage, and I know he's big and fast, and he is no slouch as a boxer. He made my head sing, and I know he wasn't hitting with anything like all he had."

Conacher at the Plate

On January 29, 1926, Lionel Conacher and the Pittsburgh Pirates were in Toronto to face the St. Pats in an NHL game that evening. The St. Pats won 3–2, but the bigger news was made that afternoon when the Toronto Maple Leafs baseball club signed Conacher and St. Pats star Babe Dye for the upcoming season.

In addition to being a top scorer in the NHL, Dye was also a minor-league baseball star. He'd spent the previous four summers playing with the Buffalo Bisons. Conacher hadn't played much baseball since the summer of 1923, and there is little doubt that he was signed mainly for publicity reasons by the local

Other Sports Too

In addition to winning honors as Canada's outstanding male athlete, Lionel Conacher also topped the poll as Canada's outstanding football player of the first half of the 20th century. He received votes as the best lacrosse player too — an honor won by Newsy Lalonde, who also received a vote as Canada's best hockey player.

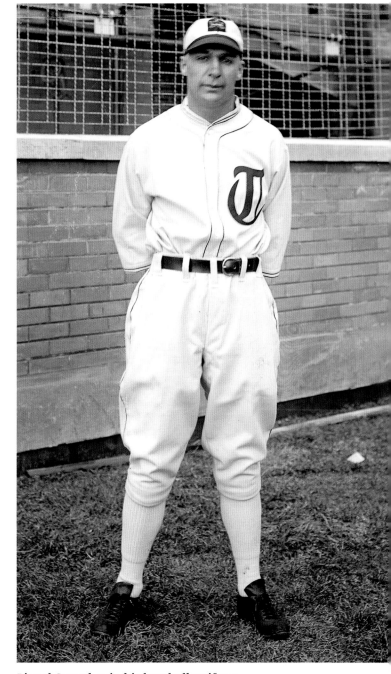

Lionel Conacher in his baseball uniform.

baseball team that would be opening the brand new Maple Leaf Stadium in Toronto that season. It was certainly a good business proposition for Conacher.

"No untried player was ever presented with a better proposition," reported the *Toronto Star*. "Under the terms of the contract, Conacher must be carried by the Toronto club all season. He cannot be sold or traded, which means that whether he makes good or not, he is sure to draw down one full season's pay."

Manager Dan Howley acknowledged that Conacher would be good for the box office no matter how much or how little he played, but he was said to have high hopes for the new recruit. "Manager Howley is of the belief that he will make something of the big fellow," noted the *Toronto Star*. "Otherwise he would not have been so keen to get him." The Leafs had a working relationship with the Detroit Tigers and shared a spring training facility with them in Augusta, Georgia. Tigers player-manager Ty Cobb was said to be "a great admirer of the great all-rounder," and it was hoped that the baseball legend would be able to help Conacher make good.

The hockey Pirates finished third in the seven-team NHL during their first season in the league in 1925–26. Conacher and Dye were already late for Maple Leafs

spring training when the NHL season ended on March 17, 1926, and Conacher would be delayed even further with his Pirates in the playoffs. Pittsburgh was eliminated in its two-game, total-goals semifinal series by the soon-to-be Stanley Cup–champion Montreal Maroons on March 23. Still, Conacher did not report to Augusta as quickly as Howley would have liked.

Dye finally showed up at the Maple Leafs' training camp on March 29. Conacher didn't report until April 6. Dye had only had one hit in 18 at-bats before that day, but suddenly went 5-for-6 with a pair of doubles. Conacher was in uniform the next day, taking batting and fielding practice with the team. The two NHL stars played together for the baseball Maple Leafs on April 8, and Conacher recorded his first hit, run (the game-winner, in fact) and putout as a professional baseball player while playing left field in a 9–8 Toronto win over the Richmond Red Sox.

Conacher and Dye broke camp with the team, though neither played in the season-opening 8–2 win in Reading, Pennsylvania, on April 14. Dye, as a proven minor-league star, was played up much more prominently than Conacher in the publicity to promote Toronto's home opener at Maple Leaf Stadium on April 28. (The game was rained out, but Dye played the next day when Toronto rallied for five runs in the bottom of the ninth to tie the score and then beat the Reading Keystones 6–5 on a squeeze play in the bottom of the tenth.)

The Maple Leafs went on to win the International League pennant that year and defeat the Louisville Colonels of the American Association in the Little World Series. But Conacher and Dye played little part. Dye had a poor season and was released halfway through the schedule. He finished the year with Baltimore and never played baseball again. Conacher didn't play his first game until May 15, when he came in as a defensive replacement in right field late in the first game of a Saturday doubleheader. He had no chances in the field and didn't come to bat. What statistics there are for the 1926 Maple Leafs show Conacher batting only three times all year.

It seems unlikely that Conacher actually spent the entire season with the Maple Leafs. A *Toronto Star* story on August 14 discusses him being on a trip to Sudbury with his wife and a brother and going fishing with future Hockey Hall of Famer Shorty Green. Later, Conacher was playing lacrosse in St. Catharines, Ontario, on September 19 during the final weekend of the International League season.

Both Conacher and Dye made their biggest splash of the baseball season on June 19, when the Maple Leafs were on the road, but they were allowed to return to Toronto for an exhibition game at Maple Leaf Stadium between the Toronto Semi Pros and Buffalo's Pullman Colored Giants. The Semi Pros featured a third future Hockey Hall of Famer in Conacher's buddy and longtime teammate Roy Worters. The team also had two other Conacher–Worters hockey teammates in Duke McCurry and Jess Spring, plus another hockey player in Chris Speyer. Conacher had a single and a triple in this game, and made two sensational catches in the outfield, but the Colored Giants rallied for an 11–10 victory.

Canada's Athlete of the Half Century

Lionel Conacher was named Canada's outstanding athlete of the first half of the 20th century in a Canadian Press poll of sports editors and sportscasters that was released at the end of 1950. Conacher received 33 votes in the CP poll. No one else received more than two:

Athlete	Sport	Votes
Lionel Conacher	All-around	33
Harvey Pulford	All-around	2
Percy Williams	Track and field	2
George Hainsworth	Hockey	1
Walter Knox	All-around	1
Tom Longboat	Marathon running	1
Cyclone Taylor	Hockey/Lacrosse	1
Joe Wright Sr.	Rowing	1

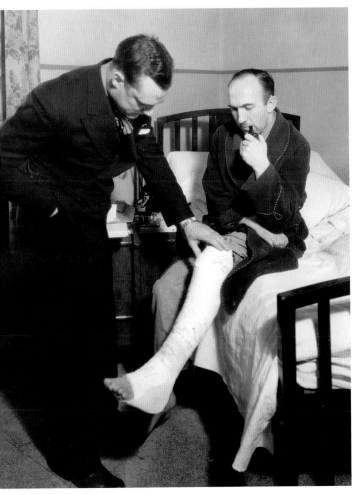

Charlie Conacher visits Howie Morenz in the hospital in February, 1937.

Morenz for Hockey

The most exciting star in hockey during his era, Howie Morenz won the Stanley Cup in his rookie season with the Montreal Canadiens in 1923–24 and later won back-to-back titles in 1930 and 1931. He was also a two-time NHL scoring champion and a three-time winner of the Hart Trophy during his 14 seasons in the NHL. Though he'd been dead for 12 years by 1950, Morenz was the overwhelming choice as Canada's greatest hockey player of the half century.

It's interesting to note that Morenz did not receive a vote for outstanding athlete, while hockey players Cyclone Taylor and George Hainsworth did. Taylor may have been considered more of an all-around athlete than Morenz, because he was also a star lacrosse

The Stratford Streak

One of several players who would become known as "the Babe Ruth of Hockey," the other nicknames attributed to Howie Morenz were all because of his blazing speed. Most famously known as "the Stratford Streak," for the town he grew up in, Morenz was also known as "the Canadien Comet" and "the Hurtling Habitant" while starring in Montreal, and "the Mitchell Meteor" for the town he was born in on September 21, 1902.

player in summer, like Newsy Lalonde. Hainsworth may have received something of a sympathy vote considering that he had died in October 1950. Here is the hockey balloting:

Player	Votes
Howie Morenz	27
Maurice Richard	4
Cyclone Taylor	3
Frank Nighbor	2
Syl Apps	1
Turk Broda	1
Aurele Joliat	1
Newsy Lalonde	1
Milt Schmidt	1
Eddie Shore	1
Nels Stewart	1

Lalonde for Lacrosse

Newsy Lalonde was the Rocket Richard of his day. One of hockey's first French Canadian superstars (although, technically, he was a Franco-Ontarian, born in Cornwall near Ontario's border with Quebec), Lalonde wasn't great as a skater, but he had a knack for putting the puck in the net. He also played the game with a nasty physical edge.

Born on October 31, 1887, Edward Cyril Lalonde was nicknamed "Newsy" after working on a Linotype print machine for newspapers in Cornwall and Woodstock, Ontario, when he was a teenager. He'd begun playing hockey and lacrosse in his hometown before 1903 and turned pro in hockey during the winter of 1906–07. He continued playing until 1927–28. It's difficult to get precise numbers for him, but in approximately 340 regular-season games as a pro, he scored about 456 goals, adding 34 more in 32 playoff games. Remembered mainly for his time with the Montreal Canadiens from 1909 to 1922, Lalonde suited up in no fewer than nine leagues that were eligible (or attempted to challenge) for the Stanley Cup. He won scoring titles (either goals or points, or both) in the Ontario Professional Hockey League, the National Hockey Association twice, the Pacific Coast Hockey Association, the NHL twice and the Western Canada Hockey League.

But for all his hockey prowess, it was lacrosse that earned Lalonde his selection as the greatest player of the first half of the 20th century. It was the sport he enjoyed most.

"Lacrosse looks like a rough game, but it really isn't," said Lalonde in a 1963 interview. "I always preferred it over hockey because it's played in the summer, out of doors where you get lots of fresh air. It's healthier."

In a Canadian Press obituary after his death on November 21, 1970, it was said that Lalonde figured he'd earned $140,000 in his pro sports career. His biggest salary in hockey was reported as $4,500 but he had once earned $6,500 playing a 16-game summer season with the Vancouver Lacrosse Club.

The Great One Says

In the book *99: My Life in Pictures*, Wayne Gretzky says that the biggest influence on his hockey career was the fact that he played lacrosse as a boy: "That's where I learned to protect myself from hard body checks. In those days you could be hit from behind in lacrosse, as well as cross checked, so you had to learn how to roll body checks for self-protection. I scored a lot as a lacrosse player, but not as much as I did in hockey."

Greatest Team

The vote for the best hockey team of the first half of the 20th century ended in a tie, with the Ottawa Silver Seven, Stanley Cup champions from 1903 until near the end of the season in 1906, and the Toronto Varsity

Grads, Allan Cup champions of 1927 and Olympic gold medalists of 1928, receiving four votes apiece. Other teams receiving votes were the Montreal Canadiens' Stanley Cup teams of 1944 and 1946, the Toronto Maple Leafs of 1932, 1942 and 1949, the Boston Bruins of 1930 and 1941, the Montreal Maroons of 1935, the Ottawa Senators of 1909, 1921, '22 and '23, the New York Rangers of 1928 and 1933, and the 1907 Kenora Thistles. Also named were Allan Cup championship teams the Winnipeg Victorias of 1912, the Toronto Granites of 1923, the Port Arthur Bearcats of 1926 and the Moncton Hawks of 1934, plus the Memorial Cup–champion Winnipeg Falcons of 1921 and Toronto St. Michael's of 1947.

The Complete Honor Roll

Here's the list of all the winners in the Canadian Press poll for Canada's outstanding athletes of the first half of the 20th century:

INDIVIDUAL ATHLETES

Male Athlete	Lionel Conacher (Toronto, ON)
Female Athlete	Bobbie Rosenfeld (Toronto, ON)
Basketball	Norm Baker (Nanaimo, BC)
Golf	Sandy Somerville (London, ON)
Hockey	Howie Morenz (Mitchell, ON)
Lacrosse	Newsy Lalonde (Cornwall, ON)
Oarsman	Joe Wright Sr. (Toronto, ON)
Football	Lionel Conacher (Toronto, ON)
Soccer	Dave Turner (New Westminster, BC)
Swimming	George Young (Toronto, ON)
Tennis	Jack Wright (Vancouver, BC)
Other (Badminton)	Jack Purcell (Toronto, ON)

MOST DRAMATIC EVENT (Tie)

Percy Williams' gold medals in 100m and 200m at the 1928 Amsterdam Olympics
Toronto Maple Leafs' rally from down 3–0 to win the 1942 Stanley Cup

Quote ... Unquote

"You call a rule infringement in that game and they give the other guy a free throw and a chance to score a point. That's too big a penalty."

— **King Clancy**, Hockey Hall of Fame player and longtime NHL referee, on why he wouldn't want to officiate a basketball game (*Montreal Gazette*, January 6, 1947)

TEAMS

Hockey	Ottawa Silver Seven, 1903–1905
	Toronto Varsity Grads, 1927 and 1928
Lacrosse	Montreal Shamrocks, 1902–1905
Football	Toronto Argonauts, 1950
Soccer	New Westminster Royals, 1929

Overlooked Excellence?

A little more than a year before the results of the Canadian Press polls were announced during December 1950, Andy Lytle, sports editor of the *Toronto Star*, in his column on October 20, 1949, quoted Montreal's Elmer Ferguson (namesake of the Hockey Hall of Fame's award for writers), discussing the multisport talents of Art Ross: "Ross was, in my opinion, the greatest and most versatile of Canadian athletes. Conacher was great, but Ross even more so. He was a star at baseball, football, lacrosse, and hockey. He was a first-class boxer, a fine trap shot, and a clever cricketer."

Best known today for the name of the trophy he donated to the NHL with his sons in 1948 to honor the leading scorer each season, Art Ross was a coach, general manager and executive with the Boston Bruins from the team's founding in 1924 until his retirement in 1954. Before that, from 1905 until 1918, he was widely regarded as the best defenseman in hockey. Hockey records have generally shown that he was born on January 13, 1886, but he was probably born on that date one year earlier.

There is little evidence to suggest that Ross actually played lacrosse or cricket, as Ferguson said. But as a young man in the early 1900s he was a good basketball player, and from about 1916 until 1920 he was one of Canada's top motorcycle racers. (Fellow future Hockey Hall of Famers Sprague Cleghorn and Jack

Art Ross and his football team in the early 1900s. Ross is standing at the back, second from the left. Frank Patrick is in the front row, seated at the far right.

Laviolette also raced motorcycles around the same time.) Later, Ross would become a pretty good bowler, an excellent golfer and a fine trap shooter.

As a baseball player, Ross played on some of the top teams in his hometown of Montreal, often with or against Frank and Lester Patrick and Sprague and Odie Cleghorn. He was a slugging first baseman and an excellent pitcher who sometimes switched from throwing right-handed to left-handed to fool baserunners or just to keep himself interested if a game got out of hand. Reportedly, he once had a tryout with a top minor-league team in Minneapolis.

Still, among all of the sports he played — even hockey — football was the game Art Ross enjoyed the most. On the night of his induction into the Hockey Hall of Fame on December 3, 1949, a Boston newspaper quoted Ross as saying: "Football, or rugby, was probably my best sport."

In Ross' day the terms "football," "rugby" and "rugby football" were used almost interchangeably. Fans today would recognize the game more as rugby than as football, but the sport in Canada was definitely moving away from its roots in England. Ross was a halfback, but when he was playing in the early 1900s, teams in Canada played with 14 men per side, not 12 (or 11 as in U.S. football). "While there were thirteen other members of his team on the field," remarked a story in the *Regina Leader* from 1916 looking back at Ross' football days, "he was reckoned fifty percent of their strength." In an era where the foot was still a big part of football, the *Gazette Times* in Pittsburgh that same year noted that Ross "could kick a ball 40 or 50 yards without much effort." When he died in 1964 his obituary said that he could kick equally well with either foot.

In 1902 Ross led his Westmount football team to the Quebec junior championship. In 1903 (with Frank Patrick as a teammate) Ross led Westmount to the intermediate championship of Canada. His fallout with the brass from the Westmount senior football team in October 1905 led to his resignation as captain, and may have helped in his decision to head west to Brandon, Manitoba, to play hockey during the winter of 1905–06. It was in Brandon that his skill as a hockey player first began to show. In early 1906, the *Morning Telegram* in Winnipeg picked up a report from the *Montreal Herald* that read: "Arthur Ross, the famous football player, is making a peach of a reputation out west as a hockeyist."

Ross would help to form and serve as captain of a football team in Brandon in the fall of 1906. But when he accepted money to play hockey professionally for the 1906–07 season, he was no longer allowed to play football, which was an amateur sport in Canada. Ross was a hockey player from then on, although after returning to Montreal to play for the Wanderers in 1908, he would continue to coach football for a few more years.

End of the Century

When the Canadian Press and Broadcast News polled newspaper editors and broadcasters for Canada's top athlete of the 20th century in late 1999, the results looked quite different from those in 1950. Hockey Hall of Famers dominated the male list:

1   Wayne Gretzky (hockey)
2   Gordie Howe (hockey)
3   Bobby Orr (hockey)
4   Lionel Conacher (all-around)
5   Maurice Richard (hockey)
6   Donovan Bailey (track and field)
7   Ferguson Jenkins (baseball)
8   Mario Lemieux (hockey)
9   Larry Walker (baseball)
10 Gaetan Boucher (speed skating)

Bobbie Rosenfeld, who had topped the women's vote in 1950, was an all-around athlete best remembered today for her success at the 1928 Summer Olympics. Among other things, Rosenfeld played top level women's hockey in the late 1920s and early '30s. No longer number one on the list, she still made the top 10 in 1999:

1. Nancy Greene (skiing)
2. Silken Laumann (rowing)
3. Barbara Ann Scott (figure skating)
4. Myriam Bedard (biathlon)
5. Marnie McBean (rowing)
6. Bobbie Rosenfeld (all-around)
7. Catriona Le May Doan (speed skating)
8. Sandra Post (golf)
9. Marilyn Bell (swimming)
10. Elaine Tanner (swimming)

Stanley Cup and Grey Cup

Only three players have ever won the Stanley Cup for hockey and the Grey Cup (first contested in 1909) for Canadian football. In addition to Lionel Conacher, there were Carl Voss and Joe Miller.

Voss was the NHL's first Rookie of the Year during his first full season in the league in 1932–33 and later, as a referee and a hockey executive, became a member of the Hockey Hall of Fame in the builder's category. Voss won the Grey Cup with Queen's University in 1924 and won the Stanley Cup with Chicago in 1938. Miller won the Grey Cup with the Ottawa Rough Riders (who were frequently referred to as the Senators at the time) in 1926 and led the New York Rangers to the Stanley Cup in 1928 after taking over in goal for coach Lester Patrick, who had heroically come off the bench to backstop the Rangers when goalie Lorne Chabot was hurt in Game 2 of the final against the Montreal Maroons.

Carl Voss as a member of the Ottawa Senators during the 1933–34 NHL season.

Two other men have their names on the Grey Cup and the Stanley Cup, but as players and executives. Normie Kwong was a star with the Edmonton Eskimos when they were champions of Canadian football in 1954, '55 and '56. Later he was a part owner of the Calgary Flames when they won the Stanley Cup in 1989. Wayne Gretzky won the Stanley Cup with the Edmonton Oilers four times in the 1980s and got his name on the Grey Cup in 1991 as a co-owner of the Toronto Argos along with the late John Candy and former Los Angeles Kings owner Bruce McNall.

The Champion of Champions?

John Bower "Bouse" Hutton was a multisport star in his native Ottawa in the late 1890s and early 1900s. Born October 24, 1887, Hutton was a goalie with the Ottawa Hockey Club from 1898–99 through 1903–04, winning the Stanley Cup his last two seasons with the team when it was known as the Silver Seven. He was also a goalie with the Ottawa Capitals lacrosse team and a fullback with the Ottawa Rough Riders in football.

It's long been said that Hutton is the only man ever to win Canadian championships in hockey, lacrosse and football all in the same year. For a long time that year was said to be 1907 — but no Ottawa teams won national titles that year. More recently the season of 1903–04 was credited, but Ottawa only won the Stanley Cup that year. The truth seems to be that while Hutton did win national championships in all three sports, they didn't all come in the same year.

In 1900 Hutton's Capitals were champions of the National Amateur Lacrosse Union, which was an eastern-based league even though it had "National" in its name. (The National Hockey Association was the same, and even the NHL until 1967.) Despite a loss in early September 1900 to the New Westminster Salmonbellies, who had already beaten three other top teams on an eastern tour, the Capitals were considered Canada's national champions when they clinched the NALU title that fall. A year later the Capitals became the first winners of the Minto Cup when they defeated Cornwall 3–2 on September 20, 1901. "Hutton," reported the *Ottawa Citizen*, "made a few wonderful stops."

Barely two months after the Capitals claimed their lacrosse championship for 1900, the Rough Riders (who had won in 1898) became champions of Canadian football. Hutton was only a part-time player with the team that season, but the *Citizen*, in reporting on the team's title on December 1, said of him: "[He] deserves special mention as a spare. For a tight corner, where headwork is required, Hutton is the individual."

Hutton wouldn't complete his national championship hat trick until he won the Stanley Cup for the first time in March 1903. However, he did win a different hockey title in 1900.

Hutton was an employee of the Canada Atlantic Railway (CAR) in Ottawa, and in 1900 he led the company team to the championship of the Canadian Railway Hockey League. This was a six-team circuit based in Ottawa and Montreal. While hardly a national title, the *Ottawa Journal* in reporting on the victory in the paper on March 3, noted that the team "includes many of the best players in the city."

In addition to Hutton, the CAR roster also featured Jim McGee, who had also played on the 1900 Rough Riders and would win the Stanley Cup with Hutton in 1903–04. Jim was the brother of Frank McGee, soon to become a superstar with the Silver Seven and a member of the Canadian Pacific Railway team in the railway league in 1900. Another future Hockey Hall of Famer on the 1900 CAR team was Bruce Stuart, who'd win the Stanley Cup with the Montreal Wanderers in 1908 and Ottawa in 1909 and '10.

No Pros Allowed

In the summer of 1904 Bouse Hutton left the Ottawa Capitals to sign professionally with a lacrosse team in Brantford, Ontario. Since hockey was officially considered an amateur sport in Canada until the 1906–07 season, the fact that Hutton had openly accepted money to play lacrosse meant he was no longer eligible to play hockey for the Silver Seven.

In the same article from Regina in 1916 that mentioned Art Ross as a former football star, several Ottawa hockey players are mentioned too. All of them also had to give up football once they became pro hockey players. Among them were three more future Hall of Famers. Alf Smith, who played hockey in Ottawa from 1895 until 1909, was said to have been a star quarterback with the Ottawa Rough Riders before openly accepting money to play hockey. Eddie Gerard was said to have been the best halfback of his time until he went pro in hockey with the Senators in 1913. George Boucher was said to have had no peer "as a runner, kicker, and all-around performer" before signing with the Senators in 1915.

Ottawa's Greatest All-Around Athlete

It's hard to argue with the choice of Lionel Conacher as Canada's outstanding athlete of the half century in 1950. Still, Harvey Pulford of Ottawa probably deserved a little more consideration than just the two votes that left him in a distant tie for second place.

When Pulford died in the early hours of October 31, 1940, a headline in the *Ottawa Journal* that day proclaimed, "Title of Canada's Greatest Belonged to Harvey Pulford." The sub-headline below added, "Magnificent Athlete Was Champion in Rowing, Football, Hockey, Boxing, Paddling, Lacrosse." Like Conacher, Pulford died of a heart attack, a series of them in his case. He was just 65 years old, but he had been in failing health for about a year.

Born Ernest Harvey Pulford in Toronto on April 22, 1875, he came to Ottawa with his parents when he was still a small child. When he was 13 years old Pulford was awarded the all-round championship of the Ottawa Model School. "This," said the *Ottawa Citizen*, "was the beginning of an athletic career which was to go on for more than 35 years."

By the age of 18 Pulford was playing with the Ottawa Hockey Club in the Amateur Hockey Association of Canada — the NHL of its time. Always a tough competitor, Pulford was a star defenseman

Harvey Pulford in his Ottawa sweater.

when the strategy of the day called for defenders to lift long, high shots from end to end to clear their own goal area of danger (like a punt in football). When strategies shifted toward rushing the puck, Pulford adapted and starred at that style too. He was captain of the Ottawa Silver Seven when they won the Stanley Cup for three straight seasons from 1903 to 1905 and defended it successfully twice in 1906 before losing the title at season's end. He played two more seasons before retiring from hockey in 1908 after 15 seasons.

According to his obituary in the *Ottawa Journal*, Pulford played football for 16 seasons with the Ottawa Rough Riders from 1893 until 1909. He won national championships in that sport in 1898, 1900 and 1902.

(The Rough Riders were also considered to have won the title in 1899, when no championship game was played due to a dispute.) Pulford is also reputed to have won championships with the Ottawa Capitals lacrosse team between 1896 and 1900. But while he did play that sport too, it appears he played only in 1898 and part of 1899, and the team did not win titles in those years. He is also credited with heavyweight and light heavyweight boxing championships for Eastern Canada between 1895 and 1898 and won various paddling championships from 1898 to 1900 while competing with the Britannia Boating Club.

In 1905 Pulford took up a new water sport at the age of 30 when he joined the Ottawa Rowing Club. It became, perhaps, his most successful sport. Pulford won numerous rowing titles in four-man and eight-man boats in the junior, intermediate and senior divisions in Canada, the United States and England until 1912. Later in life he took up squash, winning his final title in 1924 when he was approaching 50 years old by claiming the championship of the Ottawa Squash Racquets club.

Ottawa vs. Rat Portage ... Twice

The most famous Stanley Cup series from the early era when hockey's top prize was a challenge trophy is the matchup between Ottawa and Dawson City in January 1905. That series has stood the test of time because of the 14 goals Frank McGee scored for the Silver Seven in Ottawa's 23–2 victory in the final game on January 16, 1905. But the best series from the Stanley Cup's challenge era was actually held in March 1905 when the Rat Portage Thistles faced the Silver Seven in a best-of-three set that went down to the final minutes of the last game.

Rat Portage would change its name to Kenora later in 1905 and would win the Stanley Cup against the Montreal Wanderers in 1907. The Thistles first played for the Cup against Ottawa in 1903, but the young players from the small town on the shores of the Lake of the Woods in northwestern Ontario weren't ready yet. They were beaten easily in two straight games. But the team was at the peak of its powers when Rat Portage took on Ottawa again in 1905.

The Thistles were led by four future Hall of Famers: captain Tommy Phillips, Si Griffis, Tom Hooper and Billy McGimsie. All had been born or raised in Rat Portage, as had the rest of the team's skaters that year: Roxy Beaudro, Matt Brown and Theo "Tuff" Bellefeuille. Only goalie Eddie Giroux was an outsider, having been brought north to Rat Portage that season from his hometown of Toronto.

Like the Edmonton Oilers 80 years later, the Thistles emphasized offense first and were a fast-skating team whose defensemen were expected to rush the puck whenever they could. Rat Portage romped through the 1904–05 season of the Manitoba Hockey League and stunned Ottawa in the first game of their Stanley Cup series with a 9–3 victory behind five goals from Phillips.

If the Thistles were the 1980s Oilers of their day, then the Silver Seven were the 1970s Philadelphia Flyers. Like "the Broad Street Bullies," Ottawa's team was as tough as it was talented. Hometown reporters often put it down to the jealousy of the losing teams, but fans and sportswriters in cities outside the Canadian capital thought they were dirty. And they were! The Silver Seven definitely played it rough in Game 2 against Rat Portage in 1905. They probably didn't salt the ice before the game to slow down the Thistles as they were accused of, but they may have flooded the ice a little too close to the start of the game so that the surface wouldn't have time to freeze as solidly as it should have. Or it may just have been the return to the lineup of future Hall of Famers McGee and Billy

The Kenora rowing team. Tommy Phillips is in the bow seat. Si Griffis is right behind him.

Gilmour, joining other future Hall of Famers Harvey Pulford, Alf Smith and Harry "Rat" Westwick. Regardless, the Silver Seven won the second game 4–2 to set up the final game on March 11, 1905.

Befitting their status as the two best players in hockey at the time, Phillips and McGee each had three goals in the big game. But it was McGee's third goal, on a setup from Pulford with just 90 seconds left, that gave the Silver Seven a 5–4 victory and kept the Stanley Cup in Ottawa.

With the hockey season over, the summer sport of choice in Rat Portage for several Thistles players was rowing. Phillips and Griffis raced in a four-man crew with the Rat Portage Rowing Club, and in August 1905 they were in St. Catharines, Ontario, to compete for another national championship. This time it was the Junior Fours at the Royal Canadian Henley Regatta. Reaching the final, Rat Portage was pitted against the Argonaut Rowing Club of Toronto (the sports organization that had spawned the football Argos) and the

Ottawa Rowing Club — featuring their Stanley Cup rival Pulford.

There was a lot of betting on the big race, and like the final game of the Stanley Cup series between Ottawa and Rat Portage in March, this contest between Ottawa, Rat Portage and the Argonauts in August proved to be a thriller. The three boats were rarely separated by more than two lengths, and over the last 200 yards of the roughly 1.3-mile-long course the three crews all jockeyed for the lead. When they crossed the finish line, it was too close to call, and though Ottawa was declared the winner, no one was really certain.

Hockey Hall of Fame biographies of Griffis over the years always used to say that he had "successfully stroked the Junior Four at the Canadian Henley." So, had Rat Portage actually won the race?

Years later, long after he had moved to Vancouver, Griffis told the story while on a visit to Kenora. As reported in the *Winnipeg Free Press* on January 31, 1949, Griffis said that his crew did win the race, but with the finish so close there was confusion caused by the team's sweaters. The judges hoisted the Ottawa colors first, Rat Portage second and the Argonauts third. Those would be the official results. Rowing was considered a gentlemen's sport, which meant the Rat Portage Rowing Club refused to enter a protest.

But it wasn't a complete loss.

"The bookies paid off on Kenora," said Griffis with a smile.

Langway Knew ...

Rod Langway was born in Taipei, Taiwan, on May 3, 1957, while his father was serving in the United States Navy. He grew up in Randolph, Massachusetts, near Boston. Langway played football and baseball as a boy. By 1970, when Langway was 13 and Bobby Orr was leading the Bruins to the Stanley Cup, he started playing hockey with his friends. He quickly became a star in that sport too, leading the Randolph Rockets high school hockey team to the state tournament in 1973 and '75. He was also the quarterback of the school football team and a top baseball prospect as a catcher.

Colleges and universities across the United States were recruiting Langway, including Notre Dame and other big football schools. The University of New Hampshire offered a scholarship that would allow him to play hockey or baseball too. Langway accepted and played football and hockey at New Hampshire. In his sophomore season of 1976–77 he helped the Wildcats hockey team reach the semifinals of the NCAA championship tournament. That summer Langway had a choice to make after the Montreal Canadiens selected him 36th overall in the second round of the NHL draft and, two days later, the Birmingham Bulls drafted him sixth overall in the World Hockey Association draft.

"Montreal told me that I should stay in school and

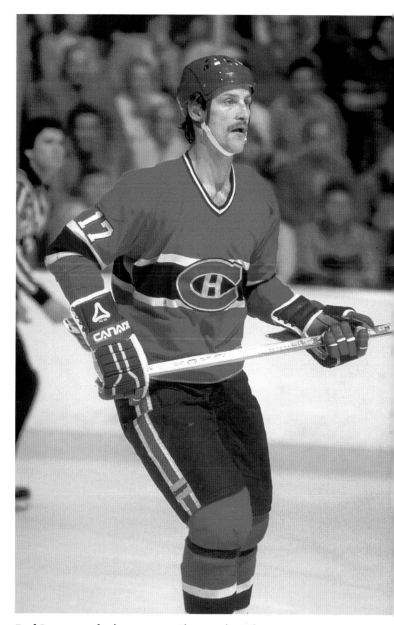

Rod Langway during game action against the Buffalo Sabres in 1982.

get my education," Langway told the *Montreal Gazette* for a story on September 22, 1978. "They were strong on defense and I'd probably end up in Nova Scotia." So Langway chose the Bulls, but he didn't get the large contract other WHA prospects did, as he told the same paper on December 2. "They weren't offering big money if you were coming out of college. But I figured I would make some money and not be in Nova Scotia."

Langway still spent time in the minors, splitting the 1977–78 season between the Bulls in the WHA and the Hampton Gulls of the American Hockey League. He had a clause in his contract that allowed him out of Birmingham if the WHA didn't merge with the NHL (the NHL wouldn't absorb four WHA teams until 1979), so in 1978 Langway signed with the Canadiens … and spent a month in Nova Scotia midway through 1978–79 season.

He was big and strong, and Montreal writers compared him to Larry Robinson, but Langway wouldn't become a star in the NHL until he was traded to Washington in 1982. Named captain of the Capitals upon his arrival, Langway would win the Norris Trophy as the NHL's best defenseman in 1982–83 — a rare feat for a defensive defenseman. He won it again in 1983–84 and finished as the runner-up to Wayne Gretzky in voting for the Hart Trophy as MVP that season.

Before Langway's arrival in Washington, the Capitals had missed the playoffs in all eight of their seasons since joining the NHL in 1974–75. They would never miss the postseason during his 11 years with the team.

Mr. Hockey's Summer Pastime

By any measure, Gordie Howe is among the greatest players in hockey history. Fans and experts may quibble about exactly where he ranks these days, but if there were a Mount Rushmore of hockey, there's little doubt that Howe's would be one of the heads carved in the rock.

From 1946 until 1971 Howe spent 25 seasons with the Detroit Red Wings. He won the Art Ross Trophy as the NHL's scoring leader six times, the Hart Trophy as MVP six times and the Stanley Cup four times. But it was his consistent greatness over such a long period that truly made him stand out. Howe was a top-10 scorer for 21 straight seasons from 1949–50 through 1969–70 and a top-5 scorer for the first 20 of those years. He was named to either the NHL's First or Second All-Star Team 21 times and played in the All-Star Game 22 times. At the age of 40, in 1968–69, he became one of the first three players in NHL history to top 100 points in a single season. (The other two — Phil Esposito and Bobby Hull — were 26 and 30 years old.)

After retiring in 1971 at the age of 41, Howe came back after two seasons away to play with his sons Mark and Marty with the Houston Aeros of the World Hockey Association, and he was a dominant player in the rival league for most of his six seasons there. Then at the age of 51, Howe returned to the NHL for a final season when the Hartford Whalers were one of four WHA teams admitted. Howe turned 52 that March, but he played in all 80 games on the schedule. His 15 goals and 26 assists pushed his NHL totals to 801 goals, 1,049 assists and 1,850 points in 1,767 games played. Howe's seemingly invincible records have since been broken, but that fact has done nothing to diminish his legacy.

Howe was such a remarkable athlete that he may well have excelled at any sport he chose to take up. Howe would occasionally take batting practice with the Detroit Tigers, and Hall of Fame outfielder Al Kaline recalled a story during a celebration of Howe's life after he passed away on June 10, 2016.

"I first met Gordie Howe back in 1956," said Kaline. "I had just moved from Baltimore here. I had just won the batting title so I figured I'd be with Detroit a few years before they got rid of me. So I moved to Detroit, bought a home, and went to my first hockey game at Olympia with a friend of mine, a guy named Frank Carlin, who also was a friend of Gordie's. So we went to the hockey game and afterwards we went out to eat.

Mr. Hockey

Because of the longevity and all-around excellence he displayed throughout his career, Gordie Howe will always be thought of as "Mr. Hockey." Still, there were many others given that name before Howe took it over. Articles from as early as 1933 show that New York sportswriters were fond of calling Rangers coach and general manager Lester Patrick Mr. Hockey. By at least 1940 Boston writers had given the name to Eddie Shore after often referring to Bruins boss Art Ross that way. Maurice Richard was occasionally dubbed "Canada's Mr. Hockey" during the 1950s, and while the earliest reference to Howe as Mr. Hockey seems to date back to 1953, Red Wings executive Jack Adams is referred to as Mr. Hockey in Michigan newspapers during the 1960s before the name finally seems to become Howe's alone after Adams died in 1968.

Gordie Howe poses for a portrait no later than 1949–50.

We went to a place called Carl's Chop House ... That was my first meeting with Gordie. We became very friendly after that. We played a lot of golf together ... and we've been friends for a long, long time."

Kaline said that Howe always wanted to come to the ballpark to take batting practice. "So one day I had him and a couple other hockey players. I think it was Ted [Lindsay] and Marty Pavelich, I'm not really sure."

Kaline remembers when Howe took off his shirt to put on a Tigers uniform. "Gordie didn't have any shoulders. His arms went right up to his neck. He had the biggest pair of arms and all the Tiger players were like, 'Man, what a beast he is!' But anyhow, he got out there, struggled a little bit, naturally so, probably never played much baseball or softball in his day — but finally he was able to hit a ball out of the ballpark, and I'll tell you what, the expression on his face looked like he just won the Stanley Cup. He was so thrilled that he finally hit a ball over the fence."

But it turns out that Howe had played a lot more baseball than Kaline knew or remembered.

In the early days of his NHL career, from 1947 through 1952, when Howe returned home to Saskatoon in the summers, he played semipro baseball with several local teams in various provincial leagues. Howe, who'd played baseball and softball since his school days, played first base, third base and the outfield. He even pitched a little too. And Howe had power. A headline in the *Saskatoon Star-Phoenix* from Tuesday, June 6, 1950, when the Saskatoon All-Stars faced the Swift Current Indians at Cairns Field in Saskatoon, declares, "TOWERING HOMERS FEATURE GAME," adding that "Willis, Howe Clear Left Field Wall."

The main article notes that "the Saskatoon round-tripper by first baseman Gordie Howe, whose hockey exploits during the winter with the Detroit Red Wings get him into the headlines many times, sailed 365 feet over the left field wall."

In the book *Gordie: A Hockey Legend*, it was noted that Ned Powers, the veteran sports columnist for the *Star-Phoenix*, liked to relate the local Howe legend of

Coach Sid Abel and Bill Gadsby during the 1952–53 NHL season.

the longest home run ever hit at Cairns Field. As the story goes, Howe launched a ball over the right field wall and onto a flatcar from the Canadian Pacific Railway rushing along the tracks that ran behind the ballpark. The ball didn't stop moving until the train reached the town of Unity, some 80 miles to the west.

By the summer of 1952 Howe was a two-time Stanley Cup champion and a two-time NHL scoring champion, who'd set a league record with 86 points (43 goals, 43 assists) in 1950–51 and tied it (47 goals, 39 assists) in 1951–52. In Detroit, Red Wings boss Jack Adams learned that Howe had been spiked in a baseball game and developed blood poisoning. According

The Great Gadsby

Bill Gadsby played 20 years in the NHL from 1946 through 1966, starring with the Chicago Black Hawks and the New York Rangers before finishing up his playing career in Detroit with the Red Wings from 1961 to 1966. Gadsby was just the second player, after Gordie Howe, to play 1,000 games in the NHL, and Gadsby and Red Kelly are the only players to play 1,000 games in careers that ended before NHL expansion in 1967. During the early 1950s Gadsby played baseball for teams in Calgary and Edmonton during the summer. He homered for the Edmonton Oilers in an 11–9 win over Howe's Saskatoon 55s in 1951, but Howe's squad won two of three games that weekend.

to *Gordie*, Adams wired Howe: "Quit baseball. Who will pay bills if you are hurt."

Howe sent a return telegram asking if Adams was serious. "I am serious," was the reply.

On July 2, 1952, the *Star-Phoenix* ran a picture of Howe under the headline "Hangs Up Spikes." The caption read: "Gordie Howe, who yesterday wound up his 1952 baseball playing for the Saskatoon Gems on orders from bossman Jack Adams of the Detroit Red Wings. Fearing that his most valuable player might be injured the Detroit general simply told Gordie to quit the diamond. He leaves the Western Canada League as its second best hitter, the last averages showing him with a .393 mark."

But Howe wasn't done with baseball just yet.

On April 15, 1953 — just 10 days after the Boston Bruins had eliminated the Red Wings from the NHL playoffs — Howe married Colleen Joffa. After their honeymoon in Florida, the *Star-Phoenix* reported on May 21, 1953, that the couple were due in Saskatoon any day. "They will spend the summer here," said the paper, "and chances are that you'll be seeing Gordie out with some softball or baseball team as long as Jack Adams doesn't hear of it."

Eight days later, the paper reported: "Interested spectators at the Saskatoon–Moose Jaw contest were Gordie Howe, the famed Detroit Red Wing hockey star, and his pretty bride, Colleen, who will be spending the summer here in Saskatoon with Gordie's parents … Howe was a member of the Gems last summer — until Jack Adams caught up with him … He didn't say whether or not he would try baseball again, but intimated he might be confining his summer sports to golf and fishing … However, he visited the dressing room after the game and began swinging a bat."

Come July, Howe had gotten into a few games, playing first base and pitching, but this appears to mark the end of his baseball career. Still, Peter Gzowski, in an article for *Maclean's* magazine in 1963, wrote that when Howe began taking batting practice with the Tigers in 1956, manager Bucky Harris was heard to remark that it would only take a few months to turn Howe into a regular in the big leagues. Unlike Bo Jackson, Howe wasn't ready to try life as a two-sport star, but as Gzowski further noted in his story, "Howe has been seen at a Red Wings practice standing beside the goal, holding his stick like a baseball bat and knocking back many of the hardest shots his teammates tried to fire past him."

Dipsy Doodle Dandies from Delisle

Six Bentley brothers grew up playing hockey in Delisle, Saskatchewan, in the 1920s and '30s. Jack, Roy, Wyatt (known as "Scoop"), Reg, Doug and Max were born between 1902 and 1920. All but Jack played together on the Drumheller Miners of the Alberta Senior Hockey League in 1938–39. (An executive member of that club, Dr. Thomas R. Ross, was a brother of Art Ross, who ran the Boston Bruins at the time.) Doug, Max and Reg would reach the NHL over the next few years, with Doug and Max enjoying Hall of Fame careers.

In addition to putting Delisle on the hockey map, most of the Bentley brothers played baseball too, starring for the hometown Delisle Gems. According to the Western Canada Baseball website, Max ran away with the batting title of the Saskatoon and District Baseball League in 1948, hitting at a .438 clip, which was more than 70 points ahead of his nearest challenger. Doug and Max dominated the batting statistics in the Saskatoon and District League in 1949, hitting .410 and .389, respectively. In 1950 Doug batted .324 for Delisle, while Max hit .296 and Bev Bentley (Roy's son, and a longtime minor pro goalie) led the league in runs scored. At the Saskatoon Optimist Baseball Tournament in

Reg, Max and Doug Bentley during the 1942–43 season.

the summer of 1951, Doug won the coveted shotgun for the highest batting average by hitting .600 during the tourney.

The Calgary Pucksters

Tiny Thompson was known to be good with his glove as a goalie with the Boston Bruins, and as a first baseman in summer he was known for his soft hands. It was sometimes said that his nickname "Tiny" (his given name was Cecil) came ironically from the fact that he was the tallest player on his midget baseball team as a teen. A future Hockey Hall of Famer, Thompson played semipro baseball for the Calgary Pucksters

Little Sweeney

"Very seldom did I recognize my name, David," explained Sweeney Schriner in a story in the *Calgary Herald* in 1983. "I'd have to apologize to people when I didn't answer them.

"When I was going to school, a milkman on our route noticed me. We had a fella named Bill Sweeney playing [baseball] here at that time. I used to copy his style. The milkman nicknamed me Little Sweeney and the name has stuck ever since."

Doug Harvey during the 1953–54 NHL season.

during the 1930s with his brother Paul, another NHL star. The team was managed by Red Dutton, also a future Hockey Hall of Famer. Among the many NHL players in the Pucksters' lineup was yet another future Hall of Famer, Dave "Sweeney" Schriner.

Gretzky, Gordie ... and Vida Blue

Wayne Gretzky met Gordie Howe for the first time at the Kiwanis Great Men of Sports Dinner in Gretzky's hometown of Brantford, Ontario, on May 4, 1972. That's when the famous picture of the two of them smiling, with Howe holding a stick hooked around Gretzky's neck, was taken. "Obviously, I was very nervous," said Gretzky for the book *99: My Life in Pictures.* "A lot of times, when people meet their idols they get disappointed, but our meeting turned out to be bigger and better than I ever dreamed. It was such a great moment for me."

Gretzky, of course, grew up to shatter many of his idol's records while establishing more than 60 of

his own during his NHL career. Gretzky was the first player to surpass Howe's NHL total of 1,850 points (en route to 2,857) and is still the only one to top Howe's 801 goals (with 894). But other than the fact that Detroit was so close to his hometown, Gretzky

The Great One

"The Great One" may seem a little grand as nicknames go, but it's hard to argue that anyone in hockey deserves it more than Wayne Gretzky. Teammates usually called him "Gretz," but in his interview with Dan Patrick, Gretzky reveals an earlier nickname. "When I played junior hockey, I was 14 years old, I was 122 pounds, and they called me 'Pretzel' because they thought I would break in half. So, that was my nickname for about a year."

idolizing Howe as a boy was somewhat strange. When Gretzky started playing hockey as a six-year-old in 1967, Howe was 39 years old and players such as Bobby Hull, Stan Mikita, Jean Beliveau and a youngster named Bobby Orr had become bigger stars. Still, in one of Gretzky's earliest interviews, which ran in the *Toronto Telegram* on October 28, 1971 (he was 10 years old but would turn 11 in January during a hockey season in which he collected 378 goals and 139 assists in 85 games played), Gretzky told John Iaboni: "Gordie Howe is my kind of player. He had so many tricks round the net, no wonder he scored so many goals. I'd like to be just like him."

Gretzky also played lacrosse as a boy and was a competitive middle-distance runner too. His favorite player in yet another of the sports he played was someone more in keeping with his age.

"If I couldn't play hockey," Gretzky told Iaboni, "I'd like to play baseball with the Oakland Athletics and Vida Blue."

The A's would win three straight World Series titles from 1972 through 1974, and at the time of Gretzky's interview Blue was fresh off a 1971 season in which he'd won the Cy Young Award in the American League by going 24–8 with a 1.82 ERA.

A few years later, Gretzky was interviewed by Peter Gzowski for *This Country in the Morning* on CBC Radio. When Gzowski asked, "You'd like to be a hockey player, wouldn't you?" Gretzky replied, "Yes. Or a baseball player. Doesn't really matter."

Gretzky was a pitcher and a shortstop growing up. He'd listen to Ernie Harwell call Tigers games from Detroit, and as he told Dan Patrick in a 2017 interview, he could pick up St. Louis Cardinals broadcasts with Jack Buck on the radio when he was in bed at night. Gretzky loved baseball. "Probably even more than hockey," he said in *99*. "It was my passion. I didn't grow up dreaming, 'I'm gonna be a hockey player,' but I did

Son Shines

Trevor Gretzky, the third of five children of Wayne Gretzky and Janet Jones, was drafted by the Chicago Cubs in 2011. Trevor spent two seasons in the Cubs' minor-league system and then two more in the Los Angeles Angels organization. He later played Independent ball in Quebec City and Trois-Rivieres. Since 2018 he has followed in his mother's footsteps as an actor and producer with several films to his credit.

grow up every night thinking, 'Boy, I wish I could play major league baseball.'"

Gretzky played with a Brantford team that won a Canadian national baseball championship when he was 11 years old. He played junior baseball with the Brantford Braves and three games as a senior with the Brantford Red Sox (one each when he was 14, 15 and 16).

But, "when I turned pro in hockey at 17," said Gretzky, "I didn't want to take the risk of getting injured in another sport, so that's when I quit baseball."

Still, as he told Patrick, if he had been good enough, "I would have taken baseball all day long."

Harvey the Wallbanger

On the Mount Rushmore of NHL defensemen, Doug Harvey would definitely be there. The greatest defenseman in the game between the eras of Eddie Shore and Bobby Orr, Harvey's seven Norris Trophy wins as best defenseman (tied with Nicklas Lidstrom) are topped only by Orr's eight. There was no Norris Trophy in Shore's day, although his four wins of the

Hart Trophy as MVP are more than any other defenseman in NHL history.

Harvey was considered too lazy to succeed in the early years of his career after breaking in with the Montreal Canadiens in 1947–48. Later, fans and experts came to appreciate that Harvey's deliberate style allowed him to control the pace of everybody on the ice. By 1958 even Eddie Shore said, "Harvey is the best I've ever seen. He's cool, he can think, and he can lift a team." Toe Blake, who played against Shore in the 1930s and '40s and was coaching Harvey at the time, agreed. "Yes, he's ahead of Shore," said Blake. "He can do more things — when he wants to."

When he was breaking into the NHL, Harvey may have been even better at baseball than hockey. From 1947 through 1950 Harvey played the outfield as a professional ballplayer with the Ottawa Nationals in the Class C Border League, roughly equivalent to High-A minor-league baseball today. Harvey hit .340 in 109 games during the 1948 season, and then improved his grip and led the league with a .351 average and 109 RBIs in 109 games in 1949.

Though he was playing in his third season with the Canadiens by 1949–50, Harvey was drafted by the Boston Braves in 1950. Writing in the *Ottawa Journal* on May 16, 1950, Bill Westwick noted that the Braves had paid the Nationals the draft price to obtain Harvey, whom "some very astute observers rated [as] one of the best prospects they had seen in many a year." But Harvey, wrote Westwick, had no interest in joining one of Boston's minor-league teams. Hockey stories have long claimed that Harvey ignored the Braves' invitation to spring training because he was playing with the Canadiens during the 1950 playoffs. Whatever the reason, Harvey did play some baseball with Ottawa through the summer of 1950, but he was a full-time hockey player by the fall … except for exhibition softball games with his Canadiens teammates in summer over the years.

Dropping the Gloves

Fergie Jenkins, the first of only two Canadians (along with Larry Walker) to be elected to the Baseball Hall of Fame, was a three-sport star growing up: baseball, basketball (he played with the Harlem Globetrotters in the baseball off-season from 1967 to 1969) and hockey. "I was an extremely good skater," Jenkins told the *Chicago Tribune* in 1991, "and I was pretty good at clearing the puck. I always played on the All-Star teams, and I made the Junior B team in Chatham."

Living close to Detroit, "everybody else," remembered Jenkins, "wanted to be Gordie Howe or Ted Lindsay." But Jenkins was a defenseman. "Doug Harvey was my idol."

Jenkins gave up on hockey when he signed to pitch for the Philadelphia Phillies (either as a minor-leaguer in 1962 or when he made the Majors in 1965), and they told him they didn't want him to get injured on the ice. "I haven't been on skates since," said Jenkins in an interview after he was traded to the Chicago Cubs in 1966.

He didn't stay off the ice for good.

In the winter following his 25-win season with the Texas Rangers in 1974, Jenkins was playing hockey in an industrial league back home — unbeknownst to his ball club. During one game an opposing player kept taking shots at him. Jenkins told the story in the book *Winners: A Century of Canadian Sport*. "I dropped my gloves and let him have it — bam — and broke all the knuckles in my right hand." Fortunately, the injury healed in time for the next baseball season.

Draft Trivia

The 1984 NHL entry draft produced five future Hall of Famers. The Pittsburgh Penguins made Mario Lemieux the first overall pick. Patrick Roy was a third-round choice by the Montreal Canadiens, 51st overall. In the sixth round, the Calgary Flames selected Brett Hull

117th overall, while Luc Robitaille went to the Los Angeles Kings in the ninth round with the 171st pick.

The fifth Hall of Famer was picked in the fourth round, when the Kings used the 69th choice to select a high-scoring Boston-area high school kid from Billerica Memorial. Tom Glavine didn't play much hockey after that season, but he did go on to win 305 games and two National League Cy Young Awards in a 22-year career with the Atlanta Braves and the New York Mets that landed him in Cooperstown.

Taylor, Ty and Wagner

Cyclone Taylor is often considered professional hockey's first superstar. In fact, it's been said that Frank Patrick, his longtime friend and teammate — and often his hockey boss as well — coined the term "superstar" to describe Taylor. He was among the first living members to be elected to the Hockey Hall of Fame in 1947.

Mainly a defenseman in his early hockey days with the Ottawa Senators (1907 to 1909) and Renfrew Millionaires (1909 to 1911), Taylor's end-to-end rushes helped lead the attack on offense while his blazing speed meant he could always get back to his own end. Later, when starring with the Vancouver Millionaires in the Pacific Coast Hockey Association, he was moved up to forward, playing at center and the old position of rover. Taylor led the PCHA in scoring five times in six seasons from 1913–14 through 1918–19. He'd won the Stanley Cup with Ottawa in 1909 and won it again with Vancouver in 1915.

Taylor also played lacrosse, and as a young man he played soccer and baseball too. In a trip to New York with Renfrew in the spring of 1910, the hockey teammates were bragging about their baseball skill. "I was playing ball one day," related Taylor, "and there were men on second and third. I came to bat with our team three runs behind and, taking a mighty swing at the

Cyclone Taylor in a 1910–11 Sweet Caporal Cigarettes black-and-white hockey postcard.

pill, landed it far out in deep center. Seeing that it was a long hit, I put my head down and ran like the wind. And would you believe it, I beat both men to the plate!"

Because of Taylor's box-office appeal on trips to the United States, the American press sometimes called him "the Ty Cobb of Hockey." The comparison is an interesting one. Both men broke into the highest levels of their game in 1905, and both quickly became stars. Each was fast and flashy, tricky and aggressive, and in the years before the darker side of the baseball legend's personality was known, Taylor enjoyed his tie to Cobb.

In Eric Whitehead's biography *Cyclone Taylor: A Hockey Legend*, Taylor told of making the trip to

Cyclone Taylor

Frederick Wellington Taylor joined the Ottawa Senators for the 1907–08 season. His first home game with his new team was played on Saturday, January 11, 1908. The Senators opened a new arena that night with a resounding 12–2 win over their archrivals, the Montreal Wanderers. Taylor starred in that game. A report in the Monday edition of the *Ottawa Free Press* noted, "Taylor came here with the appellation of 'the whirlwind of the International' tagged to him. On his performance Saturday he can well be styled the 'tornado of the [Eastern Canada league]."

In Eric Whitehead's biography of Taylor, he writes that *Free Press* sports reporter Malcolm Brice overheard Governor General Grey (of Grey Cup fame) remarking on his way out of the arena that "that new No. 4, Taylor, he's a cyclone if I ever saw one." Whitehead then writes that Brice reported in the *Free Press* that "in Portage la Prairie they called him a tornado, in Houghton, Michigan, he was known as a whirlwind. From now on he'll be known as Cyclone Taylor."

There are, however, at least two things wrong with the story. First, players did not yet wear numbers on their uniforms at this time (although Taylor would later wear No. 4 for most of his time in Vancouver). Second, reports in the *Free Press* say no such thing about Lord Grey, nor make any mention of cyclones. Still, regardless of how it actually happened, the nickname soon caught on. References show up regularly in Ottawa newspapers by February and March 1908.

He was Cyclone Taylor forever after.

Detroit from his hometown in Listowel, Ontario (some 100 miles west of Toronto), to watch Cobb play for the Tigers. The round-trip journey took nearly 24 hours by train, by ferry and on foot. Cobb likely never made a similar trek to see Taylor in action, but another of baseball's early superstars had seen him play and came away impressed. This was during Taylor's time with the Portage Lake team of Houghton, Michigan, in the International Hockey League, the sport's first openly professional organization. Whitehead quotes the account from a Pittsburgh paper called the *Evening Journal*, probably from a game on March 3, 1906:

> There was a great cheer just after the start of the game when the star of the Pittsburgh Pirates Honus Wagner appeared, accompanied by Pirates' manager-outfielder Fred Clarke. They took seats a few rows behind the Portage Lake bench. Wagner, considered the finest shortstop in baseball history, had travelled from his home in Plattsville to see the game. He is a real hockey fan, and he seemed to be greatly excited by last night's proceedings. He was on his feet many times, and afterwards said he thought the Portage Lake player, Taylor, was as fine an athlete as he has ever seen.

The World Series of Hockey

In the early days of Stanley Cup competition, from 1893 until 1913, the Stanley Cup was a challenge trophy. With travel limited to trains, and ice dependent on cold weather, seasons were short and leagues were regional, sometimes with as few as two teams, and rarely more than six.

To make the Stanley Cup open to teams from all across Canada (American teams weren't allowed to compete for the trophy until the 1915–16 season), the champions of any recognized senior provincial hockey league were permitted to challenge the current Stanley Cup champion for the prized trophy. If the challenger won (which happened only rarely), the Cup would become the possession of the new team and move with it into its league. The Stanley Cup could also change hands if the defending champion was beaten out for first place in its own league standings at the end of the season. The Cup would then go to the new league champion … who would be called on to face challenges themselves.

Because of the short nature of the hockey season, a Stanley Cup challenge series might be played at the end of the season (like a modern playoff) or before the next regular season got underway. Sometimes, Stanley Cup games were even played in the middle of the regular season. But no matter when the games took place, a Stanley Cup series in this era was never more than a best of three. Often it was a two-game, total-goals series. Sometimes, it was just a single-game, winner-take-all challenge.

Beginning in the 1913–14 season, the National Hockey Association (forerunner to the NHL) and the Pacific Coast Hockey Association signed an agreement stating that their respective league champions would meet in an annual postseason series. When the trustees in charge of the Stanley Cup gave their approval, this would be how the Cup was awarded through the 1925–26 season. During that time the champions of the NHA and later, after 1917–18, the NHL would meet the champions of the PCHA or the Western Canada Hockey League (which became the Western Hockey League in 1925) in a best-of-five championship series. Newspapers often referred to these Stanley Cup games as the World Series of Hockey.

Lester Patrick's Role

The Pacific Coast Hockey Association was launched by brothers Frank and Lester Patrick in the winter of 1911–12. The Patricks were former eastern hockey stars who'd moved west (Lester in 1907 and Frank in 1908) after their father sold his Quebec-based lumber company and established a new one near the new family home in Nelson, British Columbia. The sale of this new Patrick Lumber Company in 1911 helped finance the construction of artificial ice rinks in Vancouver and Victoria, which made the PCHA viable.

Growing up in Montreal, and later in Nelson as well, the Patrick brothers both played baseball in addition to hockey. They were good at it too. By 1914 Lester was a director of the Victoria baseball club in the B.C. capital, where he then lived. It doesn't seem like much of a stretch to say that Lester's interest in hockey helped change the way the Stanley Cup was awarded.

During October 1912 Lester visited Winnipeg, Ottawa, Montreal and Toronto on a scouting mission to sign players for the PCHA. Given the coverage the World Series between the New York Giants and Boston Red Sox was receiving at the time, it's impossible to believe that a baseball fan like Lester wasn't following the news. The best-of-seven series actually required an eighth game because one ended in a tie, and the Red Sox won the finale 3–2 with a two-run rally in the bottom of the 10th inning. One of the key plays was a dropped fly ball by the Giants' center fielder that would haunt him for the rest of his life. When he passed away 62 years later, his obituary in the *New York Times* read, "Fred Snodgrass, 86, Dead; Ballplayer Muffed 1912 Fly."

Lester's 1912 scouting tour got plenty of coverage all across Canada. On October 17 the *Edmonton Daily Bulletin* reported, "A World Series in hockey between the champions of the NHA and the B.C. league is

A cartoon advertising the Toronto Maple Leafs versus the New York Rangers at Maple Leaf Gardens in Toronto on February 24, 1934.

the idea of Lester Patrick." The next day, the *Globe* in Toronto had more to report from Lester: "My idea is to have a series of games, such as the [World Series], to decide the championship — not a series of two games, but one of seven or more, which would decide beyond all question which team is best."

It would take another year before the NHA and the PCHA signed such an agreement, and it would take until 1939 before the NHL expanded the Stanley Cup Final from a best-of-five to a best-of-seven, but there can be little doubt that the World Series of 1912 helped pave the way.

The Babe Ruth of Hockey

"The Babe Ruth of Hockey" was a term thrown around fairly regularly when Babe Ruth's home run power was revolutionizing baseball in the 1920s. Hall of Famers Newsy Lalonde, Frank Fredrickson, Joe Simpson, Billy Burch, Ching Johnson and Eddie Shore all had the term associated with their names before it seemed to settle on Howie Morenz. In later years the name was sometimes applied to Maurice Richard, Gordie Howe and even Wayne Gretzky.

One of the earliest players to be known as the Babe Ruth of Hockey was Cecil Henry Dye. Better known by his nickname, "Babe," Dye was a star sniper with the Toronto St. Pats in the early 1920s.

Dye broke into the NHL in 1919–20 and would lead the league in goals four times and points twice from 1920–21 through 1924–25. He was a pretty decent football player growing up in Toronto as well, although he was never a halfback with the Toronto Argonauts as old hockey records used to claim. He was, however, an excellent left-handed pitcher and a star left-handed hitting outfielder (like Ruth) who played high-level minor-league baseball, mostly with the Buffalo Bisons and the Toronto Maple Leafs, during most of his NHL career.

As a baseball player, Dye was good enough that the legendary Connie Mack wanted him for his Philadelphia Athletics. Hockey records long claimed that Mack offered Dye $25,000 in 1921, which is what was reported in the *Toronto Star* along with an obituary for Dye on January 4, 1962, the day after he had died. In truth, the offer came in 1923, and it appears to have been for $30,000.

Hockey stories say Dye turned down Mack's offer in order to concentrate on his NHL career, but the *Buffalo Enquirer* of August 29, 1923, makes it pretty clear that it was the Bisons who were actually offered the money to buy Dye's rights. It was also the Buffalo team that turned down Mack because the Bisons wanted players in return, not money, if they were going to give up a perennial .300 hitter. By strange coincidence, the same day the *Enquirer* reported on Mack's interest in Dye, the New York Yankees were in Buffalo to play an exhibition game against the Bisons ... and Babe Dye and Babe Ruth both hit home runs in the same game. (The Yankees beat the Bisons 13–7.)

Dye's baseball career ended after the 1926 season, and a broken leg at training camp with the Chicago Black Hawks in 1927 marked a sharp decline in his hockey career too. That appears to be when the title the Babe Ruth of Hockey passed to Morenz.

Cecil "Babe" Dye poses for a portrait as a member of the Toronto St. Pats.

Stanley Cup or Spring Training?

Babe Dye signed a contract with the Buffalo Bisons of baseball's International League on March 2, 1922. There were still six days left in the NHL's regular season, and Dye "will endeavour to get permission from the Buffalo club," read newspaper reports the following day, "to remain with the Toronto hockey team as long as his services are required for the winter pastime." The Bisons would give Dye permission to report late to spring training after the Toronto St. Pats defeated the Ottawa Senators for the NHL championship on March 13 and prepared to face the PCHA's Vancouver Millionaires in the Stanley Cup Final beginning on March 17.

Though he failed to score on the first penalty shot in Stanley Cup history in the second game on March 21 (penalty shots were not yet part of the NHL rule book, but were allowed in the PCHA), Dye set an NHL record for the Stanley Cup Final that still stands by scoring nine goals in the five-game series. He scored four in Toronto's 5–1 victory to wrap up the series on March 28, 1922. Five days later, on April 2, Dye arrived at the Bisons' training camp in Gastonia, North Carolina. A week later, on April 9, the *Buffalo Courier* reported that Dye had won the job as the Bisons' starting left fielder. "He has all the earmarks of a crackerjack ball player," the newspaper said.

Switch Hitters

Over the years plenty of NHL players have enjoyed playing baseball or softball during the summer. But only one man has ever played in the NHL and played Major League Baseball too. That man is Jim Riley.

Riley played 13 seasons of pro ball, including parts of two years in the Majors with the St. Louis Browns in 1921 and the Washington Senators in 1923. He played in just six games with 14 at-bats and had no hits but drew two walks. Riley played his only NHL season with the Chicago Black Hawks and Detroit Cougars in 1926–27, combining for just nine games and no goals. He spent the bulk of his hockey career in the PCHA with the Victoria Aristocrats (1915–16) and Seattle Metropolitans (1916 to 1924), winning the Stanley Cup with Seattle in 1917 and scoring a career-high 23 goals in 30 games in 1922–23. Hall of Fame teammates during his hockey career include Lester Patrick, Frank Foyston, Jack Walker, Gord Roberts and Hap Holmes.

Andy Kyle also played Major League Baseball and major professional hockey. Kyle played minor-league baseball from 1910 until 1921 and spent nine games in the Majors with the Cincinnati Reds at the end of the 1912 season. He had seven hits in 21 at-bats for a .333 average with a double and four runs batted in. Kyle's hockey career predates the NHL, but he scored 18 goals in 22 games for the Halifax Crescents of the Maritime Professional Hockey Association (a league that had competed for the Stanley Cup) in 1913–14. He also played in the National Hockey Association, spending a single game with the Toronto Ontarios in 1914–15 and 10 games with the Toronto Blueshirts in 1916–17, although he never scored a goal in that league.

Kyle was expected to join Toronto's NHL team at training camp before the league's first season of 1917–18, but he didn't play hockey again. During the course of his pro career, Kyle had played on teams featuring future Hockey Hall of Famers Jack Walker, Tommy Smith, George McNamara, Cy Denneny, Harry Cameron, Duke Keats, Reg Noble and Percy LeSueur.

Not Just Old-Timers ...

At 6-foot-3 and 215 pounds, Clark Gillies was one of the NHL's premier power forwards during the 1970s and '80s. He teamed with Mike Bossy and Bryan Trottier to form one of the highest-scoring lines in the

Clark Gillies on December 3, 1977, during a game at The Checkerdome in St. Louis, Missouri.

NHL and help the New York Islanders win the Stanley Cup four years in a row from 1980 through 1983. But long before he was a Stanley Cup, or even a Memorial Cup, champion (Regina Pats, 1974), Gillies was a big, strong kid in Moose Jaw, Saskatchewan, playing junior hockey with the hometown Canucks as a 16-year-old during the winter of 1969–70 and playing baseball with his buddies in the summer.

During the summer of 1970 the assistant farm director of the Houston Astros came to town. His name was Pat Gillick. Years later he would build the Toronto Blue Jays into World Series champions as part of a Hall of Fame career as a baseball executive. Gillick had spent the summers of 1956 to 1958 playing ball in Western Canada while pitching collegiately at the University of Southern California. "I knew there were a

Quote ... Unquote

"So what? He's a good dog."

— **Clark Gillies**, who posed for a photo with his German shepherd, Hombre, after the Islanders' first championship in 1980 and let the dog slurp some champagne from the Stanley Cup

lot of good players there," recalled Gillick for an article in the *Houston Chronicle* in 2020. "We were just looking for guys who were good athletes. Usually, good athletes are able to adapt to another sport."

A few years later, in 1973, the Astros would find Terry Puhl playing high school ball in Melville, Saskatchewan. In 1970 Gillick was impressed by Gillies at a one-day training camp and signed him to a contract. Gillies had never been on a plane before flying to Covington, Virginia, to join the Covington Astros at the tail end of the 1970 Appalachian League season. Nervous and homesick, Gillies hit just .077 (1-for-13 with 10 strikeouts) in five games as a catcher,

Jethro

Clark Gillies was known as "Jethro" after the muscular but dumb character Jethro Bodine on *The Beverly Hillbillies*.

outfielder and first baseman. He improved during the short summer season in 1971, hitting .239 in 35 games. Playing with future Islanders teammate Bob Bourne (of Kindersley, Saskatchewan) in 1972, Gillies hit .256 in 46 games.

"I thought they were prospects," said Gillick of Gillies and Bourne. "I think if they had concentrated (on baseball) and stuck with it, they could've gone up the ladder and had a chance to go to the big leagues. Both of them had talent. Both were good athletes, good people, and hard workers."

Gillies had already given up football at the Astros' request to concentrate on baseball, but he wasn't willing to give up hockey too. After the 1972 season Gillies and Bourne both realized that hockey was what they really wanted, but both would retain fond memories of their baseball experience.

"I think what I got out of it," recalled Gillies, "was a sense of discipline, having to go to work every day and really work every game."

A Texas Ranger

Brian Leetch was born in Corpus Christi, Texas, but his family moved to Cheshire, Connecticut, when he was just three months old. Leetch first learned to skate at a local hockey rink that was managed by his father. As a teenager he starred in hockey and in baseball. As a high school sophomore Leetch's 90-mile-per-hour fastball led the Cheshire Rams to a state

Brian Leetch of the New York Rangers skates with the puck during game action at Madison Square Garden.

championship, and as a senior at Avon Old Farms prep school in 1986 he set a school record by striking out 16 batters in one game.

"Growing up in Connecticut," Leetch told NHL.com in 2008, "one sport never played a huge part in anybody's life. Never was there a time when kids my age were playing just one sport all year round. I played baseball because my friends played." But Leetch always felt his future was in hockey. "Once I was drafted in the first round right before college [in 1986], I knew I'd have a chance to go to the NHL camps, but I just didn't know where I'd fit in at that point. I just assumed baseball would end, but a few of the [colleges] said that if I wanted to play baseball, I could and still miss a few practices in order to play hockey. I thought about it initially, but knew I wanted to play hockey."

Leetch attended Boston College in 1986–87, then joined the U.S. National Team the following year. He made his NHL debut with the New York Rangers on February 29, 1988, immediately after the Calgary Winter Olympics.

"I enjoyed baseball as a pitcher and shortstop," said Leetch, "but I don't really think it had any real effect on my hockey career, except for the fact that when it was time to play hockey again, I always looked forward to it because I missed it."

The Big E

Eric Lindros was probably never serious about a career in baseball. Still, as a 17-year-old, after playing his first season of Major Junior hockey with the Oshawa Generals, a photograph of Lindros taking a cut in the batting cage at the SkyDome (as the Rogers Centre in Toronto was called then) was included in the 1990 Score baseball card series. The front of the card lists Lindros as a third baseman with the Toronto Blue Jays. The back of the card says:

Eric is another in a growing list of multi-talented athletes who are cropping up in the sports world with increasing frequency. Unlike Bo [Jackson], Deion [Sanders] and D.J. [Dozier], however, his two sports are hockey and baseball. This makes him quite similar to a current major leaguer who excelled in both sports — pitcher Kirk McCaskill of the Angels. McCaskill was chosen in the '81 NHL entry draft by the Winnipeg Jets, and totalled 22 points in the AHL.

Eric, a big, 17-year-old power hitter, batted over .400 in high school and will be given a

Eric Lindros of the Philadelphia Flyers celebrates after a goal.

tryout by the Blue Jays. "He's an unknown quantity right now because he's so inexperienced," said one scout. "But he has all the tools to make it big."

Lindros worked out for the Blue Jays on July 5, 1990, fielding balls at third base and taking swings in batting practice. A picture the next day in the *Toronto Star* showed Lindros shaking hands with Jays manager Cito Gaston in the clubhouse. The caption notes that Gaston's advice to Lindros was "Stick to hockey."

Jarome Iginla during a game at Rexall Place in Edmonton, Alberta.

The Big Tree

Jarome Iginla's last name means "Big Tree" in the Yorba language, the native tongue of his Nigerian father. As a player of mixed heritage, Iginla occasionally faced racism while playing hockey, but he was inspired by the black players in the NHL, including Grant Fuhr, who starred with the Edmonton Oilers while Iginla was growing up in the Edmonton suburb of St. Albert, Alberta.

Iginla was a hockey star from a young age, leading the Alberta Midget Hockey League in scoring as a 15-year-old in 1992–93. He also played baseball, which was actually his favorite sport as a boy. Iginla was a pitcher, a catcher and a shortstop, and in the summer

of 1992, before he led the midget scoring stats with the St. Albert Raiders, he represented the St. Albert Cardinals at the Canadian national bantam championship and was the all-star catcher.

Shortly after being drafted 11th overall by the Dallas Stars in 1995, Iginla talked about playing baseball and hockey with Mike Heika of the *Fort Worth Star-Telegram* for a story on July 16, 1995: "There was a time when I was a bit younger when I really thought I could play both professionally. But I've realized what it takes, and I know better now."

Still, having recently watched Iginla help his junior team, the Kamloops Blazers, win the Memorial Cup, Blazers general manager Stu MacGregor told Heika that Iginla was "an exceptional baseball player" and that a week before the NHL draft, "he just threw a no-hitter for his all-star team."

The Goalies of Summer

Bill Durnan and Turk Broda became two of the greatest goalies of all time during the 1940s. In 1972 the two would pass away within two weeks of each other. Broda died on October 17 at the age of 58. Durnan was just 56 when he died on October 31. They had shared more than just being great goaltenders. Both were great softball players too.

Durnan was known for being ambidextrous, using specially designed goalie gloves so that he could grip his stick with either his left or right hand. His career was short — he starred with the Montreal Canadiens for just seven seasons from 1943–44 through 1949–50. During that time he won the Vezina Trophy six times. The award was really a team trophy in those days, going to the goalie whose team had allowed the fewest goals in the NHL. Still, Durnan was voted by sportswriters to the NHL's First All-Star Team in each of those same six seasons. He also helped the Canadiens win the Stanley Cup in 1944 and '46.

Broda's career was longer. He starred with the Toronto Maple Leafs from 1936–37 through 1950–51, with his final game played on March 23, 1952. (He missed the 1943–44 and 1944–45 seasons due to military service in World War II.) Broda was a First-Team All-Star and Vezina Trophy winner in 1941–42 and 1947–48 and would have shared the Vezina with Al Rollins in Toronto in 1950–51 under later rules. He helped the Leafs win the Stanley Cup in 1942, 1947, 1948, 1949 and 1951.

From at least 1950 through 1952, the Maple Leafs goalie led a team known as "Turk Broda and his NHL All-Stars" on summertime softball tours. Among those

Bill Durnan and Turk Broda shake hands following Toronto's win in Game 6 of the Stanley Cup Final on April 19, 1947.

joining him were Toronto teammates Gus Mortson, Jim Thomson, Sid Smith, Cal Gardner, Harry Watson, Danny Lewicki and Fleming MacKell. In a *Maclean's* magazine article that ran on February 1, 1951, Trent Frayne noted that during the two and a half years Broda served with the Royal Canadian Artillery in England, France and Holland, "his only injury was not the result of German shells; he broke an ankle in a softball game."

Before he got to the NHL (and after), Durnan was one of the top amateur softball pitchers in Canada. In an obituary for Durnan that appeared in the *Calgary Herald* on November 1, 1972, sports editor Hal Walker wrote: "His exploits as a fireballing hurler will long stand in the record book. He holds an incredible career record of averaging 15 strikeouts a game over a span of 25 years in softball. He is credited with only 14 no-hitters but I'm certain he had many more than that. He pitched for two world championship teams out of Toronto and he owned a lifetime batting average of .350."

Though it's hard to confirm Walker's numbers, it's not hard to find newspaper stories about Durnan's pitching prowess, such as this one from Montreal that appeared in the *Ottawa Journal* on June 13, 1941: "Tonight, Bill Durnan, who plays goal for Montreal's senior Royals in the Winter and pitches a mean softball game in the Summer, struck out 19 men and allowed no hits in leading the Royals to a 2–0 victory in a contest here."

In fact, it was his pitching that revived Durnan's pro hockey career. He told the story to Stan Fischler in an interview in 1969 that was later used in two of Fischler's books and in his column on NHL.com in 2020.

Durnan played hockey growing up in Toronto and joined the North Toronto Juniors in 1931–32. North Toronto was part of the Maple Leafs' system, and after Durnan enjoyed a star season playing for the Sudbury Wolves the following year, the Leafs signed him and invited him to training camp.

"I began thinking that maybe goaltending could be my career," Durnan told Fischler. But that summer, "I spent a week at Wasaga Beach with a buddy of mine. As luck would have it, we started wrestling and I wound up ripping my knee very badly. When the Maple Leafs found out about it, they dropped me. I was disillusioned and figured if that was the kind of treatment I was to get, then I didn't want any part of it."

Durnan spent the next few years playing amateur hockey in Toronto in the winter and pitching softball in the summer. Then in 1936, he went north again to Kirkland Lake. "Gold had been discovered," Durnan told Fischler. "By the 1930s, seven mines were operating — and they all sponsored sports teams, including softball… The Lake Shore Mine had heard that I was doing some good pitching in the Toronto Beaches League. I got invited to pitch for Lake Shore's softball team, then wound up playing goal for their hockey club. Kirkland Lake was a terrific hockey town, so I could play hockey and earn some money at the mine."

Durnan spent four years in Kirkland Lake and led the Lake Shore Mine Blue Devils hockey team to the Allan Cup as Canada's national amateur champions in his final season of 1939–40. After that, "I moved down to Montreal and got a job in the accounting department of Canadian Car and Foundry Company. Money wasn't a problem for me anymore, and I got a break because my boss, Len Peto, was a director of the Canadiens."

Durnan still wasn't thinking about a pro career in hockey because of his experience with the Maple Leafs, but he did spend the next three seasons playing with the Montreal Royals, who were a Canadiens farm club. "Everything was just fine," remembered Durnan, "until Peto started pressuring me to sign with the Canadiens. This was in October 1943, when I was 29, not exactly young for a goalie." But it was wartime. Players were scarce, and Durnan's job carried a military deferment because the Canadian Car and Foundry Company was making airplanes for the war effort.

"They kept pushing me to sign," said Durnan, "and I resisted at first. Somehow I managed to hold out until the day of the season opener at the Forum. I finally got the Canadiens management to give in to my wishes. I signed for the huge sum of $4,200 and found myself on a hockey team beginning to jell."

Durnan liked playing under coach Dick Irvin. "Like myself, Dick loved baseball. Whenever we'd go on a road trip, Dick would make a point of visiting the ballpark in whatever city we happened to play. He'd go out to see the empty field, just for the chance to look at a major league ballpark."

But Durnan didn't like playing for general manager Tommy Gorman. He told Fischler that Gorman was always riling up French–English tensions and threatening to replace him with Montrealer Paul Bibeault. After the war Durnan's salary climbed to $10,500, but injuries and the mental strain were beginning to take their toll. And his reflexes were slowing down. Durnan told Fischler that in January 1950 he'd told Irvin he'd be gone for good when the season ended. Then after dropping three straight playoff games to the New York Rangers in the spring of 1950, Durnan said he knew Gerry McNeil was ready to take

over, and "I told Irvin to let the kid finish the series."

Durnan officially told the Canadiens he was retiring on July 13, 1950. "I could never stand another season," he said then. "My nerves are all shot and I know it." As he would later tell Fischler, "I'm glad I went out when I did."

Hainsworth Too

A standout goalie in the 1920s and '30s, George Hainsworth had some involvement with softball after his NHL career. Out of the NHL by 1937 Hainsworth had a softball team in Kitchener, Ontario, that featured NHLers and minor-league hockey players from that city. Among those performing with Hainsworth during

Cartoon promoting the Toronto Maple Leafs hosting the Boston Bruins at Maple Leaf Gardens on January 18, 1934.

Hayley Wickenheiser skates in a game against Team Kazakhstan at the 2011 IIHF Womens World Championship.

the summers of 1938 and 1939 were the Boston Bruins' "Kraut Line" of Milt Schmidt, Woody Dumart and Bobby Bauer — all future Hockey Hall of Famers. The Boston linemates were Stanley Cup champions in 1939 and 1941 and finished 1–2–3 in the NHL scoring race the season in between. Hainsworth, however, was more active as a golfer in summer months than as a softball player. Famously unemotional on the ice, there are stories from after his playing days claiming that his antics could get much more animated when things went badly on the links.

Wicked Good

Hayley Wickenheiser is almost universally acclaimed as the greatest women's hockey player ever. She was first invited to join the Canadian national women's hockey team during the 1993–94 season when she was just 15 years old, and she helped the team win a gold medal at the World Championship in the spring of 1994.

Over the course of her 23-year career, Wickenheiser won seven golds and six silver medals at 13 Women's World Championships. She was selected to the tournament All-Star Team seven times and was the MVP four times. In 61 games at the Worlds, Wickenheiser scored 37 goals and added 49 assists for 86 points. She also played at the Winter Olympics five times, winning a silver medal the first time women's hockey was included in 1998, and following up with gold medals in 2002, 2006, 2010 and 2014. When she retired, Wickenheiser was the all-time leading women's scorer at the Olympics with 18 goals, 33 assists and 51 points in 26 games. In all, she represented Canada in 276 international games, scoring 168 goals with 211 assists for 379 points.

Early in her hockey career Wickenheiser was also an outstanding softball player, and on June 18, 2000, she was officially named to the Canadian women's Olympic softball team to compete at the Sydney Summer Games between September 15 and October 1. An outfielder, Wickenheiser had been on the bubble but earned a spot with her strong play at tournaments during the spring.

The Canadian softball team was hopeful of winning a medal but managed just one win in seven games in Sydney. Canada beat Italy 7–1 and aside from a 6–0 loss to the United States was close in all other games, losing 3–2 to New Zealand, 1–0 to Australia, 4–3 to Japan, 2–1 to Cuba and 1–0 to China to finish last out of eight teams.

Wickenheiser was just the second Canadian athlete to compete at the Summer and Winter Olympics, joining Sue Holloway, who had competed in cross-country skiing in 1976 and in kayaking in 1976 and again in 1984, when she won silver and bronze medals. Since Wickenheiser, 10 other Canadians have competed in the Summer and Winter Games, highlighted by cyclist and speed skater Clara Hughes, who won gold, silver and three bronze medals and is the only athlete in the world to win multiple medals in both the summer and winter competition.

Chapter 3

The Men
in the Nets

By the Numbers

When it comes to the greatest goalie ever, the debate these days often comes down to Martin Brodeur or Patrick Roy. Going strictly by regular-season numbers, it's hard to argue against Brodeur. He played more often and won more often than any goalie in NHL history. And it's not even close. His 1,266 games played and 74,438:30 minutes are well ahead of Roy (1,029 and 60,214:34), and his 691 wins are 140 more than Roy (551), who's runner-up in all three categories. Brodeur's 125 shutouts are tops too, and his 2.24 lifetime goals-against average currently ranks him 10th all-time (Roy is 58th) on a list that is mostly topped by goalies long before his era.

When it comes to postseason performance, however, Roy tops Brodeur in most career playoff categories, including games (247 to 205) and wins (151 to 113), although Brodeur holds a slight edge in shutouts (24 to 23). Roy did win the Stanley Cup four times to Brodeur's three, so there is also a case to be made for "St. Patrick" as the greatest goalie.

But for those who saw Terry Sawchuk perform in his prime, few would argue there has ever been anyone better. And, of course, for years Sawchuk topped the statistical lists too. His win total used to stand at 447, although a new inventory of NHL statistics completed in 2017 dropped him to 445. Sawchuk became the NHL's all-time wins leader during the 1961–62 season and held top spot for nearly 40 years

until Roy passed him in 2000–01. Sawchuk became the NHL's all-time shutout leader when he passed George Hainsworth with his 95th on January 18, 1964. After upping his total to 103 in 1968–69, Sawchuk would retain top spot for more than 40 years until Brodeur posted No. 104 by blanking the Pittsburgh Penguins 4–0 on December 21, 2009.

By George

George Hainsworth starred in the NHL with the Montreal Canadiens and Toronto Maple Leafs from 1926 through 1937. The seasons were shorter in that era, so he played just 465 games in 11 years — but he recorded 94 shutouts. That means Hainsworth had shutouts in just over 20 percent of the games he played. During the 1928–29 season Hainsworth blanked his opponents in half of his games when he set a single-season record with 22 shutouts while playing every one of the Canadiens' 44 games on the schedule. That's a record not likely to ever be broken — although offensive production across the NHL was so weak that year, with an average of less than three goals-per-game scored by both teams combined, that the rules were altered the next season to allow forward passing in all three zones on the ice.

Before he entered the NHL in 1926–27 Hainsworth spent the previous three seasons playing goal for the Saskatoon Crescents of the Western (Canada) Hockey

Terry Sawchuk pursues the puck in a game against the Blackhawks.

George Hainsworth poses in net.

League, a professional rival of the NHL for the Stanley Cup in those days. It's often been said that when the Canadiens were looking to replace the late great Georges Vezina in goal, their former scoring star Newsy Lalonde, who was playing in Saskatoon at the time, recommended Hainsworth. That may be true, or it may have been Canadiens owner Leo Dandurand who had suggested Hainsworth — who'd been playing as an amateur in Kitchener, Ontario — as a possibility to Lalonde when he was looking for goalie help in the fall of 1923. The *Saskatoon Star* from November 10, 1923, says only that "scouts strongly recommended"

Hainsworth to Lalonde, although he had signed back in mid-October at the same time that the Canadiens were negotiating with Howie Morenz in the same part of Ontario. Regardless, when the Canadiens signed Hainsworth on August 23, 1926, many newspapers across Canada reported that it was in an effort to get him for themselves ahead of the NHL's bulk purchase of players from Frank Patrick when the Western Hockey League was going out of business.

The NHL doesn't count the statistics from the WCHL/WHL, but the 10 shutouts Hainsworth recorded with Saskatoon from 1924 through 1926 were

NHL All-Time Leaders in Goals-Against Average (Minimum 100 Games Played)

Player	Seasons	GP	GA	Minutes	GAA
Alec Connell*	1924–1937	418	836	26,177:27	1.92
George Hainsworth*	1926–1937	465	937	29,104:00	1.93
Charlie Gardiner*	1927–1934	316	664	19,687:00	2.02
Lorne Chabot	1926–1937	412	857	25,403:00	2.02
Tiny Thompson*	1928–1940	553	1,179	34,176:00	2.07
Roman Cechmanek	2000–2004	212	419	12,086:16	2.08
Dave Kerr	1930–1941	430	954	26,807:22	2.14
Dominik Hasek*	1990–2008	735	1,572	42,836:22	2.20
Ken Dryden*	1970–1979	397	870	23,328:54	2.24
Martin Brodeur*	1991–2015	1,266	2,781	74,438:20	2.24

* Member of the Hockey Hall of Fame

certainly "major league" and would give him a total of 104 shutouts in his professional career. That's one more than Terry Sawchuk, which means that Brodeur didn't become the professional hockey shutout leader until he recorded his 105th by blanking Pittsburgh again (this time 2–0) three games later on December 30, 2009.

1928–29

When he earned his record 22 shutouts in 1928–29, George Hainsworth allowed just 43 goals while playing all 44 games for the Montreal Canadiens. His goals-against average of 0.92 is another single-season record not likely to be broken. Offensive production was at a record low that season, with just 642 goals in 220 games, so plenty of other goalies had impressive numbers too. No regular starter on any of the 10 teams had an average higher than 1.85 that year, and seven others in addition to Hainsworth posted 10 shutouts or more.

Roy Worters was in his first season with the New York Americans in 1928–29. He'd played the previous three years with the Pittsburgh Pirates but had reached a contract impasse with the team. Worters was suspended by NHL president Frank Calder until the financial issues were resolved after Worters was dealt to the Americans. He reportedly signed a contract with his new team for $8,500 — a huge salary at the time, especially for a goalie.

Worters made good on his new deal, posting 13 shutouts in 1928–29, which tied him with John Ross Roach of the Rangers for second behind Hainsworth. His goals-against average of 1.15 was barely behind

George Hainsworth and Roy Worters shake hands in the dressing room on February 2, 1935.

Boston's Tiny Thompson (1.1548 compared to 1.1512) for third in the league. Most importantly, Worters led the Americans to the playoffs for the first time in their four-year NHL history. Though the Vezina Trophy went to Hainsworth that year (it was merely a statistical award at the time, given to the goalie on the team that allowed the fewest goals), Worters was rewarded with the Hart Trophy as the NHL's most valuable player. The NHL didn't begin selecting players as All-Stars until 1930–31.

MVPs

In 1928–29 Roy Worters became the first of just seven goalies to win the Hart Trophy. Here's a look at the others.

1949–50	Chuck Rayner*	New York Rangers
1953–54	Al Rollins	Chicago Black Hawks
1961–62	Jacques Plante*	Montreal Canadiens
1996–97	Dominik Hasek*	Buffalo Sabres
1997–98	Dominik Hasek*	Buffalo Sabres
2001–02	Jose Theodore	Montreal Canadiens
2014–15	Carey Price	Montreal Canadiens

* Member of the Hockey Hall of Fame

Worters' Thoughts

The lack of scoring in the NHL in the late 1920s led to all sorts of proposals to increase the number of goals. Wider nets, no goalies, smaller equipment and no limits on forward passing were all ideas being discussed. On February 1, 1929, Roy Worters addressed the issue in a conversation with syndicated columnist Frank "Lank" Leonard:

> Do I think that scoring must be increased to have the sport continue to hold favour? Well, I don't just know about that. Maybe New York would like it better if goals came more often. New York must have thrills aplenty to be satisfied. But in Canada and other league cities here in America, I doubt that high scores would be popular. All sorts of suggestions have been made, but I don't believe any would meet favour excepting possibly in this city. Such changes as have been proposed would not be considered 'hockey' in cities where hockey has been played for years. To my way of thinking, there's only one thing that might increase scoring without radically changing the rules of play. That is to increase the size of the goal itself. It would make it tough for us goalies but it would increase the thrill for me."

More Than Just Numbers

No discussion of the greatest goalies in NHL history would be complete without Jacques Plante. He certainly has the numbers to back him up. Plante's 437 NHL victories from 1952 until 1973 while playing with the Montreal Canadiens, New York Rangers, St. Louis Blues, Toronto Maple Leafs and Boston Bruins still rank ninth all-time, and he was neck and neck

Shrimp

Roy Worters played 12 seasons in the NHL, from 1925 to 1937. He spent most of that time on weak teams in Pittsburgh and New York, reaching the playoffs just four times and winning only one series. Still, in addition to his Hart Trophy win in 1928–29, Worters finished top 5 in voting for MVP three other times in an era when only two other goalies (Clint Benedict and John Ross Roach, twice) ever received any votes. So, Worters was a big talent ... but he came in a tiny package. Standing just 5-foot-3 and weighing only 135 pounds, he is the smallest player in NHL history and was known by the nickname "Shrimp."

with Terry Sawchuk for the all-time lead for much of their time together in the league. Plante's 82 shut-outs rank fifth all-time, and his 2.38 lifetime goals-against average ranks among the top 20 — although no one has led the league in goals-against average more often than Plante, who did it eight times. His six Stanley Cup championships with Montreal in the 1950s are a record for goalies equaled only by the six Ken Dryden won with the Canadiens in the 1970s, and his seven wins of the Vezina Trophy have never been matched.

Despite the big numbers, it's the innovations that make Plante stand out. He wasn't the first to roam from his crease in front of the net, but he was the first to make it a regular part of his game. He didn't just charge out to control rebounds or play the puck to his forwards, as other goalies had done; he was the first to go behind his net to stop the puck from ringing around the boards on shoot-ins. Plante wasn't the first to wear a mask either, but he was the one who championed the cause. His persistence truly changed the face of hockey.

Most people considered Plante an oddball. He relaxed by knitting his own toques and undershirts and wasn't keen on socializing with his teammates. But he worked hard to perfect his craft. "So often your skilled players are not dedicated," fellow Hall of Fame goaltender Glenn Hall once said. "But Plante was." He was happy to share his knowledge with his fellow goalies too, famously mentoring Bernie Parent when they played together in Toronto for most of two seasons between 1970 and 1972. Plante wrote *On Goaltending*, an instructional book, in 1972, and became the NHL's first goalie coach in 1977, when the Philadelphia Flyers hired him to help his old teammate Parent regain his form.

International Fraternity

Vladislav Tretiak became the first Soviet player inducted into the Hockey Hall of Fame in 1989. For many, he is the greatest goalie in international hockey history. Tretiak first came to the attention of most fans in North America during the Canada–USSR Series in 1972 when he was just 20 years old and helped the Soviets push the Canadians to the final seconds of the final game before Canada won the series. He turned in another memorable performance on New Year's Eve in 1975, when the Central Red Army tied the Montreal Canadiens 3–3 despite being outshot 38–13. Tretiak retired in 1984, but Canadian fans of a certain age have never forgotten him.

The Soviets had dominated international hockey since their first appearance at the World Championship in 1954, but they never competed against top NHL stars before 1972. Most Canadians believed the NHL pros would beat the Soviets handily. Before the first game of the so-called Summit Series, played in Montreal on September 2, 1972, Jacques Plante went to the Soviet dressing room to talk to the team's young goalie. He wanted to give him tips on the NHL stars he would be facing.

"I don't know why he did it," said Tretiak from Moscow in an interview featuring him, Alexander Yakushev and Boris Mikhailov that aired on the internet program *Hockey Time Machine* in March 2021. "Perhaps he thought they were going to get 20 by me, or there was a kind of fraternal feeling. I should have asked him. I don't know. But the very fact that he... came to see me — that made me happy... Normally, no outsider would be allowed in [our dressing room], but they must have let him in out of respect."

Tretiak and Plante had met before. Tretiak remembered it happening in 1971, but in an earlier interview he had said 1969 or 1970. It was probably in Montreal in 1969, when Tretiak was playing with the Soviet

Jacques Plante makes a save.

national team on a Canadian tour. The Soviets were in Montreal to play a team of all-stars from the Canadiens' farm system on December 29. Plante was also in Montreal, where his team, the St. Louis Blues, would face the Canadiens the next day.

A few days before in Toronto, where the Soviets played on December 26, coach Anatoli Tarasov had been discussing Plante and Tretiak. The conversation was reported by Milt Dunnell in the *Toronto Star* on December 29, 1969.

"We have seen many of the NHL goalies," said Tarasov, "and we know they are good. We remember how Jacques Plante (during his retirement) beat us lone-handed in a game at Montreal [2–1 on December 15, 1965]. Our young goalies must learn through competition. That is why we used a boy who is only 17 [Tretiak] in the game at Maple Leaf Gardens."

As Tretiak recalled that first meeting in his interview in 2021, "We had a practice on the same rink as the Blues. I went into the dressing room to take a shower, and suddenly Tarasov runs in and says, 'You are taking your shower, while Jacques Plante is out there on the ice. Go take a look at how he is practicing.'"

Even growing up in the Soviet Union, Tretiak knew about Plante. "All of us goalies are very grateful to him because he saved our lives by inventing the mask. That's why I knew about him. I didn't even finish my shower. I ran there and parked myself behind the net just to watch his movements. He noticed me because there was this kid sitting there with a CCCP sweater on. So he started showing me how he'd move around the net. He also gave me his stick. That's how we first met.

"Then, of course, before Game 1, he came into our dressing room. He started speaking to me in English, and I didn't understand anything. So he started drawing. It was obviously difficult to understand anything, but just the fact that he came to see me!

"You know, there is a kind of goalie brotherhood.

I was very grateful … I often remember this meeting and am very grateful. I had the feeling that he came to give me support before a difficult battle. What a great guy.

"Canadians probably weren't pleased though."

Behind the Mask

Goalies had worn masks before Jacques Plante. Even in the NHL, Clint Benedict had worn one briefly, late in the 1929–30 season (his last year in the NHL).

On the day before that season opened on November 14, 1929, Toronto Maple Leafs goalie Lorne Chabot was struck in the face by the powerful shot of rookie hopeful Charlie Conacher. Depending on the reports, Chabot was either nearly knocked unconscious or knocked out cold entirely. Either way, he was cut for four stitches. Chabot would still play in Toronto's season-opening 2–2 tie with Chicago, but a report out of Toronto from November 13 said that owner-manager Conn Smythe intended to bring forth a motion at the next NHL meeting to compel all goalkeepers to wear masks. New rules in the NHL that season allowed forward passing in the offensive zone for the first time and limited the number of players who could "loaf" behind in the defensive zone, so Smythe felt that goalies faced a greater risk of injury than ever before.

"Manager Smythe," reported the *Montreal Gazette* on November 14, "states that several managers in the NHL are in favour of the masks for goalkeepers, but their players do not want to be the first to use the device. If all teams were compelled to do so, it would be quickly adopted."

Apparently, the Ontario Hockey Association had passed such a rule for the 1920–21 season saying that goalies "may wear a mask for protection" — although nobody appears to have done so. Despite what Smythe said in 1929, it would be many years before the NHL

Jacques Plante poses with the mask he began wearing in the 1959–60 season.

adopted similar legislation. Amazingly, even as late as 2009–10 the NHL rule book only said that "protective masks of a design approved by the League may be worn by goalkeepers." The wording was not changed to say "must be worn" until the following year.

Interestingly, in a story reported in the *Regina Leader* on February 8, 1912, the National Hockey Association (forerunner to the NHL) was said to be considering the use of face protection for goalkeepers "in the shape of a baseball mask," which some clubs in the United States were already said to be using in practice.

A handful of goalies wore wire masks like baseball catchers in international competition during the 1930s, but other than Benedict's brief experiment, NHL goalies went maskless in games until Plante wore one for the first time on November 1, 1959.

Plante had suffered the usual array of goalie injuries before then: both of his cheekbones had been fractured, his jaw had been broken, his nose had been broken several times, and he was cut for as many as 200 stitches in his face. He'd begun using a mask in practice in 1955 (this was not unheard of for NHL goalies during the 1950s) and began experimenting with different types over the next few years. During a game in the 1958 Stanley Cup Final against Boston, Plante was knocked out when he was hit directly in the forehead. After a 20-minute delay he returned to action and finished the game.

Todd Denault, in his biography of Plante, notes that Bill Burchmore, a sales rep with Fiberglas Canada, was at that game. Burchmore began experimenting with designs for a fiberglass mask. A football and hockey player at college before and after his wartime service in the Canadian Navy, Burchmore told the *Montreal Gazette* for a story on December 12, 1959: "I felt some kind of reinforced fibre-glass would stand up to the impact of hockey shots in any league. The big problem was a design that would permit the

Quote ... Unquote

"I designed it for protection, not good looks. Besides, the mask has all of Jacques Plante's facial features. If it was made for Clark Gable, it would look like Clark Gable."

— **Bill Burchmore**, Fiberglas Canada Limited, addressing criticism that the mask he designed for Plante made him look like a man from Mars (*Montreal Gazette*, December 12, 1959)

unlimited visibility required by goalkeepers. To my mind, the only solution was some kind of a mask that would hug the face as closely as possible."

Burchmore contacted Plante for the first time in August 1958: "Jacques thought that I had perfected the cage-type mask. He didn't understand plastics and thought I was crazy when I told him that it would have to be moulded if it was going to be any good. As a matter of fact, just about everyone thought I had rocks in my head. Although I had developed the use of fibre-glass in hockey sticks five years ago, even my company wouldn't go for the mask idea."

But Plante agreed to visit a plastic surgeon at the Montreal General Hospital to have a plaster mold of his face made. From that, Burchmore got to work. He made a stronger mold from poured gypsum and began to cover it with a combination of fiberglass and specially woven cloth, which was treated with heat. Then, he experimented in his basement, swinging a steel ball on a pendulum to see if his creation, which weighed 11 ounces and was less than a quarter-inch thick, could withstand the impact of a puck traveling at 100 miles per hour from 15 feet out.

Plante was impressed. Just over a year after Burchmore first contacted him, Plante wore the mask when the Canadiens began training camp in September 1959. Burchmore then had to cut the eye holes wider to allow for Plante's superior peripheral vision, but the lightweight design meant that sweat wasn't a problem. The mask didn't fog up, and its dull, pinkish color meant there was no problem with glare or shadows from the lights.

Plante was convinced and took the mask to NHL president Clarence Campbell, who approved it for use in league games. Still, coach Toe Blake and Canadiens management refused to let him wear it beyond practice and preseason games. Plante had never worn a mask since making his NHL debut in 1952, and with him in net the Canadiens had won the Stanley Cup four years in a row heading into the 1959–60 season. Why change a good thing now?

Through the first 12 games, Plante played without a mask. The Canadiens were 7-2-3 and already comfortably in first place. Plante had been in the net for every second of every game and allowed 28 goals for a 2.33 goals-against average. Then on November 1, 1959, the Canadiens were in New York to face the Rangers at Madison Square Garden. Early in the first period Plante poke-checked Andy Bathgate, who fell into the boards and cut his ear and cheek. A few minutes later Bathgate hit Plante in the face with a shot. He told Denault that it was a wrist shot and that it wasn't hard, but he had deliberately aimed for Plante's face. Plante was cut from his lip up through his left nostril. Teammates escorted him to the dressing room, his blood leaving a trail of red on the ice. Seven stitches later — and facing the prospect of using a house

Earliest Mention?

Perhaps the earliest mention of Jacques Plante and a mask comes in a Canadian Press story that appeared in several newspapers on March 1, 1948. Plante was playing junior hockey with the Quebec Citadels and posted a 5–0 shutout in a playoff win over the Montreal Jr. Canadiens the night before. But it wasn't Plante who was wearing a mask during the game. It was Citadels defenseman Len Shaw, who was wearing a mask to protect his nose while returning to action for the first time since he'd injured it two weeks before.

goalie (teams didn't carry a spare at this time) — Blake agreed to let Plante wear his mask.

Plante wound up stopping 29 of 30 Rangers shots that night and the Canadiens won 3–1. Starting that night Montreal rattled off 10 wins and a tie in the next 11 games, and Plante allowed just 13 goals. Still some of the harshest criticism of his decision to wear a mask came from his fellow NHL goalies, and Blake wanted Plante to discard it when he slumped in the second half of the season. Plante played without it in a late-season game on March 8, 1960, and the Canadiens lost 3–0. He would never play without it again. And when the Canadiens finished the season with their fifth straight Stanley Cup championship, Plante held his mask aloft in celebration.

Jake the Snake

Jacques Plante made his NHL debut when he played three games for the Montreal Canadiens on November 1, 2 and 6, 1952. (He posted two wins and a tie and allowed just four goals in 180 minutes of action for a 1.33 goals-against average.) Canadiens goalie Gerry McNeil had suffered a fractured cheekbone, and Plante had been summoned from the Montreal Royals of the Quebec Senior Hockey League (referred to in some sources as the Quebec Major Hockey League at that time) and signed to an amateur tryout contract. Plante was not yet wearing a mask, but he wore a toque he knit himself while playing for the Royals. Canadiens coach Dick Irvin would not let him wear it in the NHL.

The contract Plante signed with the Canadiens gave them his professional rights for just those three games. The terms also stated that once he played 30 games with the Royals, Plante would become available to any of the other five NHL teams, unless the Canadiens signed him to a pro contract. So, a day after his 29th game with the Royals on December 28, 1952, Canadiens general manager Frank Selke signed Plante and sent him to the Buffalo Bisons of the American Hockey League.

Plante made his Bisons debut with a 2–1 win over the league-leading Cleveland Barons on January 3, 1953. Soon afterward, Jack Horrigan of the *Buffalo Evening News* began referring to

Plante as "the Snake." The earliest reference to the nickname "Jake the Snake" that author Todd Denault found for his 2009 book *Jacques Plante: The Man Who Changed the Face of Hockey* was in a story Horrigan wrote that appeared in the *Hockey News* on February 7, 1953. The headline was "'Jake the Snake' Plante Big Boon to Buffalo Bisons." As Horrigan wrote:

Not since George Ratterman of football fame stepped off the University of Notre Dame campus into the lineup of the defunct Buffalo Bills in 1947 has an athlete captured the imagination of Buffalo sports fans as Jacques (The Snake) Plante, the fast reflexed goaltender of the American League Bisons. Superlatives often are misused in describing the play of athletes. Yet Plante has been just that — superlative — in his first games in Buffalo livery

After the AHL season ended, Plante was summoned to Montreal as a backup goalie when the Canadiens opened the NHL playoffs against the Black Hawks. After taking a 2–0 series lead, Montreal dropped three straight games, and for Game 6 on April 4, 1953, Irvin replaced McNeil with Plante, who promptly blocked 24 shots for a shutout in a 3–0 victory to tie the series. He allowed just a single goal in Game 7 as Montreal scored a 4–1 victory to move on to the Stanley Cup Final against Boston. After the Canadiens won the opener 4–2 but lost the next game 4–1, Irvin put McNeil back in the net and the Canadiens went on to win the Cup in five games.

Plante had played a big part in the Canadiens' championship in his cameo role, but he wouldn't supplant McNeil as the team's regular goalie until the 1954–55 season. By the fall of 1955 reporters everywhere were commonly referring to Plante as Jake the Snake.

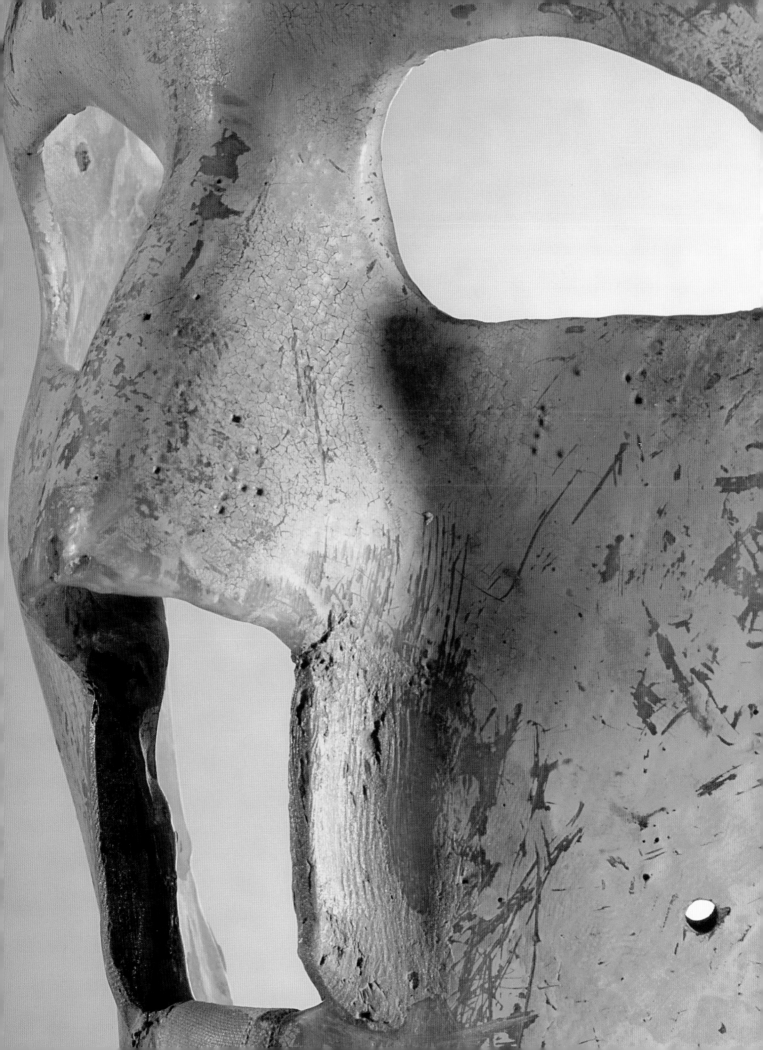

Benedict vs. Vezina

Everyone in the early days of the NHL knew that Clint Benedict and Georges Vezina were the best goalies in the young league. Along with Hugh Lehman and Hap Holmes, who spent most of their careers playing in rival leagues out west, these men were probably the best goalies in hockey history to that point. But of them, only Georges Vezina is a name most people recognize today. That is, of course, because since 1927 the NHL has presented the Vezina Trophy to the league's top goaltender.

Vezina was certainly a great one, both during the seven seasons he played in the National Hockey Association from 1910 through 1917 and then in the eight full seasons he played in the NHL through 1925 — all with the Montreal Canadiens. Still, if he hadn't collapsed of tuberculosis during Montreal's first game of the new season on November 28, 1925 (ending his career), and died a few months later — leading to the decision of Canadiens ownership to donate a trophy in his honor — the contemporaries he left behind likely wouldn't have spoken of him quite so glowingly, and he'd have faded from memory with the rest of the goalies from that era.

Benedict turned pro with the Senators in his hometown of Ottawa two years after Vezina signed with the Canadiens. He played behind another future Hall of Famer, Percy LeSueur, in the Ottawa nets during his first two seasons before taking the top job in 1914–15. He remained with Ottawa through the transition into the NHL in 1917–18 and then until 1923–24 before signing with the Montreal Maroons when they entered the league in 1924–25. Benedict remained with the Maroons through 1929–30, when he was the oldest player in the NHL at the age of 37. He spent his final season as a player with the Maroons' International Hockey League farm club, the Windsor Bulldogs, in 1930–31.

Benedict led the NHL in wins in six of the league's first seven seasons. He led or shared the lead in shutouts (not that there were many in his day) in each of the first seven seasons. No one has ever led the league in shutouts more times. He also led in goals-against average six times between 1918 and 1927. He won the Stanley Cup with Ottawa in 1920, '21 and '23 and added another with the Maroons in '26.

According to all accounts, Vezina was stoic and played a stand-up style. Benedict was a flamboyant flopper whose habit of falling to the ice to stop the puck was a big reason why the NHL changed its rules early in its first season to allow goaltenders to leave their feet. Benedict was the Dominik Hasek of his day, but he was the Martin Brodeur too, playing behind a team in Ottawa that was really the first in hockey history to emphasize defense over offense. After all these years it's impossible to know if Benedict was really better than Vezina or just played behind a better defensive team, but there are some clues.

In a feature on Vezina on January 8, 1934, that ran as part of a two-year series in the *Montreal Gazette* on the game's history called Turning Back Hockey's Pages, sportswriter D.A.L. MacDonald wrote of a story told by Leo Dandurand (the Canadiens owner in Vezina's time and the man who donated the trophy in his name) about a game between Vezina's Canadiens and Benedict's Maroons.

"It will be a close battle," Dandurand recalled Vezina saying to him. "I can hold them out at my end, Leo, but it will be tough to score against them. The best man is in the other goal, you know."

Modesty was apparently a Vezina quality, but Benedict's own teammates certainly backed their guy.

"Georges Vezina, of the Canadiens was a great goalie then," said former Senators and Maroons star Punch Broadbent in the *Ottawa Journal* on May 11, 1965. "He's honoured with a trophy; practically legend

in hockey. But we all thought there was no goalie ever better than Clint Benedict."

Writing in that same paper on June 8, 1965 (the day after Benedict was named to the Hockey Hall of Fame), *Journal* sports editor Bill Westwick told this story: "Vezina was the idol of many fans, especially the Montreal faction, but his own manager, the late Leo Dandurand, was a tremendous admirer of Benedict. There was a time when Dandurand told this reporter that he would have been very much tempted to have obtained Benedict in place of Vezina. That sounds like heresy in view of the legendary feats of Vezina, but Leo was the one to say it."

You can't always take these old sportswriters at their word, but if this story is true, it's a pretty good mark in Benedict's favor.

The NHL's First Masked Man

Regardless of a person's opinion on fighting in hockey, or the idea of letting players "police themselves" as the proponents of fighting like to say, there's no denying that hockey has always been a violent game. Perhaps it was inevitable in a contact sport played on a hard surface enclosed by solid boards and contested by men and women carrying sticks in their hands and wearing blades on their feet. As early as March 4, 1899, the *Saturday Budget Newspaper* in Quebec City, in writing about a Stanley Cup challenge from Queen's University to the champion Montreal Victorias, warned the students, "Before leaving they should order seven full suits of armour and as many coffins in order to be prepared for emergencies."

Seven, of course, because the game was played with a rover back then, and armor and coffins because, well, hockey was a violent game. No one was immune. Not even goalies. Clint Benedict spoke of the problem in a Canadian Press story about his early

days that appeared in many newspapers in late January and early February 1962:

> When those guys got in close either the puck went in the net or you did. Lots of times I went right through the back of the net. After the first couple of seasons, I lost count of the stitches they put in my head.
>
> They didn't have a goal crease in those days and the forwards would come roaring in and bang you as hard as they could. If they knocked you down, you were supposed to get back on your feet before you could stop the puck — those were the rules.
>
> I remember at least four times being carried into the dressing room to get all stitched up and then going back in to play. There were some other times, too, but I don't remember them.

Late in his career it wasn't so much the crashing bodies Benedict had to look out for as it was the flying pucks. But the old injuries still took a toll.

Benedict and the Montreal Maroons were facing his old team, the Ottawa Senators, on November 30, 1929. According to the *Montreal Gazette* on December 2, Benedict had been ailing all day with indigestion. After playing the first period he came out to start the second but was suddenly overcome. The game was held up for 10 minutes so that Flat Walsh, the Maroons backup, could get into his gear and take over. Benedict had surrendered a pair of goals, but Walsh got the win in a 3–2 Montreal victory.

Benedict would be out of action until December 29. A Canadian Press story from Ottawa on December 4 reported that medical examinations revealed he was actually suffering from an old injury received when he was playing in Ottawa several years earlier

and that a blow to the stomach in the Senators game had aggravated it. When he finally returned to action, Benedict picked up a win in a 6–2 victory over Detroit. Walsh was back in net for the Maroons in a 5–3 loss to Toronto on New Year's Day, 1930, but Benedict returned for a home game against Boston on January 4.

"Benedict had played a sensational game all evening," reported the *Gazette* on January 6, 1930, in wrapping up the Maroons' 4–2 win on Saturday night. "He robbed the Bostonese of at least a half-dozen sure goals with miraculous diving saves during the game. Benny's display was supremely courageous. He took all kinds of chances, diving head-first into the skates of onrushing Bruins, and right into the face of bullet drives."

But "about 15 minutes after the start of the third period, Benny finally paid for his bravery. He sprawled face first when [Dit] Clapper was clear in on him from the right, and took the puck square in the face. Benny dropped, and lay still as if he had been shot dead."

It took about five minutes to revive him, but after a quick trip to the dressing room for repairs Benedict returned and finished the game. He would not be so lucky against the Canadiens on January 7.

Early in that game Benedict took a Howie Morenz shot straight between the eyes and had the bridge of his nose smashed. The *Gazette* on January 8 noted that if the shot had been a half an inch to either side, "the veteran Maroon netminder would have lost an eye." As it was, "Benny dropped like a log … and he lay on the ice writhing until players of both clubs and the referees picked him up and carried him off the ice." Not only was there a trail of blood from the south goal into the Maroons dressing room, "even the wall along the corridor was splattered by the flow."

"I didn't know what happened until I woke up in the hospital," recalled Benedict in 1962.

"Some day," said the game report in the *Gazette*

back in 1930, "the league will authorize masks for net minders as baseball does for its catchers, and these accidents will be avoided."

Benedict would not see action again until February 20, 1930, some six weeks after the injury. Though the league had not authorized anything, when he returned to face the New York Americans at Madison Square Garden, Benedict was wearing a leather face mask. The game ended in a 3–3 tie.

Over the years stories have said that Benedict lost that night and threw the mask away. Others have said that he discarded the mask after three games because it obscured his view. The 1962 story reported that Benedict had had a Boston firm design a helmet with metal bars to protect his face and quoted him saying, "but it didn't feel good and I threw it away after a couple of games."

However, the contemporary game reports from 1930 make it clear that Benedict didn't just wear his mask for one, two or three games; he wore it for five. The fifth game was in Ottawa on March 4, 1930. In reporting on the game the *Ottawa Citizen* described a goalmouth scramble: "Clint Benedict was cracked on the mask he wears. The protector went in on his bad nose and it swelled up and started to bleed." (The *Montreal Gazette* says an Ottawa player fell on Benedict.) Walsh took over, playing the rest of the game for the Maroons and finishing out the season too. As for Benedict, he never played in the NHL again.

As to the mask itself, newspaper stories from the time make it clear that Benedict was not wearing a metal cage, but a leather mask like the ones injured football players occasionally wore during that era before face masks. The best description seems to appear in the *Vancouver Sun* on March 7, 1930:

He secured a heavy leather nose and mouth guard … setting a precedent for the major leagues, and setting also what may become a fashion among the much-battered goalers of the league. The mask is much like the nose-guards worn by football players, but it strapped on firmly over the top of the head and under the chin. Benedict claimed it did not interfere with his vision, which is the important factor and the main argument that has been advanced against the use of wire masks such as those employed by baseball catchers.

As to what Benedict had remembered in 1962, maybe it related to a story that appeared in numerous newspapers late in October 1932. After playing in the minors with Windsor in 1930–31 and working in the NHL as a referee the following season, Benedict was said to be contemplating a comeback, "aided by a special pair of glasses and a mask of his own design."

There is no indication that he ever played again, so perhaps that was the mask that Benedict recalled discarding so quickly.

A Hainsworth Cover-up?

Stephen Smith is the author of the 2014 book *Puckstruck: Distracted, Delighted and Distressed by Canada's Hockey Obsession*. He also maintains a website called Puckstruck, where he posts stories about hockey history. In a post from January 22, 2016, Smith wondered if perhaps George Hainsworth had worn a mask in an NHL game a little more than a year before Benedict did.

Smith presents a grisly newspaper photograph of Hainsworth lying in a hospital bed, his head swathed in bandages, after an errant shot from his Montreal Canadiens teammate Aurele Joliat had broken his nose in the warmup prior to a 1–1 tie game with the Toronto Maple Leafs on January 24, 1929. Wounded or not, Hainsworth was back in action two nights later for a 2–1 victory over Ottawa. Newspaper reports (in French) claim that Hainsworth wore "a heavy plaster" bandage over his nose. Next, the Canadiens traveled to New York for games against the Rangers and Americans.

In writing about the game against the Rangers, Harold C. Burr of the *Brooklyn Daily Eagle* told of Hainsworth wearing "from ear to ear a rubber protector across the bridge of his nose…" He also wrote of a high shot coming at Hainsworth's head, "but his mask had literally saved his face."

Had Hainsworth really been wearing a mask? Or was he merely wearing a plaster bandage as newspaper coverage from before and after the Rangers game state? Whatever it was, Hainsworth had dispensed with wearing it by the time Montreal faced Detroit on February 7.

Smith read 10 different reports of the January 28, 1929, game against the Rangers for his story, and Burr was the only one to mention a mask. Smith concluded that what Burr considered a rubber mask was really just the plaster bandage so many other writers referenced.

But then again, who knows?

Ten Years and Counting

Whether Clint Benedict was the first to wear a mask in the NHL in 1930 or George Hainsworth the year before, it wasn't until Jacques Plante in 1959 that the mask began to become a standard piece of equipment for goalies. Even then, it happened slowly. In an Associated Press story marking the 10th anniversary in 1969, Plante said, "At the time I started wearing the mask, I thought it would take about 10 years to accept it."

By that 1969–70 season Detroit's Roger Crozier, Minnesota's Cesare Maniago and Montreal's Rogie

Vachon had become the most recent NHL goalies to don a mask. But there were seven of 25 goalies on NHL rosters that were still holdouts: Gump Worsley (Montreal), Johnny Bower (Toronto), Ed Giacomin (New York), Wayne Rutledge (Los Angeles), Denis DeJordy (Chicago), Bruce Gamble (Toronto) and Les Binkley (Pittsburgh). Bower had worn a mask in practice for years and had, in fact, worn one in a game for the first time on January 19, 1969, when he came into a game in Boston after the maskless Gamble was cut for six stitches. Bower would also wear a mask in his lone game during the 1969–70 season — the last of his career — in a 6–3 loss to Montreal on December 10, 1969. So there were really only six holdouts.

Of those other six men (some of whom were also wearing them in practice), all would eventually don masks in games too, including Worsley. "The Gumper," who had famously said, "My face is my mask," would finally put one on during his final NHL season with the Minnesota North Stars in 1973–74. "I bought one for my kid," Worsley told Bob Verdi of the *Chicago Tribune* when the North Stars were visiting the Black Hawks on October 14, 1973, "then decided, what the heck, I'll wear it myself." Still, it wasn't until the following January that he started wearing the mask in games consistently.

With Worsley's conversion, the last NHL goalie to go maskless was Andy Brown, who played just 62 games over parts of three seasons from 1971 to '74. "I've used a mask in practice for the last three years," said Brown in a story in the *Minneapolis Star* on October 17, 1973, "but I've had no motivation to put it on for a game. I suppose if I get hit in the face one night that will motivate me."

Brown became the last goalie in NHL history to play without a mask when he played his final game in the league on April 7, 1974, for the Pittsburgh Penguins in a 6–3 loss to the Atlanta Flames. Brown went

Gump

His given name was Lorne John Worsley, but everyone knew him as "Gump." Worsley began his NHL career with the New York Rangers in 1952–53 and went on to play 20 more seasons from 1954 to 1974 with the Rangers, Montreal Canadiens and Minnesota North Stars. The nickname goes back to his childhood, as Worsley explained in his 1974 biography, *They Call Me Gump*: "I was about nine or ten years old. A fella I hung around with in Montreal named George Ferguson started calling me 'Gump.' I had hair that stuck up like Andy Gump, the comic strip character. The nickname came because of that."

Worsley admits it was his own fault that the nickname took over, "because when I went to play junior, you had to fill out a form and they asked for a nickname and I put 'Gump' down and it stuck."

The nickname was widely used in the *Montreal Gazette* from 1946 to 1949 when Worsley played junior hockey with the Verdun Cyclones. There are references to Lorne Worsley in those early years too, but they often appear as "Lorne (Gump) Worsley."

on to play the next three seasons with the Indianapolis Racers of the World Hockey Association … and never wore a mask in the WHA either.

Cheevers' Stitch Mask

Gerry Cheevers has told the story countless times. He wasn't much for practice in his days with the Boston Bruins and was always looking for ways to get out of it. One day a shot flipped up and hit him in the mask. It wasn't much, but he went down like he'd been knocked out. He got up and skated to the dressing room, where he lay down on the trainer's table.

"You're not hurt," said coach Harry Sinden, "so get back out there."

Bruins trainer Johnny "Frosty" Forristall drew stitches on the mask with a black magic marker.

And that's how it all started.

Cheevers' stitch mask would become an NHL classic, but it's a little tricky to figure out exactly when it all actually happened. Cheevers didn't wear a mask in a regular-season NHL game for the first time until October 11, 1967. He'd made his NHL debut playing two games with Toronto back in 1961–62, but he spent most of his time in the Maple Leafs' minor-league system until Boston claimed him after the 1964–65 season. He continued to spend most of his time in the minors until 1967–68. The mask he began wearing in 1967 did not have the stitch marks in the early part of the season, but stories about them began to appear in newspapers by January and February 1968. Still, in a Canadian Press report out of Boston in the spring of 1969, Forristall explained, "It's something Gerry and I started about four years ago."

Forristall told Leigh Montville of the *Boston Globe* in a story on March 6, 1969: "It's something I started with Gerry as soon as he came to the club. Every time he gets hit in the mask, we draw in the stitches he would have received if the mask weren't there."

Even though Cheevers didn't wear a mask in a game until 1967, perhaps he had been wearing one in practice before that. Had the tradition actually begun as far back as his first season in Boston in 1965–66? Forristall's stories seem to indicate that. But Sinden didn't become the Bruins' coach until 1966–67, and Cheevers made his first extended run with the team during the first half of that season. Did the tradition start in practice that season? "We draw stitches for both the games and the practices," Forristall said. But was he wrong about how early they had started?

"This makes the second year we've been doing

Halloween Costume

With the Flyers' orange and black team colors, Halloween references were common right from Philadelphia's NHL debut in 1967–68. With his round face and wide grin while wearing those orange and black colors, goalie Doug Favell was sometimes referred to as a pumpkin or a jack-o'-lantern from that first season too. And though Gerry Cheevers was the first goalie to decorate his mask, Favell was the first to play with a full mask paint job — just two days before Halloween in 1970.

"The Great Pumpkin rose at 8:05 Thursday night," wrote Bruce Keidan of the *Philadelphia Inquirer* on Friday, October 30, 1970. "Doug Favell, the Flyers' fabulous flake, took to the ice at that moment to face the Los Angeles Kings. The flamboyant Flyer net minder faced the Kings through the brightest orange facemask in the history of hockey."

"It's a National Hockey League first," said Favell of his mask while celebrating Philadelphia's 3–1 victory in the dressing room after the game.

"And so it was," wrote Keidan, "the first coloured mask in NHL history. And maybe the last. No one … seems quite sure if the gaudy gadget is legal or not."

But the NHL issued no ban against Favell's orange paint job, and soon goalies everywhere were painting their masks too.

this," Cheevers told Montville for the same story. "This is the second mask we've done it on. Frosty transferred last year's stitches to this year's mask at the beginning of the season."

So it would seem the stitches didn't actually start until Cheevers began wearing a mask in games in 1967–68. The practice incident may have occurred in early January 1968, since newspaper stories on January 10, 1968, reported that Cheevers was hit in the mask on a deflected shot from teammate Fred Stanfield. In a story on January 26, 1968, it was noted that Cheevers' mask was marked with 14 stitches. By late in the 1968–69 season Cheevers estimated the mask had about 100 stitches on it.

And how many of the real thing had Cheevers had sewn into his face before he started wearing a mask?

"About 100 stitches," Cheevers told Montville. "Just about the same number the mask has saved."

Saving Face

Several goalies had worn masks in games in the early days of hockey. For a while the trendy answer to who wore the first goalie mask was Elizabeth Graham, who donned a fencing mask while playing net for the Queen's University women's team in 1927 . . . reportedly under pressure from her father, who had recently paid for some expensive dental work.

But Graham wasn't the first. She wasn't even the first woman. According to Lynda Baril in her 2013 book *Nos glorieuses*, citing the original source as the *Montreal Daily Star* on March 7, 1916, Corinne Hardman of Montreal's Western Ladies Hockey Club had worn a mask in a game more than 10 years before Graham. And a month before that, the *New York Times* on February 24, 1916, reported on a game from the night before where the Union Club defeated the Knickerbocker Club 14–0 as part of a Charity Ice

Carnival for the Belgian Relief Fund during World War I. Knickerbockers goalie J.G. Milburn Jr. was replaced after the first period by J.J. Higginson, who, the *Times* noted, "wore a baseball mask."

Not exactly high-level hockey, but in 1903 Eddie Giroux (a future Stanley Cup champion with the 1907 Kenora Thistles) was experimenting with a catcher's mask — or something — with the Toronto Marlboros before the 1903–04 season in the Ontario Hockey Association. Giroux was hurt in practice on December 9, 1903, when he was hit in the face by a shot from Tommy Phillips. (Phillips would return to his hometown of Rat Portage/Kenora after the season and lure Giroux there late in the summer of 1904.)

Various newspaper stories in Toronto and elsewhere reported on Giroux wearing a baseball mask, or some kind of padded hood, over the next two weeks. Whatever it was, Giroux doesn't appear to have used it when the Marlboros played their first exhibition game in Barrie, Ontario, on December 18, 1903, nor in any games that followed during the 1903–04 season. He was said to be having trouble locating shots from the side while wearing it.

Baseball catcher's masks date back to the 1880s, and hockey goalies were quick to adopt cricket pads for added protection during the 1890s. But few opted for masks. Perhaps the earliest to do so was Edgar Hiscock of the Kingston Frontenacs, playing in the intermediate division of the OHA.

The *Ottawa Citizen* of January 23, 1899, picked up a story from the *Kingston Times* claiming that Hiscock had recently broken his nose and would be forced to wear a baseball mask in his coming games. However, nobody has yet to find a source confirming that Hiscock actually wore a mask in a game. But there is confirmed evidence of another mask-wearer a few weeks later — although this was hardly in a top-tier hockey game either.

Everett Douglas Marshall had lost his left eye
due to an errant stick in a hockey game in Calgary
on January 28, 1898. Until then, Marshall had been
a defenseman for the Calgary Press Club (he worked
for the *Calgary Herald*) and for the Calgary Volunteer
Fire Brigade. Despite the injury, Marshall continued
to referee hockey games during the winter of 1899.
There's no story as to why he chose to return to play
as the goalie for the Press team on March 16, 1899, but
the *Calgary Herald* the following day confirms that he
did: "Ev Marshall made his first appearance on the ice
this season. Playing goal for the Press team, with his
face behind a baseball mask."

Marshall played what appears to be the last game
of his hockey career for a team called the Nonpareils
against a Canadian Pacific Railway team on April 3,
1899. No mention of a mask in this one (although he
probably wore one), but his work in goal was said to
be "very fine."

Going Down in History

When the NHL began its first season on December 19,
1917, goalies were not permitted to drop to the ice to
make a save. The rules — as they had been in virtually
every hockey league there ever was up to that time
— required that goalies remain standing at all times.
But just three weeks into its inaugural season, the
NHL made a change. As the *Toronto Star* reported on
January 9, 1918:

> When Canadiens meet Torontos tonight
> in the NHL game at the Arena the hockey
> public may see Harry Holmes, the Toronto
> net guardian, standing on his left ear and
> nonchalantly booting high ones over into
> the corner, or Vezina, the French-Canadian
> wizard, sitting on the top of a goal post and

Clint Benedict poses while playing for Montreal.

batting them out like Larry Lajoie hammering out a two-sacker at the Island last summer. Anything but murder and an Ostermoor mattress goes in the nets in the pro league from now on.

It was the *Star*'s extravagant way of announcing that goalies would now be allowed to drop to the ice to stop the puck. The rule change is usually credited to Clint Benedict. "It was against the rules then," said Benedict in 1962, "but if you made it look like an accident you could get away without a penalty. I got pretty good at it and soon all the other goalies were doing the same."

Out west, in the Pacific Coast Hockey Association, brothers Frank and Lester Patrick had already dealt with this injustice. "A goalkeeper should be allowed to make any move he wants," said Lester, "just like the rest of us. He should be allowed to make the most of his physical abilities." In his biography of the Patricks, Eric Whitehead indicates that this rule change was made during the first PCHA season of 1911–12, but Craig Bowlsby (who has meticulous research to back it up) writes in his 2012 book *Empire of Ice* that the Patricks didn't actually introduce the rule officially allowing a goalie to stop a shot any way he pleased, except by throwing his stick, until the 1916–17 season.

Art Ross was in favor of the rule change. He had also introduced it in 1916–17 in the Art Ross Hockey League, an amateur organization he helped to run in Montreal. Ross was the coach, the manager and a top player on the Montreal Wanderers when the NHL's first season began, and a few days before it opened he spoke in favor of allowing goalies to drop to the ice. Though it was league president Frank Calder who announced the change on January 9, 1918, newspapers in Montreal and Ottawa noted that Ross had made the suggestion several weeks before.

Praying Benny

Clint Benedict was often called "Benny" during his career. As the story goes, crowds in Toronto would mockingly refer to him as "Praying Benny" for his habit of falling to his knees in the days before the rule was changed. The nickname stuck even afterward.

In a 1962 story about Benedict, his brother-in-law, Bruce Gibson of Ottawa, recalled the night that Toronto fans got so angry. "[They] were screaming mad," Gibson said. "They shouted 'bring your bed, Benny' and hollered at the referee for not calling a penalty."

It's hard to find any period references to corroborate this, but Lou Marsh of the *Toronto Star* confirms some of it in his column of November 5, 1930: "In the old days when goalkeepers were benched for deliberately flopping to their knees or tummies to stop or smother shots, Benny became such an adept at falling accidentally and caused so many arguments with officials that the rule was changed to allow goalkeepers to do as they pleased to stop the puck. Benedict's habit of flopping to his knees earned him the soubriquet of 'Praying Benny.'"

The papers did acknowledge that the change would give great satisfaction to the Senators and Benedict, but Calder maintained that "the idea is not to favour Ottawa or any one club, but to help the entire league, the public, the teams, and the officials … The old rule made it hard for referees, so everybody will be helped."

Gary Smith of the Toronto Marlboros makes a diving save against Ron Naud of the Peterborough Petes in 1964.

Rule Change

The Toronto Maple Leafs' two future Hall of Fame goalies — Johnny Bower and Terry Sawchuk — were out with injures on December 21, 1966, when the team was in Montreal to play the Canadiens. Bruce Gamble got the start, but after the Canadiens scored two goals by 5:23 of the first period to wipe out an early 1–0 Maple Leafs lead, coach Punch Imlach put Gary Smith in net.

A few minutes later Smith stopped a shot by Dick Duff. He caught the puck, dropped it in front of his stick and began rushing with it. Smith got within three feet of the center ice red line, then tried to make a pass. Unfortunately, the puck landed right on the stick of Montreal defenseman J.C. Tremblay, whose long shot was stopped by Leafs defenseman Marcel Pronovost.

"I was so surprised when I saw Smith that all I could think of was to shoot," said Tremblay. "Maybe I should have skated in closer."

As the *Montreal Gazette* reported, Canadiens coach Toe Blake complained about Smith holding the puck too long, but he had to laugh.

"He makes Jacques Plante look like a chicken," said Blake in reference to the nomadic former Canadiens goalie.

Fans at the Forum loved it, and Imlach would defend the move as entertaining, even though Smith was returned to Rochester of the American Hockey League on December 24 and then sent on to the Victoria Maple Leafs of the Western Hockey League. But not everyone was amused.

The same day as the reports of Smith's demotion,

a Canadian Press story had supervisor of NHL referees Frank Udvari proposing a rule change. "There's nothing in the rule book now," said Udvari, "but we may have to revise that rule. I know a goalie can hold the puck for three seconds but he isn't supposed to be carrying it like a football player. He can be out to the blue line in three seconds."

The rule change that came about, however, had nothing to do with how long a goalie could hold on to the puck but rather with where he could handle it. The new rule, now Rule 27.7 in the current NHL rule book, states, "If a goalkeeper participates in the play in any manner (intentionally plays the puck or checks an opponent) when he is beyond the center red line, a minor penalty shall be imposed upon him."

Goalies Scoring Goals: NHL

To date 12 goalies in NHL history have been credited with scoring a total of 15 goals. The first was future Hall of Famer Billy Smith of the New York Islanders on November 28, 1979. Smith was credited with a goal as the last Islander to touch the puck before Rob Ramage of the Colorado Rockies put it in his own net after goalie Bill McKenzie had vacated it on a delayed penalty.

The first goalie to actually score a goal by shooting the puck the length of the ice was Ron Hextall of the Philadelphia Flyers on December 8, 1987. Hextall was great at handling the puck and fired a long shot into an open net to ice a 5–2 win over the Boston Bruins while Reggie Lemelin was on the bench for an extra attacker. Hextall did it again in a playoff game against Washington on April 11, 1989, making him the only goalie to score two goals on direct shots.

Martin Brodeur is credited with scoring three goals for the New Jersey Devils during his Hall of Fame career. The first was a shot into an empty net in a playoff game against Montreal on April 17, 1997. On each of the other two goals (February 15, 2000, vs. Philadelphia and March 21, 2013, vs. Carolina), Brodeur was merely the last Devils player to touch the puck before an opponent put it into his own net.

Goalie Goals: Brophy vs. Moran

It was never common for goalies to rush with the puck from end to end, but it did happen on occasion. Some goalies had even scored goals. The first to do so at hockey's highest level was Fred Brophy, on February 18, 1905. He did it against a future Hall of Fame netminder: Paddy Moran of the Quebec Bulldogs.

The game in question was a strange one, with lots of goals and plenty of penalties. Moran's hometown Quebec team beat Brophy's Westmount team 17–5 in a Canadian Amateur Hockey League contest, but even with 22 goals scored (including one each for Westmount by future Hall of Famers Art Ross and Lester Patrick, who were very early in their careers), goalies Brophy and Moran were the biggest story.

"The second half was marked by very ragged play," reported the English-language Quebec City newspaper the *Chronicle*, on Monday, February 20, 1905, "but one of its greatly appreciated features was the sensational rush of Moran with the puck from his own goal the entire length of the rink. He shot on goal, which the Westmount goaler ran out to check and both goalers went into the corner in a heap. The crowd gave Paddy a great reception for his remarkable bit of play."

According to the account in the French-language paper *La Presse* in Montreal, the score was already 12–4 at the time Moran launched his attack. Westmount was one man short, but Quebec was playing with just Moran, two defensemen and one forward.

"The situation amused the public," said *La Presse* (in a translation provided by Quebec journalist Marc Durand). "Brophy, to not be left behind, returned the

Paddy Moran as a member of the Quebec Bulldogs.

compliment by scoring, after a superb race, helped by a lot of goodwill on the part of the Quebec defense."

No explanation as to what that "goodwill" entailed, but Moran was known to be a feisty competitor and not one who seems likely to have just given up the goal, no matter what the score — especially considering that Brophy had just stopped him. But as if to prove it wasn't a fluke, Brophy went end to end again to score a goal the following season, this time while playing for the Montreal AAA against the Montreal Victorias on March 7, 1906 — although his team lost by another lopsided score, this time 14–6.

Goalie Goals: Clint Benedict

A season before he made his pro debut with the Senators in 1912–13, Clint Benedict (along with fellow future Hall of Famers Eddie Gerard and Punch Broadbent) was playing with New Edinburgh, an Ottawa neighborhood team, in the Inter-Provincial Amateur Hockey Union. On March 12, 1912, New Edinburgh was on the road to open the league final against the Montreal Victorias. It would be a one-sided romp for the Ottawa team, and according to the *Montreal Gazette* the next day:

> The feature play of the whole game was that pulled off by Benedict in the second half. Stopping a shot from a Victoria forward, the New Edinburgh net guardian took a run up the ice as far as the Vic cover point position and let fly a long one at Haskell. The surprise at seeing his padded opponent so near him probably effected Haskell, for he allowed the shot to get by him, and Benedict stands on the summary credited with one goal ... The youthful goaler was deservedly cheered for the play.

Benedict's goal put New Edinburgh ahead 14–2 en route to a 17–3 victory.

Goalie Goals: Chuck Rayner

Born Claude Earl Rayner in Sutherland, Saskatchewan, on August 11, 1920, he usually went by "Chuck" — and sometimes "Bonnie Prince Charlie." Like Roy Worters a generation before him, Chuck Rayner was a Hall of Fame goalie on teams that usually weren't as good as he was.

Rayner broke into the NHL playing 12 games with the New York Americans in 1940–41 and spent

Chuck Raynor chases after the puck.

most of the next season with the team when it was known as the Brooklyn Americans. After serving in the Canadian Navy during World War II, Rayner spent eight more seasons in the NHL with the New York Rangers from 1945 through 1953. In his 10-year NHL career, Rayner's teams made the playoffs only twice, although he won the Hart Trophy as MVP in 1949–50 and led the Rangers to Game 7 of the Stanley Cup Final that spring before losing to Detroit in double overtime.

Rayner was well known for his poke check, which he would later teach to Johnny Bower, another Saskatchewan-born goalie, when Bower was property of the Rangers. Rayner was also an excellent skater, and it was not unusual to see him carrying the puck. In fact, he almost became the first goalie in the NHL to score a goal. Rayner's story is told in a Legends Spotlight on the Hockey Hall of Fame web page that is based on a Stan Fischler story in the *Hockey News* from December 31, 1982: "I got to the blue line against Toronto one night. They had pulled [Turk] Broda for an extra attacker late in the game. I stopped the puck and shot it down the ice. It bounced off the boards and suddenly, it started going straight for the empty net. Well, you could have heard a pin drop in Madison Square Garden, the people were so quiet. But at the last moment, it swerved and missed going in by just a couple of inches."

Rangers coach Frank Boucher would sometimes have Rayner move up toward center on New York power plays if he felt he could help out the offense. After all, Rayner had actually scored a goal before. He did it in a postseason all-star game on February 26, 1943, after having spent the season playing for the Esquimalt Navy team in the Vancouver Island Hockey League. The game featured the league champion Victoria Army team facing players selected from the league's other military teams as a tune-up for the Allan Cup playoffs.

Rayner remembered it as a rough game with lots of penalties, but his memory doesn't match with newspaper reports from the time. It was a wide-open game with plenty of scoring (Victoria Army won 8–4) and "not one good solid body check seen during the entire 60 minutes," according to the *Victoria Daily Times* of February 27, 1943. The summary of the game shows only one penalty throughout. The *Nanaimo Daily Times* from the same day records Rayner's goal this way: "Rayner's work in front of the nets has been one of the features of the play at the local ice palace, but last night he enacted a new role when he skated through the entire soldier club for the final goal of the match. Taking the puck from his own goal, Rayner skated straight for the opposition net and flipped the puck past goalie Art Rice-Jones, much to the delight of the fans."

The Victoria paper on March 1 said that Rayner had been tempted to take off up the ice several times during league play and had now realized his season-long ambition. "Rayner is a good skater," wrote reporter Pete Sallaway, "and can handle that goal stick better than a lot of forwards we can think of." He

quoted Rayner in the dressing room after the game saying: "I finally got a chance to show some of those forwards just how it is done. Did you notice how I faked goalie Rice-Jones out of position before lifting the puck into the net?"

In addition to future Hall of Famer Chuck Rayner in action that night, the defense for the all-stars featured NHLers Bob Goldham and Dave MacKay, while the Army team was led by center Bill Carse, who beat Rayner for a goal, and set up another, during the game. Rayner's goal was the last of the evening, coming at 14:50 of the third period. The only penalty came in the second period and went to Army's Julian Sawchuk — no relation to Terry.

Goalie Goals: Terry Sawchuk
From the *Boston Globe*, April 4, 1956:

NEW GLASGOW, N.S., APRIL 3 (AP) — The Boston Bruins continued their undefeated exhibition tour tonight with an 11–6 victory over the Pictou County All-Stars. Highlight of the game was a goal scored by Boston goalie Terry Sawchuk after skating the length of the ice in the second period. Fleming Mackell, one of four Boston players loaned to the All-Stars, scored three goals and Jerry Toppazini shot another.

Chapter 4

Off-Ice Episodes

The Plot to Kidnap Guy Lafleur

It was good to be Guy Lafleur in Montreal by the end of the 1970s. He'd grown up without much but was now making $350,000 a year. Following the first three seasons of his NHL career, when people generally thought he'd underperformed (and he had), Lafleur had rattled off six straight 50-goal, 100-point seasons from 1973–74 through 1979–80. He'd won the Art Ross Trophy for the most points in the NHL three straight times from 1975–76 to 1977–78 and helped the Canadiens win four straight Stanley Cup titles from 1976 through 1979. (He'd also won the Cup back in 1973 but hadn't been much of a factor in that one.)

So, it was good to be Lafleur. But even though he usually made it look like fun, it wasn't always easy. "I remember when I was 14, one summer [growing up] in Thurso, when one of my teachers was negotiating my contract," Lafleur told Michael Farber for a story in the *Montreal Gazette* on March 22, 1980. (This was likely when Lafleur was preparing to leave home to play provincial junior hockey in Quebec City in the fall of 1966.) "He told me, 'One day you won't own yourself.' I laughed at him. I thought he was crazy."

Farber described Lafleur's salary as "high-rent slavery." While acknowledging that Lafleur "savours it," he also noted that there was a price to pay. Lafleur couldn't take his son out in the city anymore without being mobbed. (Farber wrote that Lafleur's wife, Lise, was very sensitive about this and was angry at Lafleur for posing with their son for a magazine shoot.) Just recently, a man had stopped his car to speak with their son while he was playing in the street. A neighbor called to warn them. Lise worried that their son might be an easy mark for someone looking for ransom, or just to make headlines.

It wasn't just paranoia. Lafleur had already been the victim of a kidnap plot himself.

There had been a lot of pressure put on Lafleur from the time he arrived in Montreal. The Canadiens drafted him first overall in 1971, just one day after Jean Beliveau had announced his retirement. Lafleur was seen as the next in a long line of Canadiens superstars. He scored 29 goals as a rookie but was still seen as a disappointment. His 64 points fell behind the 77 of Marcel Dionne, whom the Canadiens had considered taking with their first choice, and his goals were well below the 44 former Junior Canadien Rick Martin scored as a rookie that year with the Buffalo Sabres.

Even after Lafleur finally broke out as a superstar in his fourth season in 1974–75, Canadiens fans were quick to turn on him when he didn't play well. He had a poor game against the Red Army in the famed 3–3 tie on New Year's Eve in 1975, after which Lafleur said he put too much pressure on himself. And he didn't perform as well as expected during the playoffs in 1976, particularly in the Stanley Cup Final, even though he led the Canadiens in scoring with 17 points (seven goals, 10 assists) in 13 playoff games and the

Le Démon Blond

To English fans, Guy Lafleur was known as "the Flower" from the translation of his last name. In French, he was "le Démon Blond" (the Blond Demon) for the way his blond hair streamed behind him when he raced up the ice.

Canadiens swept the two-time defending champion Philadelphia Flyers. Montreal fans were still critical of him.

That series wrapped up on May 16, 1976, and 12 days later, on May 28, the French-language *La Presse* newspaper in Montreal revealed that Lafleur had played the entire playoffs knowing there was a plot to kidnap him and hold him for ransom. Montreal police learned of the plot during their investigation of the $2.8 million armed robbery of a Brink's security truck that happened in the city on March 30. Lafleur was informed just as the playoffs were starting and kept under close surveillance throughout. Lise Lafleur told *La Presse* that her husband had been quite upset and lost 12 pounds during the ordeal.

Police admitted that the kidnap plot may have been a hoax, but they had taken no chances. Canadiens management was informed right away. "It was reliable information," said inspector Jean-Claude Rondou, in charge of Montreal's Criminal Investigation Bureau. "I don't think it was a hoax." About 10 days later, the informant called to say that Lafleur wasn't in danger anymore because the men who were planning the kidnapping had been arrested for something else.

"The guy wouldn't tell us who arrested them or on what charge," said Rondou. "We don't even know who the guys are."

During those 10 days or so, police had watched every move Lafleur and his family made. The Canadiens hired armed guards, and with investigations into the robbery continuing, those guards maintained their watch even after the police ended their round-the-clock personal protection. Coach Scotty Bowman was told what was going on, but neither Lafleur's teammates nor NHL president Clarence Campbell were informed. A year later, in a story in the *Gazette* on May 15, 1977, Lafleur admitted that he had told Jacques Lemaire, his roommate. "I had to tell him," Lafleur said, "because he asked me who those two guys were who kept following me around when we were on the road."

As vice president of the Canadiens, Beliveau had devoted almost all of his time to the incident. "Lafleur's home was under constant police surveillance," said Beliveau, "and he was always under guard.

"All this made it very difficult for him during the playoffs. Sometimes when he was reading criticism of himself in the papers, Guy was tempted to tell what was happening. But he had to keep it secret."

When it was all over and the Stanley Cup was won, Lafleur closed himself in a broom closet in the dressing room at the Philadelphia Spectrum in order to be alone with his emotions. Two days later, after teammates celebrated with champagne and began leaving the victory parade, a police escort led Lafleur to his car before he sped away.

When the story finally broke at the end of May, Lafleur told Canadiens PR director Claude Mouton: "I'm going away. Don't give my phone number to anybody. I don't want to talk about it anymore. I've been through hell once and that's it." Lafleur was finally able to relax when police made arrests in the robbery case on June 1.

Mrs. Beliveau

It wasn't easy to be married to the biggest new star in Montreal. Elise Beliveau faced constant rumors about her marriage during the 1950s. "I don't know who starts these stories," the 24-year-old Mrs. Beliveau told Angela Burke of the *Toronto Star* in an interview from Quebec City that appeared in the paper on March 27, 1956.

"Even before we were married, I had girls calling me saying Jean was out with some other woman. Sometimes he was sitting in our living room at the time." Mrs. Beliveau — referred to as Lise throughout the story — believed jealousy was the root of the many rumors. "Last year, when my mother was very ill and I came home to Quebec City often to visit her, everybody said Jean and I were separating. This year …I hear that I am supposed to be having a romance with a wrestler and these other interests are keeping me in Montreal. It seems that you just can't win."

Elise Couture had met Jean Beliveau over five years earlier on a blind date. They had been married more than three years. In an interview with the *Montreal Gazette* on December 10, 2020, she admitted that she knew nothing about hockey at the time but that her mother was a fan — although she had doubts about her daughter dating a hockey player.

At the time of the 1956 interview, Mrs. Beliveau was again in Quebec City while the Canadiens were on the road. "None of the wives of the players travel with the team," she said. "It's not really encouraged." But that didn't stop the rumors, including ones that claimed she wanted her husband to give up hockey.

"Why, he loves the game. On our first date he took me to see a hockey game in which he was playing and afterwards we went dancing. I like hockey too. At one time I was nervous for Jean when he played, but now I don't allow myself to worry…

"Jean and I are happy and in love," she said. "I am returning to Montreal and Jean [tomorrow]."

Jean Beliveau and Elise Couture, his future wife, in front of the Colisee in Quebec City.

The happy couple remained married until Jean Beliveau passed away on December 2, 2014. And she is still devoted to the Canadiens. As the team prepared to launch the Covid-19-delayed 2020–21 season in January 2021, a video was released pretending to show Elise Beliveau preparing the dressing room at the Bell Centre for their return.

Mike Bossy Death Threat

On April 22, 1981, *La Presse* in Montreal reported that Mike Bossy had received a death threat that January during his pursuit of 50 goals in 50 games. Many English-language papers jumped on the story.

According to the report, Bossy had received death threats from the boyfriend of a young woman he had counseled to kick her drug habit. Police patrols were increased in the area of Bossy's North Port home on Long Island, and private security guards were assigned to him. Bossy's agent, Pierre Lacroix, was quoted as saying, "I was staying with him at the time, and the suspense lasted through the last three games [of the chase for 50 in 50]."

More than the death threat itself, the *La Presse* story focused on Bossy's desire to leave New York. With the threat on his life coming so soon after John Lennon had been shot and killed in December 1980, Bossy was said to be musing about leaving the New York area if he had to live under such conditions. Bossy, who'd grown up in the suburbs of Montreal, was said to be hoping to return to his native province to play for the Canadiens or the Quebec Nordiques.

As for his own take on the ordeal, in his 1988 autobiography *Boss*, Bossy said the death threat was later assumed to have been a prank made by a disgruntled fan of Maurice Richard.

"Lindsay and Howe Will Be Shot"

In March 1956 the Detroit Red Wings and Toronto Maple Leafs met in the first round of the playoffs. The Red Wings were two-time defending Stanley Cup champions but had dropped to a distant second place in the regular-season standings, 24 points behind Montreal, after seven straight years of first-place finishes. The Leafs, who had fallen on hard times since the death of Bill Barilko in 1951, had squeaked into the playoffs for the first time in three seasons despite a record of 24-33-13.

The first two games of the series were tight. Detroit rallied on third-period goals by Gordie Howe, Johnny Bucyk and Alex Delvecchio to win the first game 3–2 on March 20. Game 2, on March 22, was a penalty-filled affair won 3–1 by the Red Wings. Ted Lindsay was cut above the eye in a fracas with the Leafs' Tod Sloan, who had to be helped off the ice later with a shoulder injury that would sideline him for the rest of the series. Leafs general manager Hap Day was critical of referee-in-chief Carl Voss, who he said had told him after the game that he'd tried to get his on-ice officials to call more penalties but couldn't get them to do it.

"If that is the situation," said Day, "Voss is to blame."

Detroit boss Jack Adams agreed that stricter control would have prevented "the outbreak of woodchopping" involving Lindsay, Sloan, Howe, Marc Reaume and Dutch Reibel in the second period.

Game 3 was scheduled for Toronto on Saturday night, March 24. That afternoon death threats were made against Detroit's two biggest stars. One threat was phoned into the sports department of the *Toronto Star*. "Lindsay and Howe will be shot if they play tonight," said a male voice. The threats were repeated three times to Red Wings officials in Hamilton, where the team was staying at the Royal Connaught Hotel.

"We have adequate protection at the Gardens," said Day. "I will confer with [rink manager] Henry Bolton over the threats, but they seem to stem from some crank."

Day recalled an incident in the 1930s when Leafs goalie Lorne Chabot was threatened with shooting if he didn't throw a game in New York City, but that game went on without incident. The *Star* also noted that threats had been made against NHL president Clarence Campbell if he attended a game in Montreal

Gordie Howe and Ted Lindsay of the Detroit Red Wings are served a meal by Ted's mother.

the year before, but did not mention his suspension of Maurice Richard, nor the punch to Campbell or the smoke bomb that went off inside the Forum that set off riots in the streets outside.

"[The] players will not be informed of the threats," said Red Wings coach Jimmy Skinner, "and Lindsay and Howe will play. Does anyone really think for one second that Gordie Howe tried to hurt Tod Sloan? Our men have been boarded and hurt scores of times and we have had injuries too."

The players must have been told, however, as a report in the *Globe and Mail* on March 26 noted that although Lindsay and Howe laughed off the telephone threats, a special detachment of plain-clothes officers

guarded them inside Maple Leaf Gardens. And the two Detroit stars played brilliantly.

" 'They're getting old,' is a comment we've occasionally heard this winter," wrote *Globe* columnist Jim Vipond. " 'They're not the same old Gordie and Ted ...'

"They're not the same, huh? That could be, but only because they're better! You can hate 'em. Threaten to kill 'em. Scream at 'em. But when it comes down to facing facts, Mister Howe and Mister Lindsay are still two valuable hockey players to have around in time of need."

With the Leafs leading 4–2 approaching the midway point of the third period, Howe scored at 9:11 and Lindsay at 14:25 to tie the game. And then, a

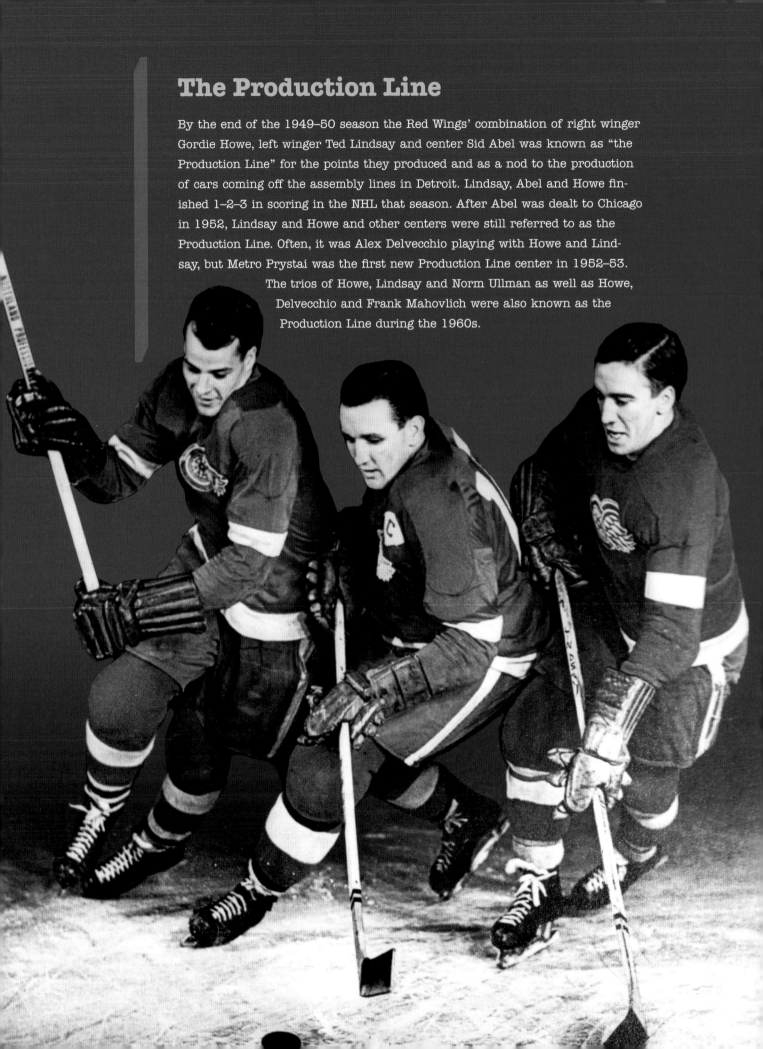

The Production Line

By the end of the 1949–50 season the Red Wings' combination of right winger Gordie Howe, left winger Ted Lindsay and center Sid Abel was known as "the Production Line" for the points they produced and as a nod to the production of cars coming off the assembly lines in Detroit. Lindsay, Abel and Howe finished 1–2–3 in scoring in the NHL that season. After Abel was dealt to Chicago in 1952, Lindsay and Howe and other centers were still referred to as the Production Line. Often, it was Alex Delvecchio playing with Howe and Lindsay, but Metro Prystai was the first new Production Line center in 1952–53. The trios of Howe, Lindsay and Norm Ullman as well as Howe, Delvecchio and Frank Mahovlich were also known as the Production Line during the 1960s.

few minutes into overtime, Howe fired the puck into the Leafs end. Bob Goldham picked it up and passed out front to Lindsay, who slammed the winning goal past Toronto's Harry Lumley at 4:22 for a 5–4 Detroit victory. As the last player off the ice a few minutes later, Lindsay waved to the crowd and then cocked his stick, rifle-style, and as Vipond wrote, "mock machine-gunned his tormentors." According to Rex MacLeod in the *Globe*, "His pose was so realistic that a few fans and some sports writers scurried for cover."

"I can afford to laugh when it's all over and we've won," said Lindsay in the dressing room. "That was the first time I ever can recall scoring the tying and winning goals in a playoff game. But it happened at the right place."

Up 3–0 in the series, the Red Wings would beat the Maple Leafs in five games but then — facing the Canadiens in the final for the third straight spring — would lose the Stanley Cup to Montreal in five games.

Canadiens Motel Fire

In the spring of 1971, the Montreal Canadiens had been surprising Stanley Cup champions thanks to the stellar play of Ken Dryden, who won the Conn Smythe Trophy as playoff MVP. Having played just six games in the regular season before taking over in the playoffs, Dryden was still classified as a rookie when 1971–72 rolled around and would win the Calder Trophy as the NHL's best freshman that season.

Though they wouldn't win the Stanley Cup again in 1972 (they would in 1973), the Canadiens were on a roll as the playoffs approached. A 5–1 win in St. Louis on March 9, 1972, gave them eight wins in a row as part of a streak of 11 wins and a tie in a 12-game stretch. Dryden was key to the win that night, as the Blues outshot the Canadiens 38–16 through two periods but trailed 2–1. Goals by Peter Mahovlich and

Guy Lafleur 33 seconds apart early in the third period put the Canadiens in control, but it was Dryden's 45 saves (St. Louis outshot Montreal 46–28) that bailed them out of trouble. Still, it would be a few of Dryden's defensemen who made some much bigger saves in the wee hours of the following morning.

At 1:51 a.m. on March 10 a fire broke out in a room on the fourth floor of the main motel complex of the Hilton Inn near Lambert Field (the St. Louis International Airport), where the Canadiens were staying. The fire, wrote the *Gazette*'s Ted Blackman, who was there, was the result of a drunken smoker who had fallen asleep with a lit cigarette and was the first man out of the building. The blaze was contained to just that room, but the fourth floor filled with smoke, and members of the Canadiens were credited with helping firemen — who many on the scene felt had done a poor job — with evacuating about 100 motel guests. Serge Savard was cut for 18 stitches and treated at a local hospital. Five other guests were treated for injuries as well.

Savard and several teammates were in a dining room when the fire alarm went off. "It sounded," wrote Blackman, "like a deep-throated cricket." Some players weren't even aware what it was. Others figured it was a prank. But when assistant general manager Floyd Curry rushed in and told them that coach Scotty Bowman was trapped upstairs, the players raced for the fourth floor. Savard cut his ankle kicking out a glass panel trying to reach Bowman's room. Choking on smoke, Savard thought Bowman was doomed.

Teammate Dale Hoganson found a flashlight and made his way into the coach's room. "I couldn't see two feet in front of me, the smoke was so thick... I managed to find the bed and I felt on it, but Bowman wasn't there. I had to leave because I couldn't breathe. I thought Scotty was dead somewhere."

In actual fact, Bowman had crawled out onto

The 1971–72 Montreal Canadiens.

the fourth-floor ledge, where he was contemplating whether or not to jump. "I didn't think I could make it for another five minutes," said Bowman later, "but I hung on after seeing the ladder."

Bowman had been on the phone when the alarm sounded. He went out to the hall, but the smoke drove him back inside. He left the door open and hollered to Curry, who was asleep in a room across the hall. Curry was able to break the window in his room, and he and another man climbed down a ladder to safety. Bowman, meanwhile, had managed to kick open the sliding glass door to a balcony. Team trainer Bob Williams instructed the coach to lie flat on the ledge while he and Rejean Houle commandeered a ladder for that side of the building. Bowman managed to skitter down, his face blackened and his body shaking.

J.C. Tremblay of the Canadiens had once been a volunteer fireman in his hometown of Bagotville,

Quebec. He made four trips up and down the ladder to the fourth floor, helping at least six people to the ground safely. "He saved my life, he was wonderful," said one woman in a sooty dress. Guy Lapointe rescued at least four others. "I guess I'm just a frustrated fireman," said the defenseman, whose father was a fireman in Montreal.

The players were able to laugh about it once they realized everyone was all right, but Bowman had another strange incident at the airport in Montreal later that night when he was caught in an elevator that kept running up and down without opening its doors.

"I've become conditioned to misfortune after what's happened this year," said Bowman of a season filled with fires, bomb scares and blizzards. "But you know where I'll be [Sunday] morning and night? In church."

Hockey Night in Moscow

It wasn't exactly life and death at Moscow's Intourist Hotel in September 1972 — although some members of Team Canada may have felt it was — but there were definitely some strange goings-on.

After four games in Canada, the series with the Soviets moved to Moscow for the final four games from September 22 to September 28. The Canadians had managed only one win and a tie back home and had been booed loudly in the final game in Vancouver. But after losing the first game in Moscow, Team Canada would rally to win the last three games and take the series.

Yet it wasn't easy on so many levels.

Canadian diplomat Patrick Reid of the Department of External Affairs had accompanied the team to Moscow. He recalled the hotel incidents during a series of interviews with Patrick White for a story first published by the *Globe and Mail* in 2012 for the 40th anniversary of the Summit Series.

"No question there was a campaign to interrupt the slumber of the team," he said.

"At night," said Brad Park, "the intercom would start playing music. You would try to turn it off, but you couldn't."

"That phone kept ringing and I'd pick it up and there'd be nobody on the other end," remembered Phil Esposito. "So, I finally got fed up and ripped the thing right out of the wall. This was in the middle of the night. A few minutes later, someone knocked on my door: They'd come to fix it. I couldn't believe it. Try getting Bell Canada or AT&T to do that."

One of the more memorable stories only emerged later. It was the tale of a Team Canada player or players finding a lump beneath the carpet in their room and unscrewing what they believed was a listening device — a bug — on the floor ... only to have a chandelier in a ballroom come crashing down on the floor below them.

Phil Esposito and Alexander Gusev during Game 2 of the 1972 Summit Series.

In his book *Pal Hal* about Harold Ballard in 1989, Dick Beddoes attributed this incident to Frank Mahovlich. Other stories mention Gary Bergman, but the most popular versions involve Wayne Cashman and Esposito.

"Somehow me and Cash got blamed for it," Esposito told White. "People say it was me. So from then on, I said it was me. It makes for a good story."

For his part, Alan Eagleson believes there was no chandelier incident. "It was made up!" he told White. But Reid insisted he saw it. "It happened," he said. "I was present when some ostentatious hotel employees carted away this chandelier in a series of pieces."

Still, it may just be an urban myth. Dating back to

Quote ... Unquote

"We came to show our hockey. That's all ... I know that Canadians have said that they had to unscrew chandeliers, thinking they were bugged."

— **Vladislav Tretiak**, Hockey Time Machine, March 26, 2021

"Someone ate their meat and drank their beer."

— **Alexander Yakushev**, adding to the story

"Well, the meat part might be true, but not bugging through the chandeliers! Who would listen in? For what purpose? These were fairy tales."

— **Vladislav Tretiak**

at least 1965, jokes have been told and stories have appeared in books that tell the same tale about foreign diplomats in the Soviet Union or just Americans traveling abroad. Richard J. Bendell is the author of *1972, The Summit Series, Canada vs. USSR — Stats, Lies and Videotape: The UNTOLD Story of Hockey's Series of the Century*, which was originally published in 2012. He was never able to find any evidence confirming the story. If it actually happened, he believes it must have involved something a lot smaller than a large chandelier, such as a candelabra-style light fixture.

Then again, it may never have happened at all.

Where's the Beef?

Provisions Team Canada brought to Moscow definitely went missing from the Intourist Hotel in 1972. "We weren't about to trust our food to them," Alan Eagleson told Patrick White for his *Globe and Mail* story. "We brought over our own beer — 500 cases. And we brought 800 to 900 steaks."

Much of the food disappeared.

"I had to look into the case of the stolen steaks," said Gary Smith, who worked at the Canadian Embassy in Moscow at the time. "I think it was likely some guy involved with the hotel, rather than someone thinking the Canadians wouldn't be able to play without their steaks."

"I was back to Moscow a number of years ago, on

Team Canada prior to Game 2 of the Summit Series on September 4, 1972.

a Team Canada trade mission," said 1972 defenseman Rod Seiling on *Hockey Time Machine* on January 28, 2021. "I was sitting at a table, and we got talking about 1972 … and our beer disappearing, and our steaks being cut in half. I'm sitting at the table with this gentleman, and he said, 'Oh, yeah, that's all true, I know all about it. I was selling it on the black market.'"

Lalonde Saves Lives

On New Year's Day 1953, the *Vancouver Province* ran a *B.C. Magazine* insert that featured Newsy Lalonde reminiscing about his long career in hockey and lacrosse with sportswriter Eric Whitehead. Lalonde recalled that his father hadn't been pleased with his early interest in sports in his hometown of Cornwall, Ontario:

Going back nearly 60 of my 65 years, I can't say I made my early choice of games with the family blessing. My father, Peter, didn't hold much stock in games. He was a shoemaker, worked hard for a living, and figured the only way to get along was to get a decent trade and stick with it. Later on, when I started whipping off to the arena and rinks to play hockey and lacrosse, he used to get pretty mad … My father figured I should be more

Newsy Lalonde poses for a photo.

interested in learning the print business with my home town paper, the *Cornwall Freeholder* … My father never wanted to hear about the games. He stayed pretty sore at me for wasting my time with sports. But he had his soft side, too, and I saw it once in a while. Like the time I came home after helping the Cornwall Rovers beat the Stars for the city [lacrosse] championship, and I went into the shop kind of quiet and there was my father bragging about me to his customers. He shushed up fast when he saw me.

Lalonde told Whitehead that his mother was always more supportive of his sports career, although she used to worry that he would get hurt. His father did too. But as Whitehead wrote, "Peter and Rose Lalonde raised a tougher nut than they ever imagined."

On Saturday, February 23, 1918, during the NHL's first season, Lalonde was called away from the Montreal Canadiens and summoned home to Cornwall because his father had fallen ill. When he arrived home around 10 o'clock that night, he found the house filled with coal gas — a dangerous hazard when homes were heated by burning coal. Lalonde immediately threw open all the windows and doors, which allowed the gas to escape and thereby saved the lives of his wife, his parents and a niece, who were all in danger of asphyxiation. He then rushed to the telephone to call a doctor, who attended to what a story in the *Toronto World* newspaper three days later referred to as "the near-victims, all of whom were very sick from the fumes."

Lalonde himself had little to say to reporters about the incident, but "neighbours of his parents spoke freely and gave him all credit for his prompt action."

A Snowball's Chance

On March 4, 1971, 18 inches of snow fell on Montreal in the space of just 12 hours. As a result, mayor Jean Drapeau asked NHL president Clarence Campbell to suspend the game that night between the hometown Canadiens and the Vancouver Canucks. The Canucks, who were already in the midst of a season-long 12-day road trip, went on to play in Minnesota and Buffalo on March 6 and 7 before extending their trip another two days to play a rescheduled game back in Montreal on March 9. The result of that game was a 3–3 tie, giving the first-year expansion team its only point on its seven-game eastern swing.

Reports at the time noted that NHL games had been canceled before, in the wake of the deaths of King George V and King George VI of England and the assassinations of U.S. president John F. Kennedy in 1963 and of Martin Luther King in 1968. Another game had been canceled in 1950 when heat inside the Boston Garden caused fog over the ice. But it was generally noted that the Canadiens–Canucks game was the first in the NHL ever to be canceled by weather. Bill Westwick, longtime sports editor of the *Ottawa Journal*, knew that wasn't true.

"After reading for the third time the uncorrected claims that in the recent snow storms a major league hockey game was cancelled in Montreal by weather 'for the first time in the history of the National League,'" Westwick wrote on March 10, 1971, "the urge must be strong among just a few remaining members of Ottawa's one-time almost unbeatable National League teams to say: 'It just ain't so.'"

Westwick then spun the incredible tale of the Senators' ill-fated train trip to Montreal on February 20, 1924, an account that is more than backed up by Ottawa newspapers from the time.

The Senators, who had won the Stanley Cup in 1920, '21 and '23, were packed with future Hall of

Famers. The roster boasted Clint Benedict in goal, George Boucher, King Clancy and Lionel Hitchman on defense, plus forwards Punch Broadbent, Cy Denneny, Jack Darragh and Frank Nighbor. Only Nighbor (out with a leg injury) was missing when the Senators decided to catch an earlier train to Montreal because of the threatening weather. "All the players were rounded up and ordered to board the Canadian National express, which left Ottawa at noon," reported the *Citizen* on February 21, 1924.

But trouble was already in the air. The train was late arriving from Pembroke because of the snowstorm and didn't pull out of Ottawa's Union Station until 1:30 p.m. It had barely gotten out of the city before it was held up again, awaiting a snowplow to be sent ahead and clear the track. This time the train got as far as Rockland, Ontario, about 25 miles (40 km) east, where it was delayed again due to a freeze-up in the water tank.

"There was no great danger that the Ottawas would be delayed," reported the *Citizen*, "until shortly after Hawkesbury [another 37 miles / 60 km] was passed." Just a short distance farther, near Cushing Junction, "a terrific blizzard" was raging. Another snowplow had gotten stuck and the train couldn't get through. By then it was a little after five o'clock.

At this point the CN train was about six or seven miles from the nearest telephone or telegraph, and even if one could be reached, most of the lines were down. As a result, some 6,000 fans would be kept waiting at the Mount Royal Arena in Montreal a few hours later, wondering where the Senators were as game time approached at 8 p.m. The crowd sat, singing, for about two hours until the game was postponed and rescheduled for the following night.

Meanwhile, members of the train crew and some of the passengers were desperately trying to clear the snowdrifts, but they were blowing back onto

Cy Denneny as a member of the Ottawa Senators, circa 1923–24.

the tracks faster than they could be removed. "Jack Darragh, [King] Clancy, Cy Denneny, and [team trainer Cozy] Dolan manned the shovels for a time, but the battle against the elements was hopeless from the start and after two hours work, a complete surrender to the storm had to be admitted."

From 5:30 p.m. until 2 a.m., the players and other passengers were stranded on the train, with practically no provisions. Finally, a plow was able to get through and clear the tracks enough to get everyone back to Hawkesbury. Manager Tommy Gorman and several players went out to find food, but the blizzard had forced all the local restaurants to close. CN officials were able to confiscate a big box of bread intended for a local business, while Clancy found a load of biscuits. Teammate Spiff Campbell had been able to find some eggs and butter.

None of the adults on board was going to starve, but a young mother had a baby that she was taking to the Royal Victoria Hospital in Montreal. Her supply of fresh milk was gone and there was none on the train. The conductor volunteered to head out again into the raging storm, and Clancy and Denneny insisted on going with him. They managed to find a farmhouse and awakened the farmer, who turned over what milk he had. An hour after leaving, the group was back on the train with the milk, but during their travels Denneny fell down a well and had to be hauled out. There are no further details, except that "he and Clancy were all in" by the time they got back to the train. Westwick in 1971 would report that Denneny "fell in a well or some such hole but wasn't badly hurt."

Finally, sometime after 4 a.m. the line was cleared sufficiently for the train to depart Hawkesbury. Montreal was only about 60 miles (100 km) away, but it wasn't until 8:30 a.m. that the train finally arrived.

The Senators slept the day away at the Windsor Hotel before showing up at the Forum for game time.

Aurele Joliat and Sprague Cleghorn (twice) scored in the first period for the Canadiens, and that proved to be all the scoring in a 3–0 Montreal victory. The Senators were said to have never really been in the game, and the Canadiens' victory moved them ahead of the Toronto St. Pats and Hamilton Tigers into second place in the four-team NHL. Three wins in their final four games would give the Canadiens a playoff spot, where they then knocked off the first-place Senators with 1–0 and 4–2 victories in the NHL final. Montreal went on to beat the Vancouver Maroons of the PCHA and the Calgary Tigers of the WCHL in two straight games each to win the Stanley Cup.

Money Matters

At a Lions Club sports dinner in Ottawa in 1965, Punch Broadbent discussed the money available to players like him during his pro career, which stretched from 1912 to 1929 with the Ottawa Senators, Montreal Maroons and New York Americans. He'd originally signed for $1,800.

"Of course, we didn't play a lot of games then," said Broadbent, "and you could hold a job on the side because we practiced at night. Later, I got $6,000, plus a playoff bonus, but that was in the last year when I went to New York."

Broadbent was traded from Ottawa to Montreal when the Maroons joined the NHL in 1924–25, winning the Stanley Cup the following season and playing with the team again in 1926–27. The Maroons were known as a big money team, and many of the players became friendly with various financial experts in Montreal. In the stock market boom of the 1920s, there was plenty of money to be made … on paper, anyway.

"I had my score up to $200,000," said Broadbent, "but despite warnings, tried for an even quarter million. Then came Black October [in 1929] and the roof fell in. But some of the Maroons lost up to half a million. It was an incredible era, and hockey was almost secondary."

Gambling in Toronto: 1915

A story out of Montreal on February 22, 1915, appeared in several newspapers across Canada the next day. It was about bribes (and other efforts) made to players in the National Hockey Association by gamblers.

The news broke when players on the Quebec Bulldogs told their story while passing through Montreal on their way back home after a game in Toronto. The article claimed that Harry Mummery of the Bulldogs and team trainer Dave Beland had been offered bribes before a Saturday night game on February 20, 1915, to let the Toronto Shamrocks win.

"As far as I know," said NHA president T. Emmett Quinn, "a well-known business man of Toronto approached Mummery and offered him $1,000 if he would throw the match and let the Shamrocks win. All the betting in Toronto, where I was myself on Saturday, was on the Quebeckers, and this man and some of his friends, it is said, were trying to make a killing on the Shamrocks."

"Mummery," said Quinn, "told the man he must be crazy, and reported it to manager Mike Quinn. Beland was also approached but only offered $50. He also reported the matter to Manager Quinn."

It was said this was not the first time something like this had happened in Toronto. Another report mentioned attempts to bribe players on the Canadiens and the Toronto Blueshirts. No names were mentioned, but Harry Cameron of the Blueshirts — a future Hall of Famer — was cited in a different vein.

"Last week," said president Quinn, "a gambler in Toronto invited Cameron of the Toronto team

out, and induced him to break training [i.e., got him drunk] with the result that he was unfit to play that night. It was found out the gambler and his friend had bet a large amount on the opposing team."

More details on Beland were reported in Montreal on February 23, and this story appeared in the *Ottawa Citizen* the next day:

An alleged briber approached trainer Dave Beland, of the Quebec team, with inquiries about the condition of his team. Securing information, he invited the Quebec trainer into the bar, and after a social drink, asked him to take a flask of Player's whiskey to the rink. This Beland refused to do, and it is claimed the bartender was overheard to say he 'could not mix such a drink' as that asked for. It was presumed that some drug was ordered to be placed in the liquor. Later in the night, Beland was handed a flask of whiskey, but smashed it on the dressing room floor.

The *Citizen* also picked up a Toronto report claiming that the businessman alleged to have offered the bribe to Mummery wasn't actually from Toronto, but was a gambler who'd recently begun betting on hockey games in the city. It was said that he had lost $2,000 the week before when the Shamrocks had upset the Blueshirts — in the game in which Cameron was "unfit to play" — and was looking to win back his money.

Meanwhile, on February 23 the *Toronto Telegram* reported that NHA president Quinn had instructed all club managers "that any player shall be expelled who has been proven guilty of offering, agreeing, conspiring, or attempting to lose any game of hockey or in being interested in any wager thereon." Quinn vowed that he was going to take action to stop this sort of thing, but the last word on the incident appears to have come from Toronto's Lol Solman, owner of the Arena Gardens on Mutual Street, a few days later on February 26, 1915.

Solman refused to take the incident too seriously. "From what I can make out," he said, "the matter has been greatly exaggerated and has been given more prominence in the papers than it is entitled to."

"Yes," said Solman, when asked if he thought gambling was hurting the game. "Gambling will kill any game and it must, of course, be stopped as far as possible at the Arena." But the case had not been turned over to John William Seymour Corley, Toronto's prominent crown attorney, because Solman didn't believe such action was warranted.

"It has been greatly exaggerated," he said again. "If any legal action is taken it is up to the NHA."

The Bull Ring

Gambling may or may not have been stamped out at Toronto's Arena Gardens back in 1915, but it would become prevalent at Maple Leaf Gardens. Perhaps not as soon as its opening at the start of the 1931–32 season, but definitely not long afterward.

Conn Smythe certainly wasn't averse to gambling. As he would tell it, Smythe took the money paid to him in the fall of 1926 by the New York Rangers (who'd fired him after he built their roster upon entering the NHL) and bet it successfully on a couple of football and hockey games. By February 1927 he had used the proceeds as his share in the purchase price when he put together a syndicate to buy the Toronto St. Pats, whom he renamed the Maple Leafs. A few years later, on September 20, 1930, Smythe won about $10,000 betting on a long-shot horse he owned named Rare Jewel. He used that money to aid his purchase of King

Clancy from the Ottawa Senators. After obtaining Clancy, Smythe made a gamble of a different sort when he went ahead with plans to build Maple Leaf Gardens during the height of the Great Depression.

Even if there wasn't gambling at the Gardens right from the start, there would soon be a so-called bull ring of bookies operating from a promenade behind the blue seats at one end of the rink. Hockey had been relatively free of gambling scandals, with nothing on a par with the 1919 Black Sox or other baseball indignities through the years, but fans of the game were definitely making bets. A Chicago newspaper called *Collyer's Eye and the Baseball World* provided plenty of details in an issue on December 1, 1934. The paper noted that reports on hockey gambling were up all around the NHL early in the 1934–35 season. "There are even rumours that efforts have been made to [bribe] some of the goaltend[er]s."

Montreal was said to be the longtime center of hockey gambling, but it was much quieter there that season than New York. Detroit was labeled as the new hot gambling mecca, with Boston only lukewarm. Nothing is said about Chicago or St. Louis (where the Ottawa Senators had recently located), but it was noted that there was plenty of action on NHL games in non league centers such as Kansas City and the Minnesota cities of Minneapolis, St. Paul and Duluth. There were plenty of details about Toronto too: "Toronto is a spot where one can get a bet down at any time. In fact, in the bull ring at Maple Leaf Gardens they will give you anything you want in the line of wagering accommodations, though they deal the nuts on Leafs. You can bet on goals, the most shots, or penalties. One favourite wager is that Leafs will score as much in one period as the other team does in the whole game."

Other stories from other sources indicate Toronto was so rife with gambling that fans were known to place wagers on whether the next spectator hit with a puck in the stands would be a man or a woman.

Efforts weren't made to clean out the bull ring in Toronto until 1946, after Maple Leafs star defenseman Babe Pratt was expelled from the NHL for gambling. But even at that, in an article about the Gardens in *Maclean's* magazine on March 1, 1958, John Clare wrote, "In an emergency, as at playoff time when the public need for the service is greatest, the bookies have been known to drift back and ply their trade with the same discretion and high ethical standards that made them a tradition in less censorious times."

Gambling in Toronto: 1946

On January 29, 1946, Maple Leafs defenseman Babe Pratt was expelled from the NHL for gambling by league president Red Dutton. He was given the right to an appeal. Pratt, a winner of the Hart Trophy as MVP in 1943–44 and a future member of the Hockey Hall of Fame, was said to have persisted in gambling despite frequent warnings over the previous two seasons.

"I have evidence that Pratt was gambling," explained Dutton to Toronto reporters in a long-distance call from the league office in Montreal. "He had been warned by the Toronto club about gambling before. In fact, all Toronto players had been warned. So had the other clubs of the league."

Dutton explained that he had appointed an investigator, who had brought him evidence against Pratt. When the player and the league president had spoken about it, "Pratt admitted he had been gambling." He insisted that he had only ever bet on the Maple Leafs to win, and Dutton said he had found no evidence "that Pratt has ever wagered against his own team." He even said that Pratt had told him about an unsuccessful effort to bribe him to throw a game, although he had not reported it at the time. "I want to emphasize,"

added Dutton, "that there is no scandal in connection with this case. Pratt is being disciplined for violating rules against gambling."

Pratt would later explain that he was offered $1,500 by a Toronto gambler to throw a game against the Montreal Canadiens but had dismissed it as a joke. He was a popular player and reaction to his suspension was mixed. Lionel Conacher, out of the pro sports business for nearly a decade by then and a former chairman of the Ontario Athletic Commission, believed Pratt's suspension was proof that hockey players needed a union.

"The time has come," said Conacher, "when a flock of antiquated laws on sports should be flung on the ash heap" and that players "should have an organization that would protect them. It's about time hockey players quit being stupid. How long are they going to allow officials to push them around?" Conacher added that if similar rules about betting on yourself had been enforced when he was playing with the Montreal Maroons during the 1930s, the entire team "would have been tossed out of the league en bloc."

Pratt made his appeal at a meeting of NHL governors in New York on February 14, 1946. Conn Smythe of the Maple Leafs excused himself from the vote after he and fellow governors Bill Tobin (Chicago), Jack Adams (Detroit), Art Ross (Boston), Lester Patrick (New York) and Tommy Gorman (Montreal) had listened to Pratt's story. Though it had been speculated that the governors would uphold Dutton's original expulsion, the league president himself made a call for leniency and the penalty was lifted.

By that time Pratt had missed five games and had been forfeiting his salary since January 29. He was reinstated with a warning from the governors to the entire league that there would be immediate expulsion with no chance of appeal for any other player consorting with gamblers.

*Game action between the Boston Bruins and the New York Rangers
in Game 4 of the NHL Semi-Final on March 26, 1940.*

"I'm glad the ordeal is over," said Pratt. "I made a mistake and nobody has suffered any more mentally, physically, and financially than I have. It's a lesson to me and to every other player in hockey. Now all I want to do is go out and lift those Leafs into the playoffs." But Toronto, who had won the Stanley Cup in 1945 and would do so again in 1947, wound up missing the playoffs in 1946. After the season Pratt was traded to Boston, where he would play the first half of 1946–47 before being sent to the minors.

Pratt finished out his career in the Pacific Coast Hockey League in 1951–52. He would later coach on the West Coast as well. Remaining in Vancouver, he became a goodwill ambassador with the Canucks in the 1970s. Popular with the public until the end, Pratt died at the age of 72 on December 16, 1988, after suffering a heart attack in the media lounge at Vancouver's Pacific Coliseum midway through the second period of a game between the Canucks and the Calgary Flames.

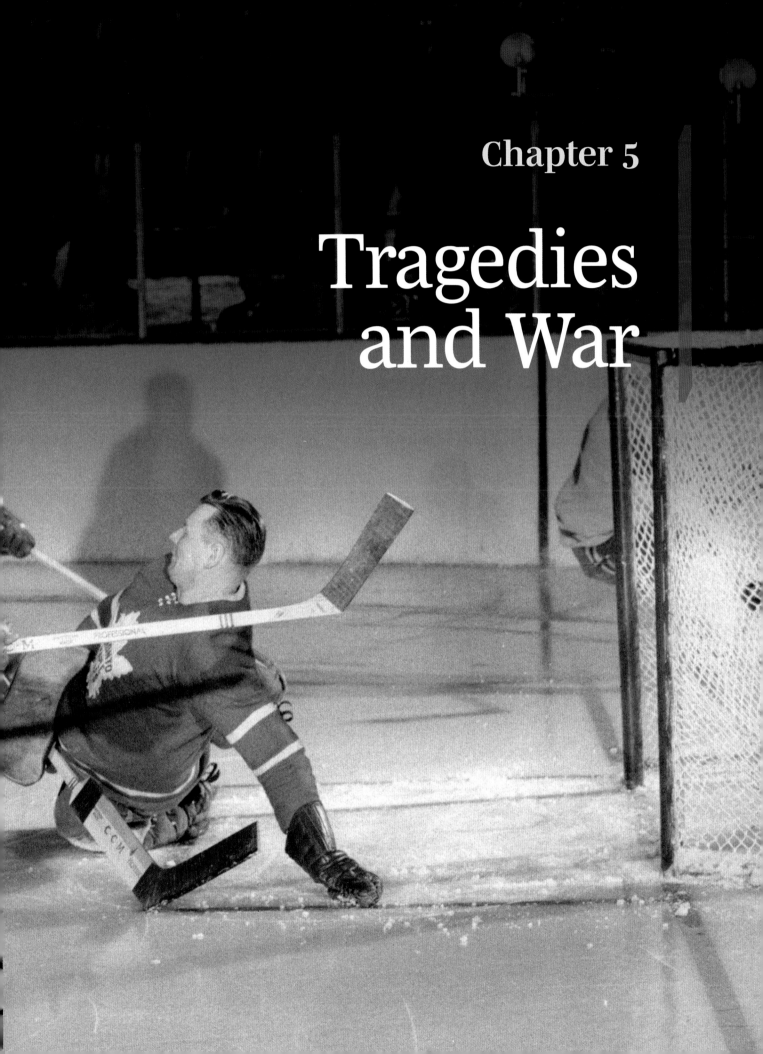

Chapter 5

Tragedies and War

Hod Stuart's Sudden Death

In his day Hod Stuart was considered the best defenseman in hockey. When players in Canada first got paid in 1906–07, Stuart's salary for that season (somewhere between $1,200 and $1,500) was the highest in the game.

Born in Ottawa on February 20, 1879, William Hodgson Stuart was the son of William Stuart and Rachel Hodgson. His father was a well-respected contractor and the captain of the Ottawa Capitals lacrosse team. His younger brother, Bruce, is also in the Hockey Hall of Fame. As a young man, Hod played football and hockey in Ottawa at the end of the 1890s, but he moved to Quebec City in 1900 on a contracting job for his father. He played hockey there too and met his future wife, Marguerite Cecilia Loughlin, whom he married in 1901. By 1907 they had two young children.

Stuart had yet to emerge as a hockey star while playing in Ottawa or Quebec, but did so quickly after 1902 when he began to play in the United States, where players were already allowed to earn a salary. Stuart played in Pittsburgh in 1902–03 and for the Portage Lake team in Houghton, Michigan, the following season. In 1904–05 Stuart played for the Calumet Miners on Michigan's Upper Peninsula during the first season of the International Hockey League, hockey's first openly professional organization. He spent most of the 1905–06 season with the Pittsburgh Pros, but then, unhappy with the refereeing in the IHL, he jumped his contract in December 1906 and signed with the Montreal Wanderers in January 1907. Canadian fans needed convincing of Stuart's talent upon his return, but the press reports from Montreal were soon just as glowing as they had been in Pittsburgh.

Stuart was not yet with the Wanderers when they defeated a team from New Glasgow, Nova Scotia, in a preseason Stanley Cup challenge at the end of December in 1906. He joined the Wanderers in time for their first regular-season game on January 2, 1907, and starred in the team's Stanley Cup series with the Kenora Thistles two weeks later. The Thistles won, but the Wanderers bounced back to finish their regular season with a perfect 10-and-0 record. Stuart was a big part of Montreal's winning the Cup back from Kenora in a rematch at the end of March, but he died on June 23, 1907, at the height of his hockey career. He was just 28 years old.

After the season Stuart had returned to Ottawa but was soon at work for his father's construction company overseeing a building project in Belleville, Ontario. On a leisurely Sunday he spent the morning canoeing with friends. In the heat of the day, around three o'clock that afternoon, they returned to the waterfront. Stuart was a strong swimmer, and he jumped in from the Grand Junction dock to cool off, swimming about a quarter-mile to a nearby lighthouse.

There was a small platform around the lighthouse, about six or eight feet above the water, and those

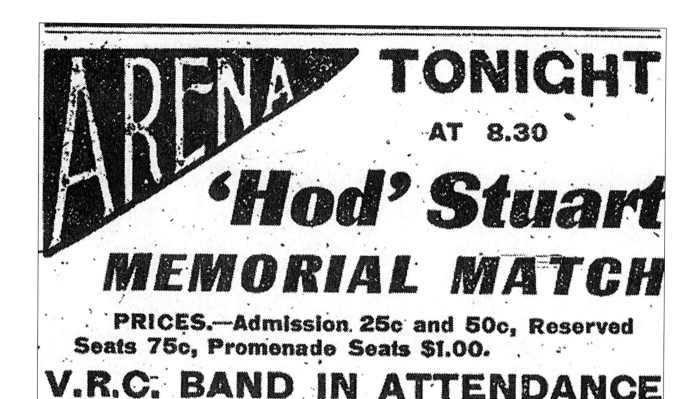

Newspaper advertisement for the memorial all-star game held to benefit Stuart's family, January 2, 1908.

watching from the dock saw Stuart climb up and rest for a few minutes before diving in again. He didn't resurface. Unaware of how shallow it was in certain places around the lighthouse, Stuart struck his head on a jagged rock just two feet below the waterline. He suffered a fractured skull and a broken neck and was said to have died instantly.

On January 2, 1908, a memorial all-star game was played to raise funds for Stuart's family. The following is taken from the final paragraphs of an eight-page commemorative booklet created for the game:

> Hod Stuart died young, too young to have made sufficient provisions for those dependent upon him. He was only twenty-eight, but in his short life he had set an example of true

sportsmanship that is worthy of emulation by the young men of this country.

To be a great hockey player is perhaps not the highest thing that a man may aim at in this world. But to be a good and true sportsman, an upright man, a faithful friend, a loving husband and father, is an ambition worthy of anyone.

Hod Stuart was all of that.

The Hod Stuart Memorial Match

The Hod Stuart Memorial pitted a team of all-stars from the Eastern Canada Amateur Hockey Association against Stuart's former team, the Montreal Wanderers. It is often cited as the first all-star game in hockey history, and sometimes as the first in any sport. But it wasn't. The Ontario Hockey Association had contested an east–west all-star game at least as early as 1904. (The OHA wasn't considered quite on a par with the ECAHA in terms of talent, but it was a huge organization, and its senior champions had challenged for the Stanley Cup, as the Toronto Marlboros had done just a month before the 1904 OHA all-star game was played.)

Sometimes, the Hod Stuart Memorial is noted as hockey's first fundraising game, but it wasn't that either. A game had been played in Hawkesbury, Ontario, on March 21, 1900, to raise money for the families of Canadian soldiers fighting in the Boer War.

Still, the Hod Stuart Memorial was likely the first all-star game played at hockey's truly highest level, and it may have been the first to raise funds for a single family … which, of course, was the most important object of the evening. The lineups on the night of January 2, 1908, were:

Not surprisingly, the All-Stars were slow to blend as a team. The Wanderers jumped out to a 7–1 lead by halftime and hung on for a 10–7 victory. A crowd just over 3,800 (barely more than half the capacity of the Montreal Arena) had paid ticket prices ranging from 25 cents and 50 cents for standing room and rush seats to 75 cents for reserved seats and $1 for promenade seats. With everybody waiving their expenses for the evening, a total of $2,010.65 was raised for Stuart's widow and her two young children.

Fallen Heroes: Davidson and Richardson

It must have seemed impossible during the summer of 1914 that the assassination of a little-known archduke in Sarajevo on June 28 would soon lead to the most horrific war the world had ever seen. Yet, as old alliances increased the tensions already being felt by European powers, that soon became the case.

Wanderers	Position	All-Stars (Team)
Riley Hern*	Goal	Percy LeSueur* (Ottawa)
Art Ross*	Point	Rod Kennedy (Montreal Victorias)
Walter Smaill	Cover	Frank Patrick* (McGill/Montreal Victorias)
Pud Glass	Rover	Joe Power (Quebec)
Ernie Russell*	Center	Grover Sargent (Montreal AAA)
Cecil Blachford*	R Wing	Eddie Hogan (Quebec)
Moose Johnson*	L Wing	Jack Marshall* (Montreal Shamrocks)

* Member of the Hockey Hall of Fame

George Richardson in uniform, 1914.

Scotty Davidson as a member of the Toronto Blue Shirts.

On July 28, 1914, Austria declared war on Serbia. On August 1 Germany, which had pledged its support to Austria, declared war on Russia. Two days later Germany declared war on France and invaded Belgium to get there. Britain, which had an old treaty promising to protect Belgium, declared war on Germany on August 4. When it did, Canada, as a proud part of the British Empire, automatically found itself at war as well.

By September 1914 more than 32,000 Canadian volunteers had made their way to a hastily arranged army camp in Valcartier, Quebec. Among the first to arrive were two former hockey teammates from Kingston, Ontario: George Taylor Richardson and Allan "Scotty" Davidson.

Richardson and Davidson grew up in the same hometown, but it's unlikely they would ever have met if not for hockey. Richardson was a graduate of Queen's University, where he'd starred on the ice

and the football field. He then went to work for his wealthy family's grain brokerage business. Davidson's family was more blue collar. His grandfather was a prison guard at the Kingston Penitentiary and his father worked at the Rockwood Asylum, where the criminally insane were housed. Off the ice, Davidson was trained as a machinist. Still, his skill in hockey attracted the attention of his city's top team, the Kingston 14th Regiment, where Richardson was the star.

Davidson and Richardson played together briefly in 1908–09 before the team was renamed the Frontenacs the following year and Richardson moved into management. Davidson led the Frontenacs to provincial junior championships in 1910 and 1911, and then in 1912 he moved west and nearly led the Calgary Athletic Club to the Allan Cup as Canadian senior amateur champions. Davidson returned east in the fall of 1912 when he signed a pro contract with the Toronto Blueshirts, who were about to enter the National Hockey Association in 1912–13. He captained Toronto to the Stanley Cup in the spring of 1914. Five months later, Davidson was in the army.

Davidson had already spent two years on active militia service with the Princess of Wales' Own Regiment, the formal name of Kingston's 14th Regiment. Shortly after the outbreak of the war, Richardson, who was a captain in the regiment, formed a contingent of 80 men from the PWOR, including Davidson, who all became part of the 2nd Battalion of the Canadian Expeditionary Force. After spending most of August and September 1914 training at Valcartier, Davidson and Richardson were among the thousands who sailed for England as part of the huge convoy of Canadian ships that departed on October 3. Nearly four months of further training in the miserable cold and wet of Salisbury Plain followed before the battalion left for France on February 9, 1915. The soldiers entered the trenches at Armentières 10 days later and saw their first major action near the end of April. In June stories of their battles began to appear in Canadian newspapers. Richardson had been wounded but it wasn't serious, and on June 8 the *Toronto Star* joked that, "Capt. Richardson's friends intimate that the Germans evidently thought he was playing hockey when they stampeded so many hot shots in his direction."

The same article mentioned Davidson's job as a bomb-thrower, which was a specialized role working with grenades to clear enemy trenches. "He carries a special harness to hold the bombs," reported the *Star*. "He also carries 200 rounds of ammunition in his cartridge belt — a rifle, a spade and handle, and, as Scotty puts it, a pair of those d--- heavy English boots, which weigh five pounds. 'A fat chance to get out of any German's way have I!' writes the husky hockey lad."

Tragically, Davidson's gallows humor proved all too prophetic when he was killed in action in the early morning hours of June 16, 1915, in fierce fighting at Givenchy in the north of France. The battle is little remembered by most people today. However, Sir Arthur Currie, who would become the first Canadian to reach the rank of general, the first Canadian to command the Canadian Corps and the mastermind behind the nation-building victory at Vimy Ridge on April 9, 1917, would remember Givenchy for the lessons learned there about what was needed to finish a job.

Richardson would write a glorious, if bloodthirsty, account of Davidson's final hours for friends back home in Kingston. He said Davidson had sought him out and handed him his bayonet, his watch and a few other valuables. "George," he said, "I may never come back, but those Germans are going to catch blazes before morning."

In Richardson's telling, Davidson went out with his unit and crawled up to within a few feet of the German trenches. He hurled bomb after bomb, and even when two of his companions retreated, he kept pulling the pin and tossing his grenades until only one remained. Finally, he was captured and ordered to surrender. Davidson refused and crashed his last hand grenade against the body of a German officer, blowing him to pieces.

"We found Scotty's body the next morning," wrote Richardson, "riddled with bullets and jabbed with bayonets, but he had kept his promise, and it was apparent that his death cost the enemy dearly.

"He was," said Richardson, "absolutely fearless in the face of the greatest danger."

Davidson may well have been fearless in battle, but in actual fact Canadian military records show that he was killed when a shell fell on his trench. A *Toronto Star* story on July 5, 1915, quoted a letter from a fellow soldier saying Davidson had been killed by the accidental discharge of friendly fire, although the official records only list an exploding shell with no mention of sides.

As for Richardson, from all accounts he was beloved by his men. A biographical entry from Queen's University states: "Richardson was known as a man who would never give an order he would not readily obey himself. He often used his own money to buy extra supplies, such as warm boots, gas masks, and cigarettes for his troops." But he too paid the ultimate price when he was killed in action on February 9, 1916.

The Memorial Cup

Often referred to as "the Father of Hockey," James T. Sutherland was certainly an important figure in the early development of the game, particularly in his hometown of Kingston, Ontario. Sutherland had coached both George Richardson and Scotty Davidson. As a longtime militia member himself, he had also helped indoctrinate them with a patriotic zeal for King and Country.

In the early days of World War I, Sutherland was a one-man recruiting dynamo. Despite his advanced age of 45, he enlisted in March 1915 and would serve overseas as a quartermaster. Before departing, as the newly elected president of the Canadian Amateur Hockey Association (a position he would serve mostly in absentia), Sutherland issued a challenge to the hockey players of the nation in a statement issued on December 30, 1915:

In this, my first official note as president of the Canadian Amateur Hockey Association, I take the greatest pleasure in sending out to all officers and players in the many provincial associations connected with our governing body the heartfelt wish that the coming year of 1916 will bring to one and all the greatest amount of prosperity possible.

James Sutherland as coach of the Kingston Frontenacs team in 1899.

I feel, however, that I have a greater responsibility and duty to perform at this time, and that is to point out to the great army of hockey players and officials scattered throughout our beloved Canada, from coast to coast, how great and urgent the need is for men to come forward and rally to the defence of our common cause, and strike a blow for liberty and justice that will re-echo around the world.

Canada's athletes have responded nobly to the call in the past, and will, I am sure, continue to do so. In a few short weeks our hockey season will be over, and if there are any who have not made up their minds regarding the future course of action, let me say that, in my opinion, there should be only one conclusion, and that should be to exchange the stick and puck for a 'Ross rifle and a bayonet' and take your place in the great army that is being formed to sweep 'oppressors of humanity' from the face of the earth …

It takes nerve and gameness to play the game of hockey. The same qualities are necessary in the greater game that is now being played in France and on the other fighting fronts.

The thousands of hockey players throughout the Dominion have all the necessary qualifications. Therefore, I earnestly urge all such to 'rally around the flag.' With every man doing his bit, Canada will raise an army of brains and brawn from our hockey enthusiasts, the like of which the world has never seen.

The whistle has sounded. Let every man 'play the greatest game of his life.'

Sincerely yours,
James T. Sutherland,
President CAHA,
Captain 146th Battalion, CEF.

After the war Sutherland donated the Memorial Cup — originally known as the OHA Memorial Cup — as a tribute to Davidson, Richardson and the many other great Canadian athletes who gave their lives in battle. It has been awarded to Canada's junior hockey champion since 1919. Later, in the 1940s, Sutherland spearheaded the creation of the Hockey Hall of Fame.

Fallen Heroes: Frank McGee

Frank McGee hadn't played hockey in Ottawa in 10 years when the report of his death on the Somme was confirmed in his hometown in September 1916. The news hit hard.

"Word was received today by Mr. D'Arcy McGee that his brother, Capt. Frank McGee, had been killed in action on September 16," said the *Ottawa Journal* on September 23. "The death of Capt. Frank McGee removes one of the greatest athletes Canada ever produced. As a hockey player he was held by many to have been the greatest the game ever produced and his fame as a footballer was scarcely less bright. Frank was a member of the famous Silver Seven when they won the Stanley Cup."

A story in the *Ottawa Citizen* two days later was even more dramatic:

Once again the Capital is called upon to mourn the death in action at the front of one of its greatest athletes. Once again there exists sadness among the sporting fraternity over the passing of one whom they had learned to idolize. Once again there has been brought home with gripping grief and pain the grim reality of the present conflict of nations.

It is doubtful if the loss of any one of the splendid young Ottawans who have fallen at the front since the outbreak of war has occasioned such keen regret as that of the late Lt. Frank McGee … 'Frank McGee dead?' Thousands of Ottawans knew him. Few seemed able to believe that he too had given up his life in the struggle for freedom.

Frank McGee came from a prominent Ottawa family. His father, John J. McGee, was the clerk of the Privy council, the highest-ranking civil-service officer

Frank McGee in uniform, 1914.

in Canada. Thomas D'Arcy McGee, one of Canada's "Fathers of Confederation," who had been killed by an assassin in 1868, was his uncle. Frank was the sixth of eight children in his family. Hockey records generally show that he was born on November 4, 1882. That's the date he entered on his attestation papers when he formally enlisted five days after his birthday in 1914. But McGee was older than he was letting on. His records as a civil servant in Ottawa show he was born on November 4, 1880. Yet he was even older than that. The record of his baptism shows that it took place on November 10, 1878, and confirms that he'd been born several days earlier, on November 4.

So, McGee was in fact 36 years old when he joined the army. Military service had long been a part of his family life, including an uncle who had fought in the American Civil War and an older brother in the Boer War. But how did a man who was famously blind in one eye manage to pass the medical exam required to enlist?

The most common story told today is an old family legend. When McGee was taking his medical exam and was asked to read the eye chart on the wall, he covered his left eye with his left hand and read the chart using his right eye. When asked to read with his left eye, he raised his right hand, crossed his face and covered the same left eye again.

As the 20th anniversary of McGee's death approached in 1936, the story being told back then was quite different. Until then a story that was generally accepted to be authentic was that McGee had a friend who looked quite a bit like him take the eye exam for him. But brother D'Arcy told a very different tale to the *Ottawa Journal* for an anniversary story on September 17, 1936.

D'Arcy admitted that because of his eye, Frank was nervous about his physical, but then the medical officer asked him his name.

"Frank McGee."

"Not Frank McGee of the Silver Seven?"

"Yes, sir."

"There can't be anything wrong with you!"

The doctor laughed, gave McGee an admiring pat on the chest and passed him for the army.

However it happened, on May 5, 1915, Frank McGee embarked for England with the 21st Battalion of Kingston, Ontario. (On May 26 another brother, Charles, was killed in action.) In training overseas, McGee qualified in machine gunnery before being sent into action in France that September. He was wounded on December 17 when he was firing his

Quote ... Unquote

"Frank was a brilliant hockey player, one of the Silver Seven. The most dashing player I ever saw."

— Diary entry of Ottawa socialite **Ethel Chadwick** upon learning of McGee's death

machine gun from an armored car that was blown up by a bursting shell. As the vehicle collapsed into a deep ditch, McGee's knee received a small puncture from some part of the car. As war wounds go, it must have seemed fairly insignificant, but the knee became badly inflamed and McGee never fully recovered. Various medical reports concluded he was unfit for general service, and even by the time he'd recovered in July 1916, he was only declared "Fit for General Service (Without Marching)."

After finally rejoining the 21st Battalion in France on August 29, McGee would serve as a motorcycle dispatch rider, even though in a letter sent home to D'Arcy in Ottawa on September 4, he claimed that he had been offered a desk job safely behind the lines. He turned it down in order to be sent back to his old unit. A short time later, on September 16, McGee was killed in action fighting near the site of a former beet processing plant known as the Sugar Factory near the town of Courcelette. His military records reveal that his body was unrecovered for burial, suggesting that he had been blown apart by shellfire.

D'Arcy received a letter from Colonel Elmer Jones on October 18, telling him about Frank's last actions on the day he died. The letter was printed in the *Ottawa Citizen* on November 11, 1916:

Dear D'Arcy—I have intended writing to you ever since Frank left us, but have had a great deal to do. That is my only excuse.

Frank came back to me only two days before we went over on the morning of Sept. 15. I left him with the reserves during the first attack. But during that day I lost every officer save one, and early on the morning of the 16th Frank brought up 50 men to hold the line and to push on past Courcelette. He reported to me and I put him in command of my first line. He knew what it meant and he laughed as he went into it. He took most of his men through and reached the front trench. I had a message from him there, telling me his disposition and adding that he would gather more men and push in. He had to go up under an extraordinary shell fire. He then came back to the sugar factory and was gathering up more men there for another attack when he was killed. I need not tell you what he was like under shell fire, because you know better than I can write, but his bravery always inspired the men under him.

When he was with me first, I had learned to rely on him, but in the Somme during his last few hours he was wonderful. I can't tell you more. He was buried where he fell and where so many of my battalion lie. If I come home I will be able to tell you more, but it is harder writing than you can know.

Always faithfully yours,
ELMER JONES

Sadly, Elmer Watson Jones was killed in action himself on August 8, 1918, during the first day of the Battle of Amiens.

Joe Hall and the Spanish Flu

When Joe Hall is remembered by hockey fans today, it's usually for one of two things. One is his reputation as the roughest and dirtiest player of his time, which is why he was known as "Bad Joe" Hall. The other is that he was the player who died of the Spanish flu in the spring of 1919 when that worldwide pandemic forced the cancellation of the last game of the Stanley Cup Final.

Hockey records used to show that Joe Hall was born in Staffordshire, England, on May 13, 1882. Baptismal records from England show he was actually born the year before, on May 13, 1881, in Milwich, which was a village in Staffordshire. In 1884 the family left England and settled in Winnipeg. The earliest days of Hall's hockey career are tough to determine. He may have been playing junior hockey in Winnipeg as early as 1897, when he would have been 16 years old. He was definitely playing intermediate hockey in Brandon, Manitoba, by 1898 and was a star on the Wheat City team that won the Manitoba intermediate championship in 1902. Hall turned pro when he signed with the Portage Lake team in the International Hockey League in 1905–06 and won the league championship that year. He returned to Brandon in 1906–07 when Canadian hockey teams were first allowed to openly pay their players.

Hall bounced around for the next few years before finding himself playing for the Quebec Bulldogs of the National Hockey Association in 1910–11. Mainly a forward in the early part of his career, Hall was a high-scoring defenseman with Quebec in 1911–12 and helped the Bulldogs win the Stanley Cup that season and the next. When Quebec chose not to ice a team after the NHL replaced the NHA in 1917–18, Hall joined the Montreal Canadiens. At age 36 he was one of the oldest players in the new league.

Hall definitely played a rough game, and maybe even a dirty one, but there were many players over the years who believed his reputation for violence was overblown. In an undated story from the *Winnipeg Free Press* circa 1912 from the Joe Hall scrapbook at the Hockey Hall of Fame, Hall himself maintained, "I'm one of those fellows able to take care of himself if anybody starts anything, but I don't think I am as bad as I am painted."

Joe Malone was among those who felt that Hall's "Bad Man" label was simply a bad rap. Malone was a teammate of Hall's in Quebec and Montreal for nine seasons. He wrote in *The Hockey Book* for Bill Roche in 1953 that "[Hall's] type of play was not of the mean sort. He checked heavily for the sheer sport of bodily contact, and he was always ready to take as well as to give … There were plenty of huge, rough characters on the ice in Hall's time, and he was able to stay in there with them for about 19 years … Just the name, plain Joe Hall, should stand down through hockey history as a symbol of pluck, aggressiveness, and courage. The addition of 'Bad' is, and always has been, unfair and wrong." Malone would later say that he was saddened when he learned of Hall's death not just because he had lost a friend but also because he believed that his longtime teammate never got the chance to outlive his reputation.

Malone offered his assessments many years after Hall's death, but Hall had many supporters even during his playing days. In another story from the Joe Hall scrapbook (from January 21, 1913), sportswriter C.C. Stein of the *Winnipeg Tribune* wrote:

> Joe is a living example of that old and true saying. 'Give a dog a bad name,' etc. Just as long as Hall plays hockey he will carry the appellation of the 'bad man of the game.' He can't get away from it. In his early days, Hall

Joe Hall posing in 1919.

was a rough and ready customer, willing to mix it any time no matter how big his opponent was. Experience taught him a lesson and Joe has tried to play clean hockey. Any number of players, prominent in professional circles, will tell you that Hall never roughs it anymore, except on occasions when he is forced to retaliate for self-defensive purposes."

Another writer makes a similar argument in an uncredited story circa 1913:

On the defence Joe Hall is an artist. He is not a heavy defence man as they go but Joe has the knack. He knows how to make the best use of himself and he makes the best use of his knowledge. He has a bad name which sticks to him as closely as a poor relation ... but he does not deserve the tithe of criticism that is handed out to him. The whole trouble is that no referee thinks he is doing his duty unless he registers a major or a minor against the Brandon man. There are far dirtier players in the [NHA] today but they get away with it.

All that being said, Hall's 100 penalty minutes in 21 games in 1917–18 ranked second in the NHL that first season, while his 130 minutes in 16 games in 1918–19 were almost triple what anyone else had. Still, as wild as he could be on the ice, Hall was always popular with teammates and opponents away from the rink. And even at age 37, he played a big part in Montreal's winning the NHL championship in 1919 and earning the right to travel west to face the Pacific Coast Hockey Association champion Seattle Metropolitans for the Stanley Cup.

The 1919 Stanley Cup series opened on Wednesday night, March 19. Playing under familiar PCHA rules (which still included a rover and featured a long-established 60-foot center-ice passing zone, as compared with the 40-foot zone that had only just been introduced to the NHL that season), the Mets romped to a 7–0 victory. The Canadiens got even with a 4–2 win under NHL rules three nights later but were crushed 7–2 under PCHA rules in Game 3 on March 24. The Mets were now just one win away from taking the best-of-five series.

Of Game 4 on March 26 sportswriter Royal Brougham of the *Seattle-Post Intelligencer* wrote, "They may play hockey for the next 1,000 years, but they'll never stage a greater struggle than last night's." The game ended in a 0–0 tie after 20 minutes of overtime. It should have been played to a conclusion, except that PCHA officials erroneously believed NHL rules called for just one overtime session. The next game, replayed under NHL rules on March 29, was another long overtime contest. The Canadiens stayed alive by overcoming a 3–0 deficit to win 4–3 on a goal by Jack McDonald at 15:57 of OT.

Seattle's Cully Wilson collapsed to the ice at the end of the game and had to be helped to the dressing room. Amid the concern for him and the excitement of Montreal's victory, few people seemed to notice that Hall had not returned to action after coming off the ice midway through the second period. When it was reported that Hall was running a fever, people assumed that, like Wilson, he was simply suffering from exhaustion. After all, as bad as the Spanish flu had been in the city earlier in the year, there had not been a single flu-related death in Seattle during the entire month of March.

The final game in the series was set for Tuesday, April 1, but by then the Canadiens were too sick to play. The day before, owner George Kennedy and players Newsy Lalonde, Louis Berlinguette and Billy Coutu had also developed fevers. It wasn't just because they were exhausted. The Canadiens had come down with the Spanish flu. (Stories circulated that they had caught the disease in Victoria, but that was probably because so many Victoria players had been sick during the season. It seems highly unlikely the Canadiens had even been in Victoria.)

On the morning of April 1, the Canadiens had five sick players among their nine-man roster. Kennedy still hoped to save the final game. He wanted to borrow players from Victoria to replace his sick men. Seattle coach-manager Pete Muldoon didn't agree. He thought it would give his own team an unfair advantage and it wouldn't be right to win like that. Because it was the Canadiens who couldn't play, some people thought Seattle should win the series by default. PCHA president Frank Patrick said the league did not want to claim victory that way. So there would be no champion declared for 1919. For the first time in hockey history, the Stanley Cup was called off. No winner would be declared that season.

Though the series was over, the eyes of hockey fans were still on Seattle. Only now, instead of waiting to get the score, people were waiting for medical reports. Telegrams and telephone calls whirred across the wires between Seattle and Montreal. Newspapers all across Canada did their best to keep readers up to date. It wasn't easy because the news changed fast.

On the night of April 1, when they should have

been playing the final game, Hall and McDonald were taken to Providence Hospital. Their temperatures were nearly 105 degrees (41°C). The other Canadiens who were sick stayed in their beds at the Georgian Hotel.

By the morning of April 2 Odie Cleghorn was sick too. Then, on April 3, Muldoon came down with the Spanish flu. So did Seattle players Roy Rickey and Muzz Murray. Still, the news was worse for Hall and McDonald. They were both "dangerously ill," and doctors were very worried about Hall. As with a great many of the victims of the Spanish flu, his disease had developed into pneumonia. A message was sent to his family. If they wanted to see him, they'd better come quickly.

By April 4 almost everyone was getting better. Even McDonald was starting to improve. Only Hall's condition had worsened. He had been moved to the Columbus Sanitarium. His temperature had dropped a little, but it was still a dangerous 103 degrees (39°C). There was fluid building up in his lungs, and it was getting harder and harder for him to breathe. There was little his doctor could do for him.

Hall's mother, Emily, who lived in Vancouver, made it to his bedside before he passed away at 2:30 on Saturday afternoon, April 5, 1919. His wife and children hadn't made it from Brandon. They were still on the train when they got the news in a telegram. They arrived in Vancouver the next morning. Joe's mother and a brother brought his body there and Hall was buried at the Mountain View Cemetery in Vancouver on April 8, 1919.

Georges Vezina's Journey

As the Montreal Canadiens prepared for their first practice before the 1925–26 season, nobody was sure if Georges Vezina would be at the Mount Royal Arena on November 10, 1925. He would soon be turning 39 years old, and his business interests at home in Chicoutimi were taking more and more of his time. He might have been ready to retire from hockey.

Vezina, in fact, was not in Montreal for that first practice. Goalie Alphonse "Frenchy" Lacroix was there instead. Knowing that Vezina was near the end of the line, the native of Newton, Massachusetts (who had played for the 1924 U.S. Olympic team) had been invited to Montreal on a tryout. He would soon sign with the Canadiens.

But on the night of November 10 Vezina sent a telegram to Canadiens owner Leo Dandurand. The *Montreal Gazette* reported the next day that Vezina had "practically assured the local management of their chances of again having him in the nets this year." On November 12 the *Gazette* confirmed that Vezina would be returning and that he was expected to be on hand by November 18, when the Canadiens played an exhibition game with the Victoria Cougars of the Western Hockey League. (The Cougars — who had beaten Vezina and the Canadiens to win the Stanley Cup on the West Coast back in the spring of 1925 — are the last non-NHL team to win hockey's top prize.)

It wasn't until November 16 that Vezina arrived in Montreal, reporting in time for practice that day. It was said that the 1925–26 season would definitely be his last, and that he had turned out only because he felt that he had given the Canadiens the impression that he would be with them again that season. It would, indeed, be Vezina's last season — but for all the wrong reasons. He would play just one league game for the Canadiens that year and would die on the night the Montreal Maroons won the NHL title at the end of the season.

Vezina had originally signed with the Canadiens in December 1910. His contract that winter called for $800. It was the team's second year of existence, having been created for the inaugural season of the National Hockey Association in 1909–10. From the time they signed Vezina until his last league game on November 28, 1925, no other goalie would man the net for the Canadiens. Counting league games and playoffs, he suited up for 367 consecutive games (328 regular season and 39 postseason) over more than 15 years, establishing himself as one of the best goalies in hockey and leading the Canadiens to their first two Stanley Cup titles, in 1916 and 1924. Vezina was calm and quiet on the ice and off — one of his nicknames in French was "l'Habitant Silencieux" — and even when the NHL changed the rules to allow goalies to drop to the ice, he preferred to remain standing.

"He was the coolest man I ever saw, absolutely imperturbable," wrote Frank Boucher, the great Rangers captain and Hall of Famer, in his autobiography, *When the Rangers Were Young.* "He stood upright in the net and scarcely ever left his feet; he simply played all his shots in a standing position."

According to stories, Vezina began playing goal as a boy, but only while wearing boots. It wasn't until he was 16 years old, or maybe even 17, that he began wearing skates. Born on January 21, 1887, he played his first game for the Chicoutimi Hockey Club early in 1905. "He was a good goalie," according to a translation of a 1926 article in the Montreal newspaper *La Patrie,* "but he had never skated before. The first games he played with Chicoutimi, he struggled to stay in control on the ice but he learned very fast." Mikael Lalancette, author of the 2021 Vezina biography *L'Habitant Silencieux,* believes the article is credible because the reporter had talked to Georges' brother Pierre and his wife, Marie-Stella.

It's long been said that Vezina came to the attention of the Canadiens when they played an exhibition game in Chicoutimi during the 1909–10 NHA season. The date that is often given is February 17, 1910. The

Georges Vezina as a member of the Montreal Canadiens.

score is usually said to have been 11–5, but sometimes 1–0. Lalancette has newspaper clippings confirming the game was actually played on Sunday, February 20, 1910, and that the score was 11–5. It's usually said that Joseph Cattarinich (a future owner of the Canadiens and a member of the Hockey Hall of Fame in the Builder's category) played against Vezina that day, or that he had as a member of the Montreal Nationals

Chicoutimi Cucumber

To English-speaking hockey fans, Georges Vezina was "the Chicoutimi Cucumber," which comes from the combination of his hometown and the expression "cool as a cucumber." According to online sources, the phrase was first recorded in the poem *New Song on New Similes* by the British poet John Gay before his death in 1732. Mikael Lalancette believes it was Elmer Ferguson of the *Montreal Herald* who coined the nickname. The first reference to Vezina as the Chicoutimi Cucumber that Lalancette found is from 1914. English translations of Vezina's French nicknames include "the Chicoutimi Boy," "the Chicoutimi Wonder," "the Chicoutimi Carpenter" and sometimes "the Silent Habitant."

back in 1905. Cattarinich was one of three goalies the Canadiens used in 1909–10, but Lalancette's newspaper clipping shows that it was one of the team's other goalies, Teddy Groulx, who faced Vezina in 1910. Lalancette says that it had been Henri Menard facing Chicoutimi back in 1905. Still, it may well have been Cattarinich who recommended Vezina to new Canadiens owner George Kennedy in the fall of 1910.

Vezina and his brother Pierre were both with the Canadiens for preseason practice in December 1910, but only Georges was signed. (Pierre played one game for the Canadiens in 1911–12.) The team had finished last in the NHA with a 2-and-10 record in 1909–10 and had surrendered 100 goals in those 12 games. Vezina

made his league debut in a 5–3 loss to the Ottawa Senators at home on December 31, 1910, and won his first game with a 4–1 victory over the Quebec Bulldogs on January 7, 1911. The Canadiens finished the season with an 8-and-8 record, and Vezina allowed just 61 goals in 16 games — the fewest goals against in the NHA that year. The Canadiens would remain contenders for the rest of his career.

The final hockey season of Vezina's life got underway in Montreal on November 18, 1925, two nights after the Victoria Cougars had beaten the Montreal Maroons 3–1. The Canadiens led Victoria 1–0 after one period and 2–1 after two, but the Cougars came back to beat Vezina and the Canadiens 5–3. The report of the exhibition game in the *Gazette* noted that the Canadiens "lacked condition" and "faded away" in the third period. "Georges Vezina, in goal, still has eagle eyes," the paper said. "He was fooled in the final period as Victoria broke through the staggering tired defense, but in the early stages of the game, when his protection was stronger, he saved many a rush by smart net guarding." The *Victoria Daily Times*, while noting that Montreal fans and sportswriters were referring to the Cougars as "the greatest team that ever came out of the west," reported that "the veteran Vezina was called on to do some snappy work."

The Canadiens would open the regular season at home against the Pittsburgh Pirates on Saturday night, November 28. The New York Americans were looking to play an exhibition game with the Canadiens in Hamilton before the season opened, but on November 21 the *Gazette* said the plans had fallen through, adding that "Vezina is under the weather with a severe cold." Other newspapers said Dandurand had told them "his veteran goalkeeper was ill in bed."

The Legends Spotlight about Vezina on the Hockey Hall of Fame website reports that he performed well but was noticeably gaunt through the preseason. Still, he played in the season opener against Pittsburgh despite a high temperature. After a scoreless first period, Vezina left the ice bleeding from the mouth. He collapsed in the dressing room, returned for the start of the second period, then collapsed again and had to leave the game. "In the arena, all was silent as the limp form of the greatest of goalies was carried slowly from the ice," wrote one journalist. Lacroix would finish the game, which Pittsburgh won 1–0.

Interestingly, there do not appear to be any reports from the time, in French or in English, claiming that Vezina returned to start the second period. These only began to appear in the years afterward. In the immediate days after the game, some newspaper reports out of Montreal from December 1 (when the Canadiens visited Boston and beat the Bruins 3–2 behind Lacroix) still indicated that Vezina was only suffering from a severe cold. But on December 4 a Canadian Press dispatch reported that Vezina's doctor had ordered him out of hockey for good. He'd left his teammates the day before (a Thursday, prior to a game with the Maroons that the Canadiens lost 3–2) and returned by train to Chicoutimi. A special report to the *Ottawa Journal* that day mentioned his "rapid decline," adding, "friends and associates are stunned and the doctors are baffled. The medical men say they are amazed that Vezina is living today." A diagnosis of tuberculosis was officially reported in newspapers on December 5, with the papers making comparisons to the great baseball pitcher Christy Mathewson, who'd died of the same disease two months earlier.

Georges Vezina died on Saturday, March 27, 1926. A funeral was held on March 30 and he was buried at the Chicoutimi cemetery. The entire town was said to be in mourning, and thousands of people turned out to pay their last respects.

Vezina's Last Game

The game report in the *Montreal Gazette* on November 30, 1925, states, "Vezina was [a] shadow," adding, "the veteran goalkeeper started the game with a high temperature. He was pale and haggard looking as he turned shots aside in the first period. At the rest interval it was decided to replace him... He remained in the dressing room with only his pads off, hoping to pick up a little and get back into the game. But he was not in condition." There is no mention of him returning to the ice to start the second period.

The game report in the *Pittsburgh Sunday* Post on November 29 is very different. It states that the Pirates "were holding their own and pressed Vezina" in the second period and that Lacroix only replaced him to start the third. Then again, the *Pittsburgh Gazette Times* on November 29 reports: "Play opened faster in the second period. Pittsburgh tested Lacroix, former United States Olympic goal keeper, who replaced Vezina in the Canadiens net. Vezina had to retire through illness."

Information on NHL.com shows that Vezina played 20 minutes and Lacroix 40 in the game against Pittsburgh on November 28, 1925. However, while the original game sheets list both Vezina and Lacroix on the roster, there are no notations to indicate what was the actual time of the change in goalies.

Leo Dandurand's Statement

Leo Dandurand issued these words on December 4, 1925, as reported in newspapers the following day:

> While it was not until today that his team-mates knew Vezina was through, the management knew it last night, and the fact that the news was kept from the other players was Vezina's last act of devotion to the club he

loved so well. 'Perhaps they will play better if they think I am going on. When I'm not on they will soon forget about me in the excitement of the play,' he said.

While Vezina thus left without bidding farewell to his teammates, there was a touching scene when Dr. Dube and he broke the news to me. The doctor ordered him home immediately. I had known from the first Vezina was not the Vezina of old. He did not look well when he reported, but assured me he would improve. That, too, was typical of him. But he lost weight in an alarming fashion and it was not by accident that we signed Lacroix.

I saw Vezina was nearly done and though he insisted on going through his last game with a temperature of 102 degrees and even then gave a good account of himself, he never recovered. Perhaps his insistence on playing that game spelled his doom. He was taken to bed that night, stayed there for a week, then when doctors examined him, it was found he had lost 35 pounds since coming to the city. Further examination revealed his lungs were in bad shape. Poor Georges has the slayer of Christy Mathewson to fight.

Vezina reported at the usual hour at our dressing room yesterday morning and sat down in his usual corner in the outer room. I glanced at him as he sat there, and saw tears rolling down his cheeks. He was looking at his old pads and skates that Eddie Dufour had arranged in Georges' corner, thinking probably that Vezina would don them last night. Then he asked one little favour — the sweater he wore in the last world's series. Then he went. He saw [15] years of professional hockey service, all with our club.

All My Children

At the time of his illness, it was widely reported that Georges Vezina was the father of 17 children. Some reports claimed the number was actually 22. That's the total so often cited even today, although some sources have claimed as "few" as 14 children and at least one credits him with 24.

The exaggerated totals of Vezina's children were first provided by Leo Dandurand, who was just having fun with the stereotype of small-town French Catholics. In truth, Vezina and his wife, Marie Adeline Stella Morin, had only two children who lived. Tragically, there were six others who died in the first hours of life, and one son, Robert, who died at three months.

Of the two children who lived, Jean Jules Vezina was born in 1912. A second son was born on March 31, 1916. That was a night after the Canadiens defeated the Portland Rosebuds 2–1 to win their first Stanley Cup title, and though this son was formally christened Joseph Louis Marcel Vezina, he was usually known as Marcel Stanley.

Georges Vezina Benefit Game

While the NHL champion Montreal Maroons were playing (and defeating) the Victoria Cougars of the Western Hockey League for the Stanley Cup in early April 1926, another WHL team had also come east to play exhibition games with NHL teams. On April 1 the Saskatoon Sheiks were defeated 4–3 by the Ottawa Senators. Former Canadiens star Newsy Lalonde wore black armbands on his Sheiks jersey that night in memory of Georges Vezina. He received a thundering ovation when he appeared on the ice in Ottawa.

The next day Leo Dandurand announced that the Sheiks would play the Canadiens on Sunday, April 4, in a benefit game for Vezina's widow and children. A crowd of 3,500 attended the game at the Mount Royal

Arena and saw the Canadiens defeat the Sheiks 7–3. Close to $3,000 was raised that afternoon.

The money for the Vezina family came from more than just the gate receipts. Aurele Joliat of the Canadiens won a fierce auction for the goalie stick Vezina used in his final game with a bid of $200, while Canadiens executive Louis Letourneau paid the same amount for a puck used that same night. James Strachan of the Maroons paid $200 himself to drop the puck for the opening faceoff, while Boston Bruins manager Art Ross and his friend Lester Patrick (owner-manager of the Victoria Cougars) paid $25 each to be the referees. Other financial contributions included $50 from NHL president Frank Calder and $100 from the New York Americans. Before the game started, players from both teams lined up at center ice, while the crowd stood and removed their hats as a band played "Nearer My God to Thee."

The Vezina Trophy

Word had been circulating in the hockey world during the 1926–27 season that the Montreal Canadiens management was planning some sort of lasting tribute to Georges Vezina. At a banquet for Canadiens superstar Howie Morenz in Montreal on March 12, 1927, Leo Dandurand — after a toast to the man of honor — announced that a trophy in Vezina's memory would be presented to Montreal's new goalie, George Hainsworth. It was Hainsworth who received the award because the Canadiens had allowed the fewest goals in the NHL during that season. The trophy, said Dandurand, would be presented annually from then on to the goalie on the NHL team that allowed the fewest goals. Three days later, at an NHL meeting in Montreal, the league accepted the donation of the Vezina Trophy by Dandurand and his partners, Louis Letourneau and Joe Cattarinich. Hainsworth would win it in each of the next two seasons as well.

George Hainsworth pours a bottle of Canada Dry ginger ale into a glass in the dressing room.

Through the 1980–81 season, the Vezina Trophy would be awarded to the goalie or goalies (playing a minimum of 25 games) who played for the team allowing the fewest goals during the regular season. Since then the Vezina has been awarded to the NHL's best goalie as voted by the league's general managers, while the William Jennings Trophy has gone to the goaltender(s) on the team allowing the fewest goals.

The Morenz Cup?

In a daily column he wrote for Toronto's *Globe and Mail* newspaper during the 1936–37 season, Charlie Conacher noted on February 12, 1937: "It is the ambition of every forward to make his goals and assists reach a larger total than that of any of his rivals. I know I was always under the impression that there was a trophy for realizing this ambition until I finally was successful. Then, the year I led the league I found that with the honour went no prize that I could keep for later years."

In his column a day later — while admitting that the NHL's maximum salary of $7,000 was a lot of money — Conacher added that, in addition to a trophy, a cash bonus for winning the scoring title would be nice too.

Over the next few weeks Conacher responded to many letters he received commenting on his trophy and bonus suggestion. Most fans were against it.

Nearly a month later, in his March 16 column, Conacher printed the contents of a letter he received from a Toronto man named Bob Mitchell: "I have read a great deal about your thoughts toward having a trophy for the leading scorer of the NHL … Wouldn't it be a fitting tribute to the late Howie Morenz if the NHL Governors donated a trophy called the Morenz Cup to be presented to the leading scorer of the NHL each season."

Morenz had passed away on March 8, 1937, several weeks after suffering a career-ending broken leg in a game on January 28. Conacher had been advocating for a benefit game for Morenz (and a players' injury fund too) since his February 15 column and was pleased to report that the governors had committed themselves to such a game, though it would not take place until November. But none of the NHL governors ever stepped forward with a Morenz Cup. It would take until the 1946–47 season before the NHL finally awarded a $1,000 bonus to the league's scoring leader. It was another year until Art Ross and his sons donated a scoring trophy.

Death Comes to Charlie Gardiner

Charlie Gardiner was only 29 years old and at the height of his fame when he died on June 13, 1934. A two-time winner of the Vezina Trophy in his seven-year NHL career, and a three-time First-Team All-Star (along with a Second-Team selection) in the first four seasons that All-Stars were named, Gardiner's death came just 64 days after he lead the Chicago Black Hawks to the Stanley Cup. He is the only goalie to captain an NHL team to the championship.

Charles Robert Gardiner was born in Edinburgh, Scotland, on December 31, 1904. His family came to Canada when he was seven, with ship's records showing they arrived in Quebec City aboard the *Scandinavian* on June 9, 1912. The family was en route to Winnipeg, where Gardiner would grow up. Often known as Chuck instead of Charlie, he rose through the hockey ranks in his new hometown. When he was 21, Gardiner turned pro with the minor-league Winnipeg Maroons. Two years later, in 1927–28, he was in the NHL with the Black Hawks.

Chicago was in only its second NHL season when Gardiner signed. The team was weak, but its new goalie was often praised for his strong play. People liked his positive attitude. He could sometimes be heard shouting encouragement to his teammates or joking with fans. After two dreadful seasons Gardiner led Chicago to the playoffs in 1929–30. In 1930–31 the Black Hawks reached the Stanley Cup Final but lost to Montreal. Gardiner earned his first All-Star nod that year, but the best — and the worst — was yet to come.

After winning the Vezina Trophy for the first time in 1931–32, Gardiner developed a tonsil infection early in the 1932–33 season. He stopped 34 shots in a 4–1 win over the Maroons in Montreal on December 22, 1932, but was rushed to the hospital after the game. Still, he was able to catch a train to Toronto with his teammates the next day. Gardiner was prescribed whiskey and

Chicago Black Hawks manager Tommy Gorman and goaltender Charlie Gardiner in 1934.

quinine, according to a story in the *Chicago Tribune* on December 24, but it was said that he wasn't much of a drinker and didn't like the taste of his medicine. Still, he led the Black Hawks to a 2–1 win over the Maple Leafs that night, with newspapers reporting he made 55 saves to just 18 stops for Toronto's Lorne Chabot.

Though he never missed a single game, Gardiner wouldn't really recover from his illness.

In her book *Before the Echoes Fade: The Story of Charlie Gardiner*, Antonia Chambers writes that in January 1934 the Black Hawks were on a train back to Chicago when Gardiner felt an intense pain in his throat that spread to the rest of his body, notably his kidneys. When he woke up on the train in the morning, he had trouble seeing, with black spots obscuring his vision. This was Gardiner's first uremic convulsion. Uremia, simply put, is the condition of having components of urine in the blood. This would essentially be what killed him.

Gardiner's poor health would plague him throughout Chicago's playoff run to the team's first Stanley Cup title in 1934. Perhaps it had for the entire season. Still, newspaper reports after his death noted that he

had "dodged about laughing between the posts, joking with railbirds as much as ever." He returned home to Winnipeg after the season, where newspapers would report that, instead of resting, he had "plunged into his usual round of activities" and had gained 13 pounds, which aggravated his kidney condition.

In reporting Gardiner's entry to the St. Boniface Hospital on June 13, 1934, the *Winnipeg Tribune* said that he was in a coma, but that his condition was thought not to be too serious. His doctors said only that a long period of rest was "absolutely essential to his complete recovery" so that he could take his place between the Hawks posts next season. But that evening, a series of uremic convulsions brought about a brain hemorrhage resulting in his death.

Tributes to Gardiner flooded in from friends, teammates, opponents, reporters and NHL executives. One story, widely reported on June 14, 1934, said that Gardiner's tragic death "recalled the equally tragic passing" of Georges Vezina: "The trophy bearing his name, gift of the club for whom he played, was awarded this spring to Gardiner, whose sudden death at Winnipeg yesterday shocked the hockey world."

The Strange Case of Terry Sawchuk

On December 19, 1959, *Maclean's* magazine ran a story by Trent Frayne called "The Awful Ups and Downs of Terry Sawchuk." The subtitle of the article stated, "For the moody veteran who's 'the greatest goalie of all,' life on the ice and off is just one crisis after another." On the ice, of course, were the standard strains most players faced — goalies most of all, knowing that their mistakes, more than anyone else's, could cost their team the game, or the series. And their bonus money. But there was more. "Injuries, domestic crises, illness, accidents, five medical operations, illogical trades, and the abnormal tensions of his pressure-cooker occupation have plagued him."

Frayne wrote that Sawchuk's playing weight had fluctuated from a high of 228 pounds to a low of 162 over his 10 years in the NHL. Sawchuk estimated that he'd had 250 stitches in his face alone, including three in his right eyeball. A childhood football injury had left his right arm two inches shorter than his left, and he couldn't straighten it. Each summer he'd had some bone chips removed. "He estimates he's had sixty chips taken out," wrote Frayne, "twenty-two of which he keeps in a small jar at home." As a 10-year-old boy, Sawchuk had seen his older brother Mike die of a heart ailment at 17. His other brother, Roger, died of pneumonia as an infant.

Just over 10 years after Frayne's article, in the spring of 1970, Sawchuk had finished up his 20th full season in the NHL. After 12 full seasons in Detroit, with a pair in Boston sandwiched in between, Sawchuk had played in Toronto, Los Angeles and back in Detroit before landing in New York for 1969–70. That season he played just eight games for the Rangers as a backup to Eddie Giacomin and parts of three more in the playoffs. Sawchuk was divorced by then (he and his ex-wife, Pat, had seven children), and at the start of the season he had rented a house with teammate Ron Stewart in Atlantic Beach, Long Island, where most of the Rangers lived during the season. Stewart was a former teammate from Sawchuk's time in Toronto. Both were divorced, and both probably drank too much. Each tended to get combative when they were drunk.

On the night of April 29, 1970, Sawchuk and Stewart were out at a local pub when they began arguing (and shoving each other) about their responsibilities regarding the end of their rental term. The argument continued back at the house. Stewart's girlfriend, Rosemary Sasso, a registered nurse, and Ben Weiner, a friend of Sawchuk's, were there. Even so, it's never been clear whether Sawchuk fell across Stewart's knee or onto a barbecue grill, but it was instantly clear that something was wrong. Sasso called Dr. Denis Nicholson, and Sawchuk was taken to Long Beach Hospital. Tests revealed he had suffered damage to his gall bladder and liver. He underwent surgery to remove his gall bladder and had another operation a few days later to repair his liver.

The story didn't become public until May 22, when reports appeared in New York papers. Sawchuk was still in the hospital on Long Island, while Stewart was at his summer home in Barrie, Ontario, north of Toronto. Red Burnett of the *Toronto Star* (an evening paper at that time) contacted Stewart. In a front-page story in the *Star* on May 22, he denied any part in the accident. "It's news to me," said Stewart. "I'm going to telephone New York and find out how it got started." When Burnett asked if he remembered wrestling with Sawchuk that evening, Stewart replied: "I certainly do not. Offhand, I can't recall what I did on that day. How could a story like that get started?" Burnett wrote that New York reports quoted a Long Beach policeman saying that the two hockey players were "horseplaying" on their lawn fairly late on the night of April 29 when Stewart apparently tripped Sawchuk by accident.

On-ice portrait of Terry Sawchuk facing "more rubber than roadkill on the I-94."

The next day, in a story special to the *Star* from New York, Shirley Walton Fischler (wife of sportswriter Stan Fischler) had an exclusive interview with Sawchuk from his hospital room. In it, Sawchuk said that after three weeks in hospital recovering from his injuries, he would never again be able to play major professional hockey: "I'm retired, man. Look at me. I can never come back from this. It would take more than a year to get into any kind of shape."

Sawchuk, wrote Walton Fischler, could recall little of what he'd undergone in the hospital. He seemed upset that the news had been reported in the press, and when informed of what Stewart had told Burnett, said, "It was just a fluke; a complete accident. Those writers, they'll go all out to make up those stories." A Long Island police official had said that Sawchuk was not planning to lay any complaint and had insisted that his falling over Stewart's knee was completely accidental.

Saying that Sawchuk merely nodded his head, indicating he would not discuss that any further, Walton Fischler wrote: "Seeing him is believing he will never play again. He is virtually unrecognizable as the former stone-faced veteran of 20 years as one of the NHL's most brilliant goaltenders." He was out of intensive care, but his condition was still listed as critical. "I really didn't think I was going to make it for a while," said Sawchuk. "And it was so bad that I didn't really care. They still don't know if I'll be okay. I'm full of tubes and my back bothers me."

Walton Fischler said that Rangers spokesmen insisted that Sawchuk was improving and would be all right, but she reported he had lost 20 pounds and "looks very, very ill." Any suggestions that he would be going to the St. Louis Blues next season, as had been rumored for some time, seemed impossible. "I'm through," he said.

Sawchuk soon took a turn for the worse. On May 29, the *New York Daily News* reported that he was back in critical care, but a spokesman at the Long Island Hospital the night before had declined to say when he had returned to the critical list. On the night of May 29 Sawchuk was transferred to New York Hospital. Tests there found internal bleeding and Sawchuk once again underwent surgery to further repair his liver. Following the surgery, Sawchuk regained consciousness briefly but died in his sleep from a blood clot on May 31, 1970. He was just 40 years old.

A funeral for Terry Sawchuk was held at Our Lady of LaSalette Catholic Church in suburban Detroit on June 3, 1970. Representatives from 10 of the NHL's 14 teams were there, including many members of the Rangers (Stewart among them), as well as former teammates Gordie Howe, Red Kelly, Sid Abel, Marcel Pronovost, Johnny Bower, Frank Mahovlich and George Armstrong.

Stewart would face charges for Sawchuk's death. Prior to a grand jury investigation in Mineola, New York, both Sasso and Weiner claimed that Sawchuk was already ill before the altercation. "Terry was spitting up blood," said Sasso in a story by Stan Fischler in the *Toronto Star* on June 4, "and I was pleading with him to see a doctor, but he wouldn't." This was about two weeks before the scuffle. Weiner had similar recollections. "He was at our house one night during playoff time and he mentioned that he had been spitting up blood, but he didn't know what it was." Stewart's lawyer, Nicholas Castellano, suggested Sawchuk "may well have suffered an injury before the end of the (hockey) season."

When the Nassau County Grand Jury met on June 8, 1970, Sawchuk's death was ruled "completely accidental" and Stewart was cleared. The exact cause of the injury remained unknown, according to District Attorney William A. Cahn, but "the case, so far as any further criminal investigation by this office, is closed."

Chapter 6

Hockey Players in Strange Places

Miami Screaming Eagles

On June 29, 1971, a small headline appeared above an article in the sports pages of the *Miami News*. "World Hockey Association may include Miami."

"Miami," began the article by reporter Jonathan Rand, "has been mentioned as a possible franchise site in the World Hockey Association, which was conceived six months ago as a rival to the established National Hockey League with plans to begin league play in October, 1972."

The WHA was the brainchild of Gary Davidson, the first president of the American Basketball Association (ABA), and Dennis Murphy, former general manager of the ABA's Floridians franchise. "Hockey has grown a great deal," said Davidson. "The National Hockey League has been very restrictive in its expansion and there are several major cities without hockey. Miami happens to be one of them."

Herb Martin was a local Miami businessman. He was responsible for building the huge Atlanta Merchandise Mart shopping center and a similar Merchandise Mart in Miami. Back in 1968 Martin had been a runner-up in the bidding to buy the Floridians basketball team. He already had new construction underway in Miami: the Executive Arena Center, an office building and arena complex that was also to feature a health club, a shopping mall and restaurants. The project, being built off the Palmetto Expressway near the airport, was expected to be complete by August 1972.

"We're going to have hockey," said Martin, who had researched the feasibility of putting the game in the Miami area and was encouraged by the results. "We have two approaches we can take — toward the National Hockey League or the new league ... Negotiations in one direction strengthen us in the other direction. We must keep our dual position and look to both leagues. That's just good business."

Though the NHL would expand again soon enough, adding a second New York franchise in the Long Island suburbs and moving south into Atlanta, league president Clarence Campbell didn't seem too concerned with Miami or too worried about the WHA. "As far as the NHL is concerned, they're welcome," said Campbell in an Associated Press report picked up by the *Miami Herald* on September 24, 1971. "There are four leagues representing 35 cities in professional hockey now, which evidently is not sufficient to satisfy the demand. We're pleased to know the other league plans to take up this shortage."

A day later the *Miami News* reported that Martin had been one of 11 owners granted franchises in the

Dennis Hull was one of the players drafted by the Miami Screaming Eagles.

Bernie Parent as member of the Philadelphia Blazers during the 1972–73 WHA season.

WHA, but in early October came clarification that no franchises had been officially awarded yet. Then on November 1 the new league was officially launched with teams in Miami, New York, Dayton (Ohio), Chicago, Winnipeg, Calgary, Edmonton, San Francisco, Los Angeles and St. Paul. Before the WHA began play in October 1972, Dayton would be relocated to Houston, and San Francisco would move to Quebec City. Calgary would be dropped, but additional franchises would be placed in Ottawa, Cleveland and New England.

Martin confidently predicted on November 1 that his 15,000-seat Executive Square Garden would be ready when the WHA began play, even though construction had been held up until the franchise was official and completion of the rink was not expected now until late September. "We'll be cutting it very close," he said. "We're all priced out and ready to go to contract. I even know what a Zamboni is." Interestingly, the *Miami News* on November 2, while quoting Martin and noting that a Zamboni was the machine required to clean the ice, spelled it "zomboni."

That probably wasn't a good sign.

It's unclear exactly when Miami's WHA franchise took on its nickname, but it was in place by at least December 21, 1971, when the Screaming Eagles became one of the first WHA franchises to take on personnel with the hiring of its first general manager. It was a big-name signing.

Sort of.

Lester Lee Patrick, known as Lester Patrick Jr., or Les Patrick, was the grandson of the late Hockey Hall of Famer and legendary pioneer of the game, Lester Patrick. His father, future Hall of Famer Lynn Patrick, was currently the vice president of the NHL's St. Louis Blues. Les Patrick, who was 31 years old at the time, had — according to the *Miami Herald* — skated on the ice at Madison Square Garden as a two-year-old when his father played with the Rangers and his grandfather ran the club. He'd been born in New York less than six weeks before the Rangers won the Stanley Cup in 1940 and was said to be the first American ever named general manager of a professional hockey franchise.

Les Patrick had been the business manager of the Los Angeles Kings when he was hired to head up the Screaming Eagles. He claimed to be unconcerned about finding talent to stock his team. "There are plenty of hockey players out there," he said. "Not all of them are of NHL caliber, but then not all of those in the NHL are players of NHL caliber before expansion."

Word soon spread that Miami was interested in Boston Bruins star Derek Sanderson, but there would be no player acquisition before the WHA's first draft, held in Anaheim, California, over the weekend of February 12–13, 1972.

Nearly 1,000 players were picked during the 70 rounds that made up that first WHA draft, but before that every one of the 12 teams was allowed to select four players each for a special "negotiation list." The Winnipeg Jets made Bobby Hull their first selection in this predraft round. Miami's picks included Sanderson, Jude Drouin of the Minnesota North Stars and Bill White of Chicago, but their first pick — and a primary target of the WHA — was Toronto Maple Leafs backup goaltender Bernie Parent. Other Screaming Eagles selections that weekend once the regular draft got underway included Jean Potvin, brother of future Hall of Famer Denis Potvin, and Bobby Hull's brother Dennis, plus Andy Bathgate and Jacques Plante.

Parent was known to have been talking with Miami in late January even before the negotiating lists had been determined. He'd been acquired by the Maple Leafs from the Philadelphia Flyers during the 1970–71 season and had sat out a week of training camp in Toronto in the fall of 1971 before signing a new two-year contract said to be worth nearly $80,000. Miami offered him a five-year deal originally said to be worth $600,000, with reports later saying that the offer had been increased to $750,000 by the time the Screaming Eagles announced that Parent had become the first NHL player to sign with the WHA on February 22, 1972.

On Sunday, February 27, Parent and his wife flew down to Miami for a 90-minute press conference.

"Good afternoon. It is an honour and pleasure to be here," said Parent. "I'm looking forward to next year with the Screaming Eagles. I'd just like to say, you have great weather here."

The Parents returned to Toronto that same night, and he was with the Leafs for practice on Monday morning. "I plan to play for Toronto as well as I can for the rest of the season," said Parent. "If I'm in goal and they are winning, they'd be stupid not to play me."

At the time of the draft two weeks earlier, Jonathan Rand in the *Miami News* wrote that "While all 12 World Hockey Association franchises drafted some players who probably won't be signed and others who definitely won't be signed, Miami Screaming Eagles general manager Les Patrick drafted at least two players with whom he should have little trouble agreeing on contract terms." Those players were his brothers, Glenn, then a member of the Columbus Golden Seals in the International Hockey League, and Craig, then with the Baltimore Clippers of the American Hockey League. But neither brother would sign with Miami. Perhaps because Les Patrick was relieved of his duties as general manager on March 23, 1972.

No clear reason was given for the firing. Martin said only that "Patrick has been relieved of his responsibilities with the club for conduct inconsistent with his position as general manager." Apparently, Patrick's five-year, five-figure contract had never been finalized. Martin indicated that the general manager's misconduct was primarily on a personal level and that "it involved him and not the club as a whole."

But soon enough, the club as a whole was coming apart.

On March 28 the *Miami Herald* reported on a lawsuit filed by the president of Miami's Merchandise Mart to halt construction of the new arena. Two weeks later zoning problems related to parking spaces jeopardized completion of the Executive Square Garden. When Martin failed to post a $100,000 bond with the WHA on the weekend of April 15–16, the team was in jeopardy too. A headline in the *Miami News* on April 28 announced, "The Screaming Eagles are close to death." That same day Davidson sent a letter by registered mail notifying Martin that his club's franchise agreement in the new league had been terminated and that membership in the league had been forfeited.

Plante and Parent

Bernie Parent grew up in Montreal idolizing the Canadiens and their great goalie Jacques Plante. After beginning his NHL career in Boston and Philadelphia, Parent was traded to Toronto in 1971 where he got to play with his childhood hero. "I learned more from him in two years with the Leafs than I did in all my other hockey days," said Parent. Both goalies would wind up in the Hockey Hall of Fame.

Plante was 43 years old when the World Hockey Association was formed. Parent was 27. Plante, who had 79 shutouts at the time, claimed he was more interested in trying to stick around the NHL long enough to challenge Terry Sawchuk's career record of 103 shutouts than in accepting lavish offers from the rival league — although he would eventually jump to the Edmonton Oilers in 1974.

In speaking with Jim Vipond of Toronto's *Globe and Mail* for a column on February 16, 1972, Plante, who was the Leafs' starting goalie with Parent as his backup, said he hadn't been approached by the WHA. "No," he said, "but I understand I've been drafted by Miami, the same club that has Bernie. I guess they want me as his understudy."

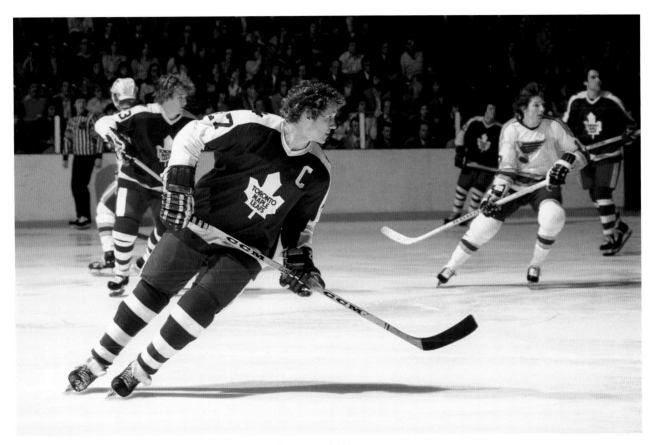

Darryl Sittler during a game at St. Louis Arena in St. Louis in 1977.

On May 31, 1972, the Miami franchise was offered to Philadelphia. Pro hockey would finally come to Miami more than 20 years later when an NHL expansion team was awarded in December 1992. The Florida Panthers began play for the 1993–94 season.

The NHL Comes to Miami

Less than a month after the World Hockey Association pulled the plug on the Miami Screaming Eagles, the NHL came to town … if only for one night. On May 26, 1972, 13 NHL players — including future Hall of Famers Gilbert Perreault, Darryl Sittler and Ken Dryden — filmed a skills exhibition followed by a 30-minute mini game at Miami's Polar Palace ice rink.

A crowd of approximately 1,000 fans (the *Miami News* reported 1,200 while the *Miami Herald* reported about 750) paid $5 each for the privilege of attending.

Whatever the size of the crowd actually was, the rink was said to be filled to capacity, with some 3,000 people turned away. The ice surface at the Polar Palace was at least 80 feet short of the standard NHL length of 200 feet, and as for the competition, "It was like seeing a prize fight in a phone booth," said *Herald* sportswriter Bill Sheldon, "but hockey-starved fans came away pleased." According to Jonathan Rand in the *News*, "the slapstick was heavier than the slap shots, but it was the only ice in town and the hockey-hungry fans were grateful to be fed."

The night began on a strange note when it was

announced that the national anthems of the United States and Canada would be played, but it wasn't O Canada the fans heard.

"I walked into a record store and told the guy to give me the Canadian national anthem," said Polar Palace owner Carl DeAngelo. What he received was a two-part instrumental that began with "Alouette" and concluded with what a fan in the stands with a French accent explained was "a French song which means 'The Cowboy Goes Around the Mountain.'" The public address announcer apologized to the Canadians in the audience, but nobody seemed offended.

In addition to the three future Hall of Fame players, the NHL lineup that night included goalie Jim Rutherford of the Pittsburgh Penguins (a future Hall of Fame builder), Mike Walton of the Stanley Cup–champion Boston Bruins, Doug Jarrett of the Chicago Black Hawks, Red Berenson of the St. Louis Blues, Ed Van Impe of the Philadelphia Flyers and Pat Quinn of the Vancouver Canucks. After filming the skills competition in their own NHL uniforms, the players split up into two sides dressed in blue and gold outfits. The teams for the evening were dubbed Fort Lauderdale and the Screaming Eagles.

When the game began the two teams were playing with just four skaters a side. With the small ice surface, that was soon reduced to 3-on-3. Even with the film lights, the rink wasn't bright enough to make it safe for the goalies to face many hard shots, but the small arena heated up to such an extent that the ice was soft and slow and the players were drenched in sweat. An empty-net goal late in the game gave Rutherford's Fort Lauderdale team a 5–3 win over Dryden's Screaming Eagles.

Before the game Dryden had told Jonathan Rand that "it's not going to be much … It's too small and you can't see a bloody thing. You're really not going to get the flavour [of NHL hockey]; you're not going to get any sense of speed or excitement." Still, the fans enjoyed it.

"We haven't seen a game in 20 years," said Miami resident Edward Shepard, a transplant from Timmins, Ontario, who attended with his wife.

"I bought a half dozen tickets," said former Brooklyn prep school player Allen Benowitz. "I think the Screaming Eagles would have been a big hit here."

Early Miami Hockey History

Perhaps the earliest mention of a hockey league in Florida appears in the Sunday edition of the *Detroit Free Press* on September 18, 1938. In a story from Hancock, Michigan, dated the previous day, the Detroit paper notes: "Joseph Springer, the Chicago hockey promoter representing the Tropical Ice Hockey League of Miami, Fla., and the Southern Pacific Coast Hockey League, Los Angeles, is expected to make his annual tour of the Upper Peninsula this month. He has sounded out prospects via mail."

Two days later the first appearance of an article that would run in papers all across North America over the next three weeks provided more details of the proposed Florida hockey circuit:

> MIAMI, Fla., Sept. 19 — Sports enthusiasts who like sunshine and ice sports as well, will have both in Miami this Winter, with an artificial indoor rink measuring 78 x 165 feet. Opening December 1, the rink will be the home of the Miami entry in the newly-formed Tropical Ice Hockey League, composed of teams representing Jacksonville, Miami Beach, Coral Gables, and one adding international flavor from Havana.

As it turned out, there would be no Jacksonville team. There was, however, talk of a team from Nassau in the Bahamas. On November 4, 1938, the *Miami*

News reported that an application for membership was received from a group of Canadians who had been sent down to the islands by the Royal Bank. But when the league began on December 10, there were just the Miami Clippers, the Miami Beach Pirates, the Coral Gables Seminoles and the Havana Tropicals, who would all play out of the new Metropolitan Ice Palace in the Miami suburb of Coral Gables. The Tropicals would have no connection to Havana beyond the Cuban flags they wore on their hockey jerseys. The four teams played a 14-game season, which wrapped up with an all-star game on February 16 featuring the league-champion Seminoles (who were 12–2 on the year) facing a lineup picked from the three other teams.

No major stars played in the Tropical Hockey League during its one and only season of 1938–39, although 18-year-old Bob Dill from St. Paul, Minnesota, who played with the Clippers and on the all-star team, would continue to play professionally until 1952. Dill played 76 games in the NHL with the New York Rangers from 1943 to 1945. Lachine, Quebec, native Frank Mailley played for the Miami Beach Pirates and would play one game with the Montreal Canadiens in 1942–43. His coach in Miami Beach, Stan Jackson, had played 85 games in the NHL with the Toronto St. Pats, the Boston Bruins and the Ottawa Senators from 1922 to 1926.

Among the biggest names in Miami that winter was Mike Goodman, who was a playing coach with the champion Seminoles. Although little known today, Goodman had played high-level amateur and minor pro hockey since 1918 and had starred on the first Olympic gold medal hockey team, Canada's Winnipeg Falcons, back in 1920 with future Hockey Hall of Famer Frank Fredrickson.

Tropical Hockey Hall of Fame

Two Hockey Hall of Famers did take part in the Tropical Hockey League during its one season of play. Former NHL star King Clancy refereed a few games while in Miami recuperating from an operation in January 1939. More notably, Bullet Joe Simpson served as coach of the Miami Clippers.

Joe Simpson was born in Selkirk, Manitoba, on August 13, 1893. He once claimed that he could skate as soon as he learned to walk, and he played top amateur hockey in his hometown and in Winnipeg from 1912 until 1916. Simpson won the Allan Cup as Canadian amateur champion with the Winnipeg 61st Battalion team in 1916 before serving two years in the Canadian army during World War I. He was back in his hometown playing hockey in 1918–19 and led the Selkirk Fishermen to the Allan Cup final that season, losing to a Hamilton Tigers team that featured future NHL teammate and fellow Hall of Famer Shorty Green.

Simpson went professional with the Edmonton Eskimos of the Western Canada Hockey League in 1921–22, a pro circuit that rivaled the NHL and the Pacific Coast Hockey Association for the Stanley Cup at that time. Simpson and the Eskimos were defeated by the Ottawa Senators for the Cup in 1923.

In 1925 Simpson entered the NHL with the New York Americans, and though he never put up the offensive numbers in the NHL that he had in his four seasons with Edmonton, Simpson became a fan favorite in New York with his fearless end-to-end rushes. He later coached the Americans from 1931 to 1934 and then the Minneapolis Millers of the American Hockey Association from 1936 to 1938. Simpson's friendship with Bob Dill in Minnesota was how Dill ended up playing hockey in Miami.

Simpson would remain in Coral Gables for the rest of his life after coaching the Clippers in 1938–39, dying at the age of 80 on December 26, 1973. Mike Goodman

"Bullet Joe" Simpson as a member of the New York Americans.

Bullet Joe

Harold Edward Simpson appears to have gone by the name of Joe throughout his entire hockey career — although the name Harold sometimes appears in stories about him in Winnipeg newspapers. The nickname "Bullet Joe" is generally said to be a reference to his speed on the ice, although his biography on NHL.com also credits his battlefield experience in World War I. It's hard to confirm either story, but the name doesn't appear to have been in widespread use until about 1923, so certainly after his military service.

A newspaper advertisment for a hockey match at the Coral Gables Arena.

also remained in Coral Gables until he passed away on July 17, 1991 at the age of 93.

Although the Tropical Hockey League lasted just one season, hockey in the Miami area didn't disappear. Simpson managed the Ice Gardens in Coral Gables in 1940, and he and Goodman, who had been training local players for two years, helped launch the two-team Metropolitan Miami Hockey League that season. "We have at least a dozen lads," Goodman told the *Miami Herald* for an article on October 27, 1940, "who never had a pair of skates on before December of '38 and now they're good enough to play before the public." In 1941 the two transplanted Manitobans offered a three-team summer loop known as the Palm Tree League. "The sport has been gaining in popularity in leaps and bounds in Miami," said Simpson in a story for the *Brooklyn Citizen* on August 19, 1941.

The Americans' entry into World War II put an end to hockey in the Miami area, but in 1952 there were plans to revive hockey at the Coral Gables Arena. A three-team summer league was arranged, with Goodman and Simpson both volunteering to help. So did Art Coulter, another future Hockey Hall of Famer, who'd starred with the Black Hawks and Rangers in the NHL from 1932 to 1942 and now lived in the Miami area after growing up in Winnipeg. This new league ran from early June until early August and featured mainly minor pro and U.S. college players. Hot weather often led to foggy conditions inside the rink, but the caliber of play was said to be pretty decent. "Of the 40 odd players now available, and all residents of the Miami area," reported the *Miami*

News on June 15, 1952, "11 are quite good according to Ted Lindsay, the all star left winger of the Detroit Red Wings; Carl Voss, formerly of the Chicago Black Hawks and now referee-in-chief of the [NHL], and Bullet Joe Simpson."

On May 21, 1953, the *Star-Phoenix* newspaper in Saskatoon, Saskatchewan, reported that Gordie Howe was honeymooning in Coral Gables with his wife, Colleen, when he was enticed into a hockey game with Lindsay. The team they were with was reported as the Miami Eagles, but it seems there would be little more hockey in the Miami area until the talk of the Screaming Eagles nearly 20 years later.

Ireland and the World

Fred Whitcroft is the only member of the Hockey Hall of Fame who was born in Ireland. (Geraldine Heaney, longtime member of the Canadian national women's team, was born in Belfast, Northern Ireland.)

Genealogical records show that Whitcroft was born in Milford, County Donegal, Ireland, on December 20, 1882. His mother (born Elizabeth Bond) had relatives who'd lived in Canada since 1868 and were living in Port Perry, Ontario, by 1871. Before Whitcroft was even a year old, his family left Ireland for Canada. They arrived in Quebec City on November 4, 1883, aboard the Allan Line Steamship Company's *Parisian* out of Liverpool. The shipping company's records show they were headed to Port Perry, about 50 miles northeast of Toronto.

Whitcroft lived in Port Perry for just a few years before the family moved another 40 miles to the east and settled in Peterborough in 1892 or 1893. It was in Peterborough that Whitcroft honed his talents for lacrosse, baseball and hockey. He won the Ontario Hockey Association junior title with the Peterborough Colts in 1901, and after playing in Midland, Ontario, in

1904–05 he returned to Peterborough and captained his team to the intermediate championship in 1906.

In February 1907 Whitcroft left Peterborough again, joining the Kenora Thistles midseason to replace another future Hall of Famer, Billy McGimsie, who'd suffered a career-ending injury in an exhibition game just days after the Thistles had won the Stanley Cup over the Montreal Wanderers in January. Whitcroft helped Kenora defend its Manitoba Hockey League title, but the Thistles lost the Stanley Cup in a rematch with the Wanderers that March.

Whitcroft was recruited to Edmonton in the fall of 1907 to play for and manage the new professional hockey team there. (This team has been incorrectly referred to as the Eskimos over the years, but it was officially known as the Edmonton Hockey Club and was usually called the Edmonton Seniors or the Edmonton Professionals circa 1907.) Whitcroft led his Edmonton club on two Stanley Cup challenges, but the team was defeated by the Wanderers in December 1908 and the Ottawa Senators in January 1910. After the Ottawa series, Whitcroft joined the Renfrew Millionaires, where he would play alongside other future Hall of Famers Frank and Lester Patrick, Cyclone Taylor and Newsy Lalonde during the inaugural season of the National Hockey Association, forerunner of the NHL.

Whitcroft retired as a player after the 1909–10 season, returned to Edmonton and took a job with an Alberta real estate company. He also took an interest in ranching and mining on properties he owned outside the city and later got involved in the oil business. By 1920 the Whitcrofts had moved to Vancouver, where Fred would own and race horses when he and his wife weren't traveling the world on business and for pleasure.

On April 18, 1931, the *Victoria Daily Times* newspaper reported that Whitcroft and a partner, George Adams, had taken over a well-known mining property

The jersey worn by the Montreal Wanderers during their 1908 Stanley Cup win.

on McKee Creek near Atlin, British Columbia, just south of the B.C. border with Yukon. Formerly operated by the Delta Gold Mining Company, it had already yielded more than $1 million in gold. Around the beginning of July, Whitcroft and his 19-year-old son, Jack, went north to Atlin to join his partner. Sadly, Whitcroft died in Atlin on August 9, 1931. The cause was heart disease. He was only 48 years old.

A Record for Ringers

The team Fred Whitcroft helped put together in Edmonton for the 1907–08 season was a good one. According to the *Edmonton Journal*, recapping the season in its March 24, 1908, edition, the team won 19

of 22 league games playing against teams from nearby Strathcona and North Battleford, Saskatchewan. They also played and won five exhibition games.

The *Journal* reported that Whitcroft "carries off the honours for the season's play," scoring 49 goals in 16 games. Among his teammates, only Harold Deeton (25 goals in 16 games) and Hay Miller (21 in 15) came close. Still, the competition that season likely wasn't what Whitcroft was used to, certainly not in Kenora and probably not in Peterborough either. Likely the best team Edmonton faced that season was Portage la Prairie of the Manitoba Hockey League. When they defeated them in three straight games in mid-March, Edmonton decided to challenge the defending champion Montreal Wanderers of the Eastern Canada

Amateur Hockey Association for the Stanley Cup. A copy of the letter issuing the challenge was reported in the *Edmonton Journal* on March 23, 1908.

P.D. Ross, Esq.,
Trustee Stanley Cup,
Ottawa, Canada:

Dear Sir, — On behalf of the Edmonton Hockey Club, champions of the Inter-Provincial Hockey League [Alberta and Saskatchewan], we herewith issue a challenge for the Stanley Cup, now held by the Wanderer Hockey Club, of Montreal.

If our challenge is accepted we would like to have the games arranged to be played as early as possible next season, and would suggest that the best two out of three games decide the challenge. Kindly let us hear from you at your earliest convenience in regard to this matter.

Yours truly,
J.A McKINNON
President,
HAROLD DEETON,
Secretary.

Eager to press the team's case, McKinnon traveled to Ottawa in June to speak to trustees Ross and William Foran in person. In late August McKinnon received a letter from Foran saying that he'd notified the Wanderers that Edmonton's challenge had been accepted. (A two-game, total-goals series would be played in late December, just before the start of the 1908–09 season.) Whitcroft soon set out to recruit new players to strengthen his team.

The 1906–07 season had been the first in Canada

Didier Pitre.

in which hockey players could openly receive salaries to play the game. There had certainly been some form of "under-the-table" payment prior to that season, and teams had been known to bring in "ringers" for Stanley Cup games for several years already. But

Fred Whitcroft.

professionalism, with players hopping from team to team as the clubs openly bought up the best talent before big games, was giving hockey a bad name. Something had to be done.

In March 1908, shortly before Edmonton issued its challenge, the trustees in charge of the Stanley Cup made an announcement. Beginning the following season, they would no longer consider any player eligible to play in a Stanley Cup challenge if they had appeared on more than one team during that season. To play for the Cup, a player had to be with his team by the first day of the regular season. Transactions in those days were usually closer to free-agent signings

than our modern concept of trades, but in a sense the trustees had established hockey's first trade deadline.

But before the 1908–09 season started, Whitcroft brought new players to Edmonton from far and wide, adding future Hall of Famers Tommy Phillips, Lester Patrick, Didier Pitre and Joe Hall to the lineup. Hall wouldn't take part in the Stanley Cup series in Montreal, but Whitcroft also added eastern stars Steve Vair, Harold McNamara and goalie Bert Lindsay — the father of Ted Lindsay.

Technically, Whitcroft was abiding by the new rules. The new players were all in Edmonton before the season started, and none had (yet) played on any other teams that season. Still, newspapers mocked Edmonton's approach to team building. However, the Stanley Cup trustees realized that in a case like this, where a challenge from the end of one season had to be played at the start of the next, it would be impossible and unreasonable to expect a team to use only the same players it had used previously. "A contract lasts for a year," said Foran, "and at the expiration of that contract any club can sign up players for the succeeding season if it pays the money." Compelling a team to re-sign only its own players would actually give those players too much leverage in contract negotiations, so the Edmonton additions were understandable, if extreme.

With Whitcroft, Phillips, Patrick and Pitre, Edmonton's starting seven players now included four future Hall of Famers. But in an age before artificial ice rinks in Canada, the team played only three exhibition games before leaving town, and none with its complete lineup. The team had hoped to play the Stanley Cup games in mid-January to have more time to prepare, but at least the players had a few days to get in some practice in Montreal before facing the Wanderers in the opener of their Stanley Cup series on December 28, 1908. The home team (which boasted four future Hall of Famers of its own — Art

The Kenora Thistles pose with the Stanley Cup in 1907. Team captain Tommy Phillips sits to the right of the Cup.

Ross, Moose Johnson, Jimmy Gardner and Riley Hern) scored a relatively easy 7–3 victory.

Two nights later Edmonton regulars Deeton and Miller were inserted into the lineup to replace McNamara and Phillips, who'd broken his ankle during the first game. The team played well enough to win 7–6 in Game 2, but the Wanderers still took the series by a combined score of 13–10 to successfully defend their Stanley Cup title.

Professional Payday

Professional baseball in the United States dates all the way back to the 1860s. Pro hockey in Canada didn't get started until the winter of 1906–07 when two of the country's top leagues decided they would allow professional athletes to play alongside amateurs. This was quite the controversy in its day, and by the 1907–08 season people were already expressing amazement, if not quite outrage, at what the top stars were earning.

Tommy Phillips had played for the Ottawa Senators in 1907–08 but was living in Vancouver during the off-season. On December 15, 1908, a story in the *Vancouver World* discussed the lucrative offer Phillips had recently turned down to return to the Senators for the 1908–09 season. "Two hundred dollars a game for ten games of hockey!" the story started. "How would you like to be offered that amount? Would you refuse $2,000 for practically two months' work? There are few men who would; yet that is just what was declined with thanks the other day by Tom Phillips, the celebrated Ottawa hockey player, who is now in Vancouver."

The story then went on to explain how Phillips, longtime captain of the Kenora Thistles who'd led them to the Stanley Cup in January 1907, had received a salary of $1,600 to play in Ottawa during the 1907–08 season. But that wasn't all. "Ottawa paid Tom Phillips $1,600 cash," the story said, "with a $60 a month job [which is a pretty fair indication that a yearly salary of $720 was not a bad bit of money for a working man in 1908] and all living expenses last winter, for approximately two months' hockey, which figured out at ten league games."

In all, Phillips earned about $1,800 for a little more than two months, and the paper compared his take to the $7,500 Nap Lajoie had been paid to play for the Cleveland Indians during the American League baseball season of five months numbering approximately 154 games. "Getting down to real figures, Lajoie received about $49 every time he went on the diamond. Phillips practically cost his club … $180 every time he went out to play a league game." The hockey star, it was said, "would have received the stupendous sum of $17,720" if his season had as many games as a baseball season.

But the numbers were about to become even more outrageous.

On the same day the Vancouver paper reported that Phillips had turned down the $2,000 offer from Ottawa came news that he had agreed to join Edmonton for its two-game Stanley Cup series against the Montreal Wanderers. It was soon learned that Phillips was promised $300 per game plus a bonus of $200 if the challengers beat the defending champions.

"If Edmonton wins the Stanley Cup," trumpeted a later issue of the *Vancouver World* on December 26, "Tom Phillips will receive: $800 for two games, or $400 an hour, or $6.66 a minute, or $0.11 a second. A man is

Quote … Unquote

"I think Tom Phillips was the greatest hockey player who ever lived."

— **Art Ross**, *Boston Herald*, March 9, 1930

supposed to involuntarily wink about a dozen times a minute. Therefore every time Phillips bats an eyelash it costs the Edmonton club about 50 cents."

The paper went on to explain that the highest-paid person in Canada was the Governor-General, Lord Grey (who would soon donate the Grey Cup to Canadian football). Grey's annual stipend of $50,000 was broken down as $5.80 per hour for every hour of every day for an entire year, which meant Phillips was to be paid more per minute by Edmonton to play hockey than Lord Grey made in an hour. Sixty-nine times more to be exact. At that rate, the *World* reported that he would make just over $3.4 million in a year. "Pierpont Morgan, John Rockefeller, and Andrew Carnegie had better look out," the paper mocked.

When Edmonton lost the series, Phillips had to go without the $200 bonus. He played the entire 60 minutes of the first game despite breaking his ankle partway through it and was unable to suit up for Game 2. It's unclear if Phillips actually received the full $600 or just $300 for his one game.

A Teller of Tale Tales

There are many stories about Fred Whitcroft's abilities to spin entertaining yarns from the events in his life. Tommy Phillips first played with Whitcroft when "Whitty" joined the Kenora Thistles during the 1906–07

An Eye for Talent

Fred Whitcroft stopped playing hockey in 1910, but he remained associated with the game in Edmonton for a few more years. He coached various teams in the Alberta capital, and his former Renfrew teammates Frank and Lester Patrick used him as a scout to help supply players for the Pacific Coast Hockey Association. Among the players Whitcroft connected to the PCHA were two more future Hockey Hall of Famers: Mickey MacKay and Barney Stanley. Both were key members of the 1914–15 Stanley Cup–champion Vancouver Millionaires, along with another former Renfrew teammate of Whitcroft's: Cyclone Taylor.

season. Phillips was quoted speaking about Whitcroft in the *Vancouver Province*, on November 11, 1908:

Fred has this fellow Munchausen lashed to the third rail. He told us more hair-raising experiences than would fill a twenty-volume encyclopedia. Most of Whitty's stories were of the Jesse James variety. Once he claimed he was playing for a team in Northern Ontario. The rink was about as big as a minute and there was a bundle of money on the game. Lots of blood was spilled and Whitty drove home the deciding [goal] 10 seconds before full time. The crowd was so sore they went outside and shot half a ton of lead into the rink. Then the players thought it would be safer to slip out of the rink with as little noise as possible and used a snow chute for the purpose. The chute dropped them on to the frozen surface of a creek, and without waiting to get their clothes at the hotel they all skated to the next town, ten miles away, and caught the train there. Fred was a dandy to make the time fly on long trips.

A reporter from the *Ottawa Citizen* speaking to Whitcroft for a story on March 24, 1910, after his season with the Renfrew Millionaires, had this to say about him: "Fred Whitcroft…is recognized as the champion storyteller of the National Hockey Association. 'Whitty' will take you on a flying trip to the North Pole just as readily as he will tell you how he floated across the Rockies in an airship to sign on Lester Patrick for the Edmonton club."

The Klondike Kid

Fred Whitcroft may have spun stories about the North Pole and mined for gold near the Yukon border. And Ottawa's Frank McGee's scoring 14 goals in a Stanley Cup game against Dawson City may be the most famous hockey story relating to the Far North. But these are not the only hockey stories from the Land of the Midnight Sun. When Hall of Famer Hod Stuart was a young man, he went to the Yukon to strike it rich during the Klondike Gold Rush.

In the early spring of 1897, 10 years before Stuart won the Stanley Cup with the Montreal Wanderers in March 1907, Stuart left his hometown of Ottawa for the Klondike. He was just 18 years old at the time when he and another local man, sponsored by a group that included Stuart's father, went to seek their fortune after gold had been discovered during the summer of 1896.

In a letter written to his father on May 31, 1897

The 1906–07 Montreal Wanderers. Hod Stuart is the tallest player in the second row.
Lester Patrick is seated to the right of goalie Riley Hern.

(and reported in the *Ottawa Journal* on July 27), Stuart describes his journey from Alaska to the Yukon, which he says went through the "Chilkat Pass," likely a misspelling of the more famous Chilkoot Pass:

> We arrived here at the south end of the lake last night by boat. We have had an awful time of it. The Chilkat Pass is not a pass at all, but a climb right over the mountains. We left Juneau on Thursday, the 20th, on a little boat smaller than the ferry at Ottawa. There were over sixty aboard, all in one room about 10x14. There was baggage piled up in one end so that the floor space was only about 8x8. We went aboard at 3 o'clock in the afternoon and went ashore at Dyea [Alaska] at 7 o'clock Friday at night ... I had 48 pounds [the weight of the pack he was carrying] and my gun.
>
> We left Dyea, an Indian village, Sunday, but only got up the river one mile. We towed all the stuff up the river seven miles and then packed it to Sheep's Camp. We reached Sheep's Camp about seven o'clock at night on the Queen's Birthday [Queen Victoria, May 24].

A beautiful time we had I can tell you, climbing hills with fifty pounds on our backs …

We left Sheep's Camp next morning at four o'clock, and reached the summit at half-past seven. It was an awful climb — an angle of about fifty-five degrees. We could keep our hands touching the trail all the way up. It was blowing and snowing up there … We loaded up the sleighs with some of our stuff, about 225 pounds each, and started across the lakes. The trail was awful and we waded through water and slush two and three feet deep. We got to the mouth of the canyon about eight o'clock at night, done in. We left there that night, and pushed on until morning …

We worked two days bringing the stuff over from the canyon to the hill above the lake … We were out yesterday morning cutting down trees to build a boat … There are about fifty boats of all sorts on Lake Bennett, which is about half a mile from here …

We are now in Canadian territory after we passed the summit. I will have to catch somebody going through to Dyea to give him this letter, but I don't know how long before I can get anyone going through. This is the last you will hear from me until I get down to the Klondike.

Another letter, written on June 28, appears in the *Ottawa Journal* on October 12, but there's not much news after that. However, on April 7, 1898, the *Journal* notes that Stuart was among the first Ottawa parties in the gold fields and that his father "has learned from time to time that his son has been doing well."

Astoundingly, Stuart's father had left for the Klondike himself the night before that story was printed, having contracted to build the Bank of Commerce building in Dawson City. By September 1898 father and son were back in Ottawa.

Hod Stuart failed to find his fortune in gold, but he soon found fame playing hockey, if only for a little while.

The Wonder from Down Under

Australia hardly seems like hockey country, but the history of the game there dates all the way back to the early 1900s. The first indoor skating rink in Australia opened in the city of Adelaide on September 4, 1904. A month later, on October 4, two teams adapted a game known as roller polo to the ice. Newspapers advertised it as a polo match before the game but called it a hockey match the next day.

The first true hockey game in Australia was played in Melbourne on June 9, 1906. This was a game between a local team and a team of American sailors from a ship called the USS *Baltimore*. The game ended in a 1–1 tie. Hockey in Australia truly began to take off after a new rink opened in Sydney in 1907. By 1909 there was an annual national tournament. Australia has been a member of the International Ice Hockey Federation since 1938 and even had a hockey team at the Winter Olympics in 1960.

The country's top league is a semipro circuit called the Australian Ice Hockey League, formed in 2000. Its teams play for a trophy called the Goodall Cup, which has been awarded to the national senior men's champion since 1911. Australia has had a women's national hockey team since 2000, and the Australian Women's Ice Hockey League has been playing since 2007, but the first national women's tournament was held back in 1922.

In 2014 Nathan Walker, who was born in Cardiff, Wales, but grew up in Sydney, became the first Australian player to be drafted by an NHL team. Walker had dominated the local hockey scene as a boy and

The 1914 Victoria Aristocrats. Tommy Dunderdale stands at the far right. Lester Patrick is seated in the middle.

moved to the Czech Republic as a 13-year-old in 2007 to further his career. Partway through his sixth season there in 2012–13, Walker came to North America when he joined the Youngstown Phantoms of the United States Hockey League. He signed with the Hershey Bears of the American Hockey League before the 2013–14 season and was drafted by Washington after the season. He became the first Australian to play in the NHL when he made his debut with the Capitals on October 7, 2017, scoring a goal in his first game and winning the Stanley Cup later that season. He has since played a handful of games with Edmonton and St. Louis as well.

Tommy Dunderdale never played in the NHL, but during his professional career he played in many leagues that either predated or rivaled the NHL from 1906 to 1924, including the National Hockey Association and the Pacific Coast Hockey Association. Mainly a center, but occasionally playing rover in the old seven-man game, Dunderdale is widely credited with scoring 198 goals during the 12 seasons the PCHA played, making him the top goal-scorer in that league's history. He was one of the top scorers in all of hockey for his era.

Not surprisingly, there are some inconsistencies in the accounts of Dunderdale's life and career. It's generally agreed that he was born in Benalla, Australia, some 130 miles northeast of Melbourne. Some records show he was born on May 6, 1887, while others show May 16 (which is probably correct). Some also show that he was born in Boxhill, which is probably the Melbourne suburb of Box Hill. Regardless of exactly where and when he was born, Dunderdale didn't live in Australia for long.

By 1894 the Dunderdale family had moved to Ottawa, where Tommy's father, Thomas Dunderdale, became superintendent of the Ottawa Gas Company. Canadian census records confirm the year of immigration, and newspaper accounts from Ottawa show both Tommy and his older brother Harry on the honor roll at the Central East School in Ottawa early in 1895. Those same Ottawa newspapers show the family quickly becoming involved in winter sports in the Canadian capital, taking part in ice carnivals and other skating events by 1896.

Many accounts of Tommy Dunderdale's hockey career say he began playing while attending the Waller Street School in Ottawa. Newspaper stories from January 1900 confirm that a T. Dunderdale and an H. Dunderdale were expected to be members of the Waller Street School hockey team that winter.

By the summer of 1903 their father had relocated to Winnipeg to take charge of the gas company there. By January 1904 the names T. and H. Dunderdale appear in the lineup of the Wellington hockey team, playing in a series of games with other teams at the Wesley Rink in Winnipeg and competing for the Wesley Cup. They played with or against players such as Dan Flett, Billy Breen and Barney Holden, who were all big names in the city and had or would compete for the Stanley Cup with Winnipeg teams. (Thomas Dunderdale had already been a noted bowler in Ottawa, and Harry and Tommy would earn notices in Winnipeg in that sport too.)

Tommy Dunderdale played with the Wellingtons again during the winter of 1904–05, joined the Winnipeg Ramblers in the intermediate division of the Manitoba Hockey League in 1905–06, and began his professional career with the Strathconas of Winnipeg in 1906–07. On December 29, 1909, the *Winnipeg*

Tommy Dunderdale dressed in his Victoria uniform.

Tribune reported that Dunderdale would be returning east to join the Montreal Shamrocks for a salary of $1,000. The Montreal team began that season in the Canadian Hockey Association, which soon went out of business when the Shamrocks and Ottawa Senators of the CHA merged into the new National Hockey Association. Dunderdale would play with Quebec during the 1910–11 NHA season but was one of several players from that team who were signed by Frank and Lester Patrick when they launched the PCHA in 1911–12.

Dunderdale joined the PCHA for its inaugural season as a member of the Victoria Aristocrats, who are sometimes referred to as the Capitals, or the Senators, that year. His 24 goals during the 16-game schedule trailed only fellow future Hall of Famers Newsy Lalonde, who scored 26 for the Vancouver Millionaires, and Harry Hyland, who scored 25 for the New Westminster Royals. Dunderdale's 24 goals again in each of the next two seasons led all PCHA scorers in 1912–13 and 1913–14. Victoria won the PCHA title each season, defeating Quebec in a postseason series in the spring of 1913 when the Stanley Cup was not at stake, but losing to the Toronto Blueshirts in 1914 when the Cup was on the line. In 1915–16 Dunderdale was a member of the Portland Rosebuds when they won the PCHA title and became the first American-based team to play for the Stanley Cup. Portland was defeated by the NHA-champion Montreal Canadiens, who won the Stanley Cup for the first of a record 24 times in their hallowed history.

Dunderdale returned to Victoria for the 1918–19 season, winning another PCHA scoring title with 26 goals and 7 assists for 33 points in 22 games played in 1919–20. His final season in Victoria and the PCHA came in 1922–23, when the team was renamed the Cougars. In 1923–24 Dunderdale split time between the Saskatoon Crescents and the Edmonton Eskimos of the Western Canada Hockey League in his final season as a major professional player.

Three years later Dunderdale was back in action when he suited up for several games with the Winter Garden Maroons in the three-team California Professional Hockey League, which also featured the Globe Ice Cream Company and the Richfield Oil Company (Oilers), all of Los Angeles. After a shakeup of the roster midway through the season, Dunderdale finished the year as a referee.

Despite all the moving during his career, Dunderdale continued to make Winnipeg his home. He died there on December 15, 1960.

California Dreamin'

The earliest mention of "ice hockey" in California may be in a *San Francisco Examiner* newspaper story on April 14, 1894. "The very latest in indoor games introduced for the amusement-loving San Franciscans is the game of ice polo," reported the paper. "Ice polo resembles hockey on ice as played in Canada more than any other game." On February 23, 1907, the *San Francisco Chronicle* reported that roller polo was a new game on the West Coast, saying "it is a game of ice hockey revised for roller skates."

One of the earliest reports of an actual hockey game being played in California appears in several San Francisco newspapers two years later, on February 25, 1909. The stories report that hockey players from San Francisco's Olympic Club played on a frozen pond when 97 members of the sporting club had recently made a midwinter trip to the snow-covered Yosemite valley.

By 1912 plans were underway for a 1915 world's fair in San Francisco to be known as the Panama–Pacific International Exposition, celebrating the completion of the Panama Canal in 1914 and to showcase the city's recovery from the devastating 1906 earthquake. On January 14, 1913, an article in the *San Francisco Chronicle* reported that a hockey rink would be among the exhibits and attractions at the Exposition: "An ice palace and hockey arena, which will cost $150,000 is a concession right granted to Patrick Brothers, noted hockey promoters from the north. The ice palace will cover an area 175 feet by 400 feet."

More details, including an artist's rendering of the Ice Hippodrome, appeared in the same paper on April 23, 1913.

> All sports and games of winter, including skating, sleighing, tobogganing, and hockey will be provided in a big concession secured for the Panama-Pacific International

Exposition in the form of an ice palace and hippodrome. The concession privilege has been granted to Frank and Lester Patrick, proprietors of big ice palaces in Vancouver, Victoria, and other cities of the Northwest. It will represent the investment of approximately $200,000. It is planned to bring the world's best hockey teams here during the season of the exposition.

Eric Whitehead, in his biography *The Patricks: Hockey's Royal Family*, writes that the outbreak of World War I severely curtailed plans for the exposition. Construction of the ice palace did not proceed, but after Frank's Vancouver Millionaires crushed the Ottawa Senators 6–2, 8–3 and 12–3 for a three-game sweep of the Stanley Cup Final in late March 1915, a couple of future Hockey Hall of Famers did pay a visit to San Francisco.

"Do you remember that Stanley Cup series we played in Vancouver?" asked Clint Benedict of Punch Broadbent in a gathering of old-timers reported in the *Ottawa Citizen* by columnist Jack Kinsella on April 12, 1966. "We were beaten so badly that we took the $147 share from the series and went to the World's Fair at San Francisco until the heat was off."

Early Hockey in the City by the Bay

By 1916 San Francisco did have a new ice arena, though on a much smaller scale than what the Patrick brothers had envisioned. The Winter Garden opened on October 16, 1916. Local amateur teams from the Bay area, including San Francisco's University Club and some from the nearby colleges and universities, played hockey at the Winter Garden throughout the winter of 1916–17.

Professional hockey made its California debut on March 30, 1917. The Seattle Metropolitans had just defeated the Montreal Canadiens in Seattle to become the first American-based team to win the Stanley Cup when they took on the Canadiens again in a three-game championship series in San Francisco. There was no Cup at stake in this series, but there was a $5,000 prize, to be split 60/40 between the winners and losers.

Montreal won the first pro game played in California with a 5–4 victory over Seattle. Newsy Lalonde scored three goals, including the game-winner in overtime. "San Francisco people appeared tickled over the play of both teams," reported the *Ottawa Citizen*. Seattle evened the series in Game 2 on April 2. Bernie Morris — who had scored 14 goals in the four-game Stanley Cup victory over Montreal, including six goals in a 9–1 win in the finale — scored three goals in a 5–2 victory.

When Montreal won 6–2 on April 4, the Canadiens won the series, and though they had lost the Stanley Cup to Seattle, Canadiens owner George Kennedy claimed that the San Francisco series proved he had the better team. "We finished in a blaze of glory," said Kennedy. "We have … the finest aggregation playing hockey today."

The *Ottawa Citizen* reported on the possibility of San Francisco joining the PCHA, but Kennedy didn't think that was sensible. "Frisco fans were swept off their feet," he told the *Vancouver Sun*. "The rink there is an excellent one." The ice surface was measured 210 feet by 90. "But it only holds 1,800 people."

Kennedy envisioned a different future for California hockey. He spoke of a four-team circuit with teams in San Francisco, Oakland, Sacramento and Los Angeles. "I see no reason why other California towns shouldn't relish the fastest sport on Earth," he said. Still, Kennedy admitted there was one problem.

A promotional poster for the 1917 Seattle Metropolitans.

"It would take an outlay of several hundred thousand dollars to build four rinks and get the game started. The question is — who is going to take the gamble? It might be a highly paying one at that."

A Brief History of Hockey in La La Land

Before the Los Angeles Kings met the Anaheim Ducks in an outdoor game at Dodger Stadium on January 24, 2014, Jim Thurman recapped the history of hockey in Los Angeles for the magazine *LA Weekly*.

The first game ever played in Los Angeles was on February 1, 1917, at the Ice Palace, which was an arena located at 1041 North Broadway, not far from the current site of Dodger Stadium. The Los Angeles Athletic Club, whose seven players were all Canadians, defeated the University Club 7–0 in front of a crowd reported at between 800 and 1,000 people.

Hockey in Los Angeles soon moved to a new location, the Palais de Glace, near the corner of Melrose and Vermont Avenues. By 1925 both the University of Southern California and the University of California at Los Angeles had hockey teams. At around the same time, the California Amateur Hockey Association was formed, and in early 1925 a three-team league featured the Hollywood Athletic Club, the Los Angeles Athletic Club and the Los Angeles Monarchs.

The first visit of an NHL team to Los Angeles came in April 1926 when the New York Americans faced the local Los Angeles Pros. It was supposed to be a best-of-seven series, but while leading 3–2 in the series with one game tied, the Americans departed for the east after suffering a 5–3 loss to the L.A. team on Monday night, April 19. The *Illustrated Daily News* in Los Angeles reported on April 21 that the Americans "were very peeved over the way Los Angeles fans treated them and over the fights and arguments that sprang up while they were being beaten by Los Angeles Monday night."

Nonetheless, a new arena, the Winter Garden at Melrose and Van Ness in Hollywood, opened in November 1926, and the California Professional Hockey League was born. In April 1927 the first NHL games in Los Angeles were held when the Pittsburgh Pirates and Chicago Black Hawks came west to face each other at the Winter Garden after taking on the local teams beforehand. The Black Hawks returned to Los Angeles with the Boston Bruins in the spring of 1930.

In 1938 the Pan-Pacific Auditorium hosted its first hockey games and soon became the regular home for top local talent. The Tropical Ice Gardens also opened in Westwood that year and would host the Montreal Canadiens and a Canadian Navy team in war relief charity games in the spring of 1943. By 1946 the owners of the Pan-Pacific were one of three groups bidding to bring an NHL expansion team to Los Angeles, but travel costs were considered prohibitive. Instead, the "Pan" would host two Pacific Coast Hockey League teams: the Los Angeles Monarchs and the Hollywood Wolves. Bill Barilko played for the Wolves in 1945–46 and in the early part of the 1946–47 season before joining the Toronto Maple Leafs. The Monarchs won the PCHL title in 1947 and brought Los Angeles its first hockey championship 60 years before the Anaheim Ducks brought California its first Stanley Cup title.

There would be little pro hockey in Los Angeles during the 1950s, but the city finally got a team in the Western Hockey League in 1961. The Los Angeles Blades had only one winning season through 1966–67 but were a popular attraction led by star player Willie O'Ree.

O'Ree had been the first black player in NHL history when he played a few games with the Boston Bruins in 1957–58 and 1960–61. He regularly ranked among the top goal-scorers in the WHL while playing with the Blades but never got a chance to return to the NHL when the Los Angeles Kings entered the league in 1967. Instead, he played mainly with the San Diego Gulls of the WHL until 1974.

California Girl

The only Honoured Member of the Hockey Hall of Fame who was born in California is Angela Ruggiero. She was born January 3, 1980, in Panorama City and grew up in the Los Angeles area. The future star with the U.S. women's national team wanted to play for the Los Angeles Kings when she was a girl.

Angela's father, Bill, had grown up in Connecticut and played hockey there. In 1987 he went to sign up Angela's younger brother, Bill Jr., in a Pasadena youth hockey league. There was a family discount, so Bill Sr. enrolled Angela and her sister Pam too. At age 13, Angela began playing on an all-girls team in the Los Angeles area. A year later the family moved to Harper Woods, Michigan, in Metropolitan Detroit. Though she now lived in the "Hockeytown" area, Angela wanted to play high school hockey somewhere with a strong women's program. She chose a prestigious private school, Choate Rosemary Hall, in Wallingford, Connecticut.

While still a senior at Choate and barely a month after her 18th birthday, Ruggiero was the youngest

Angela Ruggiero takes a shot while playing for team USA in 2011.

member of the gold medal–winning United States women's team at Nagano, Japan, in 1998 when women's hockey made its Olympic debut. She went on to play in three more Olympics with Team USA, capturing silver in 2002, bronze in 2006 and silver in 2010. She was named the tournament's top defender in 2002 and 2006. Ruggiero also played at the World Championship 10 times and was named the top blue-liner four times. She scored the winning goal against Canada in a shootout the first time the Americans won the title in 2005 and would win again in 2008, 2009 and 2011.

After high school Ruggiero attended Harvard and played for the university's women's team for four years, winning NCAA All-America honors four times. In her senior year she won the 2004 Patty Kazmaier Award as the best player in U.S. women's collegiate hockey. She made history on January 28, 2005, when she played for the Tulsa Oilers of the Central Hockey League and became the first woman ever to play a non-goalie position during a men's professional hockey game in North America. With her brother Bill in goal for Tulsa that night, the Ruggieros also became the first brother–sister combination ever to play on the same team in professional hockey. Angela was also a member of the Montreal Axion, the Minnesota Whitecaps and the Boston Blades in various top women's leagues before retiring in 2011.

Go West, Young Man

The following members of the Hockey Hall of Fame played for these teams in California long before NHL expansion to the state in 1967. (Not all of them were so young!)

Doug Bentley / Max Bentley / Turk Broda
San Diego Skyhawks: 1942–43

Although the Skyhawks played in various leagues from 1941 through 1950, and then again from 1960 to 1962, the Bentley brothers and Turk Broda were merely added to the roster for exhibition games involving Canadian and American army and navy personnel in the spring of 1943. All three were early in their NHL careers at the time. Broda and Max Bentley would soon leave the league for military service.

Moose Johnson
Los Angeles Palais de Glace: 1925–26
Hollywood Millionaires: 1929–30
San Francisco Tigers: 1930–31

Johnson was a star with the Montreal Wanderers in various leagues from 1905 through 1911 and then with several teams in the Pacific Coast Hockey

A cartoon depicting all the injuries suffered by Moose Johnson.

Association from 1911 through 1922. He was working out with the Portland Rosebuds of the Western Hockey League during the 1925–26 season when he signed to play for the Palais de Glace in the California Professional Hockey League in February. After playing an entire season with the Portland Buckaroos of the Pacific Coast Hockey League at age 42 in 1928–29, Johnson signed with the Hollywood Millionaires in February 1930. He played his final season with San Francisco in 1930–31.

Moose

At 5-foot-11 and 185 pounds, Ernie Johnson was very large for a hockey player of his era. He may or may not have been the first hockey player nicknamed "Moose" as Si Griffis of the Kenora Thistles was known by that name at least as early as 1907. (Griffis was also known as "Sox" although no explanation for that nickname seems to have survived.)

It's often said of Moose Johnson that he used the longest stick in hockey history, which gave him a reach of 99 inches (2.5 m). "The year I quit, they buried my stick," Johnson once said. The *Oregon Daily Journal* (Portland, Oregon), in a story about Johnson on January 24, 1915, notes: "His stick from handle to heel is five feet one inch, and the extent of reach of his entire club is five feet three inches. His arm is 31 inches in length and by standing straight up and reaching out, allowing for the holding of the stick, the tape credits him with 81 inches."

Leaning forward with his stick out, as a photo with the *Daily Journal* article showed him, perhaps Johnson's reach really did extend as far as 99 inches.

Johnson played a rugged style, and though he wasn't thought to be a dirty player, he suffered many serious injuries. He fractured his jaw early in the 1914–15 PCHA season while playing with the Portland Rosebuds and wore a leather football helmet for a few games, which may make him the first hockey player ever to wear a helmet.

Jack Walker
Hollywood Stars: 1931–32
Oakland Sheiks: 1932–33

Walker had been a star in Port Arthur, Ontario (now part of Thunder Bay), from 1905 through 1912. He signed to play with the Toronto Blueshirts of the NHA in 1912–13, and after jumping to the Moncton Victorias of the Maritime Professional Hockey League at the end of the year, he returned to the Blueshirts the following season and helped Toronto win the Stanley Cup for the first time in 1914. Walker joined the newly formed Seattle Metropolitans in the PCHA in 1915–16 and helped them become the first American-based team to win the Stanley Cup in 1917. Walker won the Cup again with the Victoria Cougars of the Western Canada Hockey League in 1925, and he would play two seasons in the NHL with the Detroit Cougars after the team was purchased by eastern interests in 1926. After returning to Seattle to play with the Eskimos of the minor pro Pacific Coast Hockey League for three seasons, from 1928 through 1931, Walker played his final two seasons in the California Professional Hockey League, ending his career in 1933 at the age of 44.

Ching Johnson
Hollywood Wolves: 1943–44

Johnson was an original member of the New York Rangers from 1926 through 1937 and was considered one of the hardest checkers in hockey. He finished his NHL career with the New York Americans in 1937–38 and then spent the next two seasons as a player-coach with the Minneapolis Millers of the American Hockey Association. Johnson spent two seasons behind the bench, from 1941 to 1943, with the Washington Lions of the American Hockey

Ching

There are a few different stories about why Ivan
Wilfred Johnson became known as "Ching." All of
these stories are quite stupid, and none of them
would be politically correct today.

One story is simply that Johnson's facial
features somehow struck people as being Asian.
Another story is that, when Johnson was a young
teenager, his father built a small dressing room
next to a backyard rink to keep Ivan and his
friends from tromping into the family kitchen
while wearing their skates. Johnson would cook
meals for his friends on the small stove used to
warm the dressing room. At a time when Chi-
nese immigrants were known mainly for their
restaurants and cooking, Johnson's friends
began calling him "Chinaman," which was
later shortened to Ching.

League, but then returned to the ice as a player just a few days after his 46th birthday when he played his first game for the Hollywood Wolves on December 11, 1943. Johnson played in 17 of 18 games for the Wolves in the new Southern California Hockey League that season, his final year in the game.

Not Ready for His Close-up?

On September 23, 1938, Hollywood movie star Clark Gable passed through Winnipeg. That August producer David O. Selznick had signed a deal with his father-in-law, Louis B. Mayer of MGM, to borrow Gable to play Rhett Butler in *Gone with the Wind*. Filming would begin on December 10, 1938, with the burning of Atlanta scene, although principal photography wouldn't begin until January 26, 1939.

Gone with the Wind was not discussed while Gable chatted with newspaper reporters and signed autographs for about 100 female fans during his brief stay in Winnipeg. The Hollywood star told reporters that he didn't know how long he'd be able to stay. "I have to get back," he said as reported by the *Winnipeg Tribune*. "I'm making a new picture."

Gable chuckled when asked what the movie was called. "*The Good Canadian*," he answered. "It's a story about a hockey player."

"Are you the hockey player?"

"Yeah — I guess I'll get by."

"Ever play any hockey?"

"Sure. I was raised in Ohio, you know. I played a bit when I was a punk of a kid. But I'm sure going to have to brush up on it."

The movie was actually going to be called *The Great Canadian*, and a few days later the *New York Daily News* noted that John Reed Kilpatrick, president of Madison Square Garden and the New York Rangers, had "placed Ching Johnson in the movies with Clark Gable."

Johnson was out of the NHL by this time. He would play and coach with the Minneapolis Millers during the winter of 1938–39, but the *Minneapolis Star* noted in a story about Johnson and Gable on November 8, 1938, that Ching was a resident of the Los Angeles suburb of Redondo Beach. The paper reported that he had been hired back in the spring to tutor Gable in playing hockey, but that filming had been delayed.

"I'd get a kick out of something like that," said Johnson. "Gable is a pretty fair skater. He's athletic, usually in good condition. It shouldn't be too hard to make a passably good hockey player out of him."

Hockey scenes were to be shot at Madison Square Garden, and the Rangers were fully on board. Phil Watson was going to double for Gable in the long shots of hockey action, and Babe Pratt, a future Hall of Famer, would double for the film's villain. On December 2, 1938, Montreal Canadiens president Ernest Savard announced that his team would provide the opposition in the hockey scenes, which would be filmed around Christmas time.

On December 10 the *Pittsburgh Press* reported on the movie, which it called, simply, *The Canadian*. It noted that for the climactic scene at MSG, "MGM is going to admit the public to this game, at two bits per head, and thus not only save money, but make money, by not having to hire a couple of thousand extras out West."

But, alas, the movie would never happen. On December 14, 1938, it was reported in newspapers across Canada that production on *The Great Canadian* had been postponed indefinitely. "Ultra-ultra sources say it's because he-man Clark Gable, billed for the lead, was none too keen about taking to the ice."

The *New York Times* of March 21, 1940, indicated that *The Great Canadian* would go into production that summer, but the movie was never made.

Index